THE RISE
OF THE
NEW
PURITANS

THE RISE

OF THE

NEW

PURITANS

FIGHTING BACK AGAINST
PROGRESSIVES' WAR ON FUN

NOAH ROTHMAN

BROADSIDE BOOKS

HarperCollins books may be purchased for educational, business, or sales promotional use. For information, please email the Special Markets Department at SPsales@harpercollins.com.

FIRST EDITION

Library of Congress Cataloging-in-Publication Data has been applied for.

ISBN 978-0-06-316000-2

22 23 24 25 26 FRIESENS-CANADA 10 9 8 7 6 5 4 3 2 1

FOR MY WIFE, JARYN. THIS WAS ALL HER IDEA.

———————

CONTENTS

CONTENTS

5

Fear of God: The Evil of Banality

6

Temperance: Sober, Chaste, and Penitent

7

Order: The Company We Keep

8

Reformation: Slowly at First, Then All at Once

INTRODUCTION

You are not fragile. You won't shatter upon contact with a thought or phrase you find offensive. If you really think you're that timid, this is not the book for you.

This is a book for grown-ups.

You will be confronted with uncomfortable subjects, antisocial behaviors, and ugly words. You will be made to think about the things you enjoy that others regard as destructive to the social fabric. And you will be asked to evaluate the ways in which your behavior affects the lives of those around you and society at large.

These are the questions that consume those who believe themselves to be so competent, upstanding, and principled that they should reorder society around their personal preferences. This book is about those very people: the busybodies, the hecklers, the moralizers, the meddlers, and the zealots. It's a book about a particular human trait, one that waxes at certain periods in history and wanes in others, but that is always with us. That is, our hostility toward the aberrant and our instinctive desire to impose consistency on our surroundings.

That human trait is present in abundance today. Possessed of an unflappable faith in their own righteousness and an unhealthy level of social anxiety, a new class of activist is busily judging almost everything you do. You're not eating right; not healthfully enough and not sufficiently conscious of the damage your habits are doing to your surroundings. You're not consuming the right media; the indecent frivolities you like so much are giving license to degenerates. You're not thinking the things you should; at least, not when you're preoccupied with diversions that distract you from the crushing pain of existence in an imperfect world, even for just a few minutes.

This meddlesomeness is not new. What is new—or, rather, unfamiliar—is that these traits are no longer the exclusive province of the Anglo-American right. Not long ago, imposing a moral framework on every aspect of life was a conservative predilection. It was the right that didn't like the music you listened to, the television you watched, or the tabloid trash you read. It was the right that identified antisocial themes in seemingly harmless entertainment products that only they, with their keen senses of propriety, could discern. It was the right that saw the world through a moral prism, and it was the right that policed violations of its preferred ethical framework with vigor.

When it was the right doing the moralizing, the left could be counted on to oppose them. American liberals reliably objected not only to conservative dogma, but to almost any social program that came at the expense of individual self-fulfillment in whatever form it took—even those forms that were self-destructive and contemptuous of accepted social norms.

For most of us, this dynamic—left-leaning libertinism versus conservative prudishness—has pertained for all our adult lives. In this young century, though, that dynamic has begun to change. Indeed, it is evolving into a form that is far more historically familiar.

As the left gravitates more toward progressivism and away from liberalism, it has assumed many of progressivism's utopian conceits. Chief among them, an all-consuming conviction that the way you're living your life is not only wrong but harmful to everyone around you. And that way of life cannot be allowed to stand.

No longer do progressives subscribe to the "new morality" that took shape in the 1960s and took over in the 1990s. A much older form of propriety is today taking its place, one that emphasizes political utility over personal pleasure. From the comedy you enjoy to the sports you watch to the sex you have (or, increasingly, don't), a particular sort of left-wing activist insists that these and many other private activities have a public dimension. They must contribute to the promotion of a wholesome society—one that is observant of their preferred pieties and advances their political objectives. Anything that fails to serve this purpose is worse than worthless; it stands in the way of progress.

The outlook I'm describing is, indeed, puritanical. Progressives are unlikely to recognize that preachy and prudish impulse in themselves, but that is vanity. Progressivism in the transatlantic world arose from the ashes of the Puritan experiment. Throughout its history, progressive thought adhered to a theory of social organization that placed the perfection of the human condition above more quotidian affairs. It was as much a moral crusade as a political program. The pursuit of purity has found a home in many American political coalitions over the centuries because it is deeply ingrained. We are all heirs to that tradition—aspiring social reformers more so than most.

The revolutionary, pseudo-religious ideas that will be explored in this book and the tactics employed to enforce them are alarming. They are rapidly acquiring adherents, and those adherents are enthusiastically imposing themselves on dissidents and silencing dissenters. In January 2019, I published a book on this very subject: *Unjust: Social Justice and the Unmaking of America*. The ethos I set out to write against in early 2017 was in its infancy at the time, but its aims were clear. The modern social-justice advocate sought to rewrite many of the fundamental precepts that underwrote classical liberalism.

This was a movement that wanted to replace the fundaments of English common law—little things like high evidentiary standards for criminal conviction and the ability to confront your accuser in court—with a system that meted out a karmic comeuppance to those who were born into the wrong identities. It wanted to remake the United States in ways that were incompatible with our pre-existing legal conventions, frustrating social-justice advocates and leading them into an abject fatalism that too often manifested itself in street violence.

These activists are, in many ways, a frightening constituency. But not in *all* ways. The social-justice enthusiasts who devote so much attention to society's most nagging ills are just as inclined to obsess over trivialities and popular culture. This is an insular movement that is easily misled by hucksters willing to cater to its members' narcissism and reinforce their assumptions about the world.

This movement's pride and sanctimony blinded it to some rather obvious political pitfalls into which it regularly stumbled. Those follies provided critics of social-justice activism with plenty of opportunities to point and laugh. That tendency has only grown more pronounced in the years since the publication of *Unjust*, which leads us to the premise of this book: Sure, the radical outlook on display is menacing. But what if it is also hilarious?

You've probably heard the new progressive ethos described as puritanical before, and mostly in a derogatory context. This book endeavors to make that case as concretely as possible, grounding the thesis in an exploration of the ways puritanical society and the stuffy Victorianism into which it evolved sought to police morality.

The New Puritans believe we are conceived in sin and must be saved. They operate with confidence toward separating the worthy and the unworthy. They believe it essential to shame and shun the unfaithful, lest their ways corrupt the rest of us. They dismiss the unenlightened, detest the heedless culture we've inherited, and long for a world cleansed of human imperfections.

They are sure they will be forgiven for whatever it takes to get us there.

I intend to establish parallels linking efforts in the Anglo-American world to guard the public morality against degeneracy throughout history, from the late sixteenth century through to today. The purpose of this book is not only to condemn and inform but to popularize this case against the new puritanism. Toward that end, early modern spelling and grammar cited in primary documents from the sixteenth and seventeenth centuries have been modernized.

The mission in which the modern left is engaged is grounded in an older value system that has survived throughout the centuries because of its manifest virtues. Those who believe in this project have gone overboard in its pursuit, yes. But their excesses are a by-product of their belief in high-minded principle and the desire to leave our children with a better world than the one into which we were born. There are no one-dimensional villains in this book, only people.

Like their puritanical forebearers, the progressive activism explored in this book does not abide forms of pleasure that distract from the great work of our time. The puritanical progressive's project—the perfection of the social compact—is not going to be fun. It is work. Its pursuit is supposed to be accompanied by discomfort, sacrifice, and quiet contemplation about the abject state in which we find ourselves.

Like their forefathers, the progressive puritans are committed to waging war on decadence, frivolity, and pleasure for its own sake. They believe that to be a mark of their seriousness, but it looks more to the uncommitted observer like fanaticism. In pursuit of what they believe will be a better world, its pursuers are making fools of themselves and immiserating their compatriots in the process.

The old Puritanism left an indelible mark on American politics and culture, but the Puritans are not remembered fondly for their efforts. Their utopian and conformist vision of how society should be structured set them up for failure. The Puritan outlook could only be maintained in a homogenized environment. It rapidly fell out of favor as the American colonies diversified and the influence of commerce broke apart the old social structures.

As Puritan power waned, its remaining true believers became laughingstocks—but not without a few growing pains. Puritanism's grasping efforts to cling to a dying way of life made for misery, encouraged inchoate moral panics, and produced its share of directionless violence along the way. This is a cautionary tale for our New Puritans. It is a lesson they will be forced to relearn, one way or another.

As the old saying goes, "Never talk politics or religion in polite company." Well, this book does both, at length, and with considerable disregard for its readers' emotional states. What you're about to read is an account of people who take themselves far too seriously. It is my fondest hope that this book exposes the New Puritans for the absurd caricatures they have become.

1

REVELATION

THE NEW RISE OF AN OLD MORALITY

F ans of Mediterranean and Middle Eastern food couldn't do better than Holy Land grocer. An immigrant-run midsize market based in Minneapolis, Minnesota, Holy Land employed nearly two hundred people by early 2020 and regularly earned rave reviews from its customer base. It was the apotheosis of the American dream when it was targeted for destruction by a mob.

Majdi Wadi, owner and operator of Holy Land and a Palestinian by birth, was a fixture in the community he served. Wadi was the subject of frequent praise in the local press. Then-Democratic Congressman Keith Ellison celebrated his establishment in a speech on the floor of the House of Representatives.[1] The small chain was lauded for its "bakery, grocery, and, our favorite part, a hummus factory" by Guy Fieri, who featured the shop on his show, *Diners, Drive-Ins, and Dives*.[2] Most important, it was beloved by the community. It seems that very affection enraged those who wanted to see this business crushed and everyone who supported it deprived of something they loved.

"Everyone that loves Holy Land," a Twitter account that associated itself with the Black Lives Matter movement averred, "this is the owner's daughter and catering manager."[3] That call to action was accompanied by evidence that Wadi's daughter, a Holy Land employee, had made racially insensitive remarks on social media the better part of a decade ago when she was fourteen and eighteen years old. "Don't spend your money here unless you support racism and bigotry," one representative Yelp review read.[4]

Does one grocery store employee's decade-old indiscretion tarnish an entire institution? That would seem irrational, but rationality is a commodity in increasingly short supply. To appease the angry crowd that had amassed around his business, Wadi then took the painful but, he thought, necessary step of firing his own child. He promised to hire diversity consultants as a gesture of submission to the industry that has formed around antibias training, and he assured his critics that his daughter would devote herself to good works for "all people of color."

"Not only as a CEO, but as a father, it is my duty and responsibility to ensure my family and Holy Land team members all demonstrate high integrity and moral compass guidelines," the embattled grocer explained.[5] It wasn't good enough.

"We can no longer in good conscience support this business in any way, shape, or form even after their apology," one particularly uncompromising reviewer declared. The controversy culminated in the property's owners terminating Holy Land's lease. It was a punishment befitting the sin: the careless parentage of a willful daughter.[6]

If this was an isolated incident, we could chalk it up to a momentary hysteria. Another scalp sacrificed to the inexhaustible outrage whipped up by social media. But it was not an isolated incident.

In the summer of 2020, fans of the professional soccer team Los Angeles Galaxy woke to the news that the team's crucial midfielder, Aleksandar Katai, had been released from his contract. His removal from the roster was not a result of poor performance on the field or even some personal indiscretion. No, Katai was cut because his wife, Tea, had posted messages described as "racist and violent" on her Instagram account.

No doubt, the messages were highly provocative and insensitive. At the height of that summer's protests, some of which devolved into violent demonstrations, looting, and vandalism, Tea posted one video of a police SUV in New York driving through a crowd of protesters attempting to block the road, captioned in her native Serbian, "Kill the shits." In other posts, she described the riotous demonstrators as "disgusting cattle" and posted an image of a person carrying a box of Nike shoes from what appeared to be a looted store and wrote, "Black Nikes Matter."

The outrage over his wife's behavior was significant enough that Katai publicly denounced his spouse. "These views are not ones that I share and are not tolerated in my family," he wrote. Katai apologized "for the pain these posts have caused the LA Galaxy family and all allies in the fight against racism." Once again, the show of contrition was deemed insufficient. The player's association with a woman of such low character had tainted him, too.[7]

These somewhat obscure incidents may have gone relatively unremarked upon by the national press, but the uprising within the Poetry Foundation—of all places—did not escape the news media's attention.

You might not assume that the rarefied ranks of professional poetry are also a hotbed of racial hatred. However, following George Floyd's murder during an arrest-related encounter with Minneapolis police in the summer of 2020, that lavishly funded literary organization could not avoid the national reckoning with the legacy of racism that activists claim haunts almost every American institution.

The foundation seemed to recognize its peril. In a four-sentence unsolicited response to the events in Minneapolis, the Poetry Foundation expressed its "solidarity with the Black community" and affirmed its commitment to leveraging the "power of poetry to uplift in times of despair." With that, the scent of blood permeated the air, and poetry's hungriest rhapsodists went on the attack.

Thirty poets cosigned an open letter posted on the internet in response to the Poetry Foundation's statement. The letter alleged that the foundation was guilty of failing to "redistribute more of its enormous resources" to the pursuit of social justice and "anti-racism." The letter soon attracted over eighteen hundred signatures.

"As poets, we recognize a piece of writing that meets the urgency of its time with the appropriate fire when we see it—and this is not it," the letter read. "Given the stakes, which equate to no less than genocide against Black people, the watery vagaries of this statement are, ultimately, a violence." These incensed poets called for an "official, public response" to their demands in one week, or else.

We can only imagine what those threatened consequences might have been because this letter had an immediate and outsize effect. Shortly after its publication, the Poetry Foundation announced that its president and board chairman would resign effective immediately.[8]

These episodes and many more like them testify to a cultural shift under way within progressive ranks. This aggressive policing and enforcement of a shared moral framework did not used to be the province of the American left. Not long ago, the forces in American politics that could not abide your lifestyle choices were amassed primarily on the right.

It was the Republican Party that engaged in sanctimonious judgmentalism and moral preening. It was right-wing political culture that wanted to limit your access to the perverting influences of musical acts like the Dixie Chicks and the comedy of subversive entertainers like Bill Maher. It was the Moral Majority who sought the banishment of the singer and songwriter Amy Grant over her divorce and remarriage.[9] It was the Christian right that did its best to anathematize Procter & Gamble for advertising on "racy" television programs and failing to back statutes that would exempt gays and lesbians from certain civil rights protections.[10]

Right-leaning institutions like the Parents Television Council, founded by L. Brent Bozell III, took the lead in the culture wars— regularly pressing the Federal Communications Commission to exceed its remit and crack down on explicit but nevertheless protected speech on the public airwaves. The conservative movement's crusades are almost quaint in hindsight. In its waning days, the PTC attacked GQ magazine for a spread featuring the adult cast members of the Fox show *Glee*, calling it borderline "pedophilia." They savaged the "MTV smut peddlers" and fundraised off *Family Guy*.[11] "Whatever would America's sex-crazed, adolescent potheads do without Seth MacFarlane to amuse them?" one overwrought solicitation read.[12]

Conservative Republicans could be counted on to stand athwart American social evolution yelling, "Stop!" They were consumed with the kind of reactionary culture warring that knows no political remedy and, therefore, no end through the conduct of politics. The tables have turned. A combination of new legal conventions that expand the bounds of what constitutes protected speech, declining interest in that mission among conservatives, and even less enthusiasm for fighting against it among progressives, sapped Bozell's organization and numerous others like it of their relevance.

This surprising condition is a product of the conservative movement's evolution as much as the left's. In 2019, abortion rates in America declined to their lowest rates since the Supreme Court's 1973 decision in *Roe v. Wade* legalizing the practice nationally. That decline was a result of rising general distaste for the procedure and the right's newfound accommodation with long- and short-term contraceptive methods.[13] Similarly, same-sex marriage rights are now a settled issue, in both jurisprudence and custom. What was only a decade ago opposed by a plurality of Americans is currently favored by a two-thirds majority—including most self-described Republicans.[14]

Donald Trump's ascension to lead the GOP signaled the right's virtual surrender in the conventional culture wars its members were still inclined to wage. From the controversy over transgender bathroom mandates (which Trump endorsed as a candidate in 2016), to divorce (the former president was on his third marriage when he ran for the White House), to universalizing access to health insurance (Trump embraced Obamacare's individual mandate requiring the public to purchase a private good under penalty of law), conservatives didn't so much lose the culture wars as much as they simply fled the field.[15]

There are still plenty of Republicans and even conservatives who would be happy to wield the levers of state power to impose their preferred morality on the public. But, as they will be the first to lament, the puritanically inclined are today a self-described minority within the right-wing bloc.

Why did progressive activists rush in to fill the void the once reflexively moralistic conservative movement left in its wake? First, we have to understand how progressivism became a totalistic philosophy with religious undertones.

The progressive world view is meliorist—that is, it embraces the belief that this world can be made better, if not perfected, through labor. The psychologist Pavel Somov attributed principled perfectionism to "Puritanical Compulsives, who can be characterized as self-righteous, zealous, uncompromising, indignant, dogmatic, and judgmental." But all and only in service to the "belief that precise, correct, and perfect solutions to all human and world problems exist."[16]

There's nothing sordid about this personality quirk. "You aren't bad for wanting to save the world," Somov concedes. Commitment to making a better world and a willingness to work toward that outcome is a commendable trait. So, too, are complimentary values like judiciousness, moderation, reverence, and self-denial; these are desirable qualities that any society with an interest in its own preservation should promote.

Like the Puritans before them, the progressive perfectionist's goals tend to be frustrated by mankind's fallible nature. So it is that the aspiring left-wing reformer often comes to resent that very nature. Ultimately, he concludes that it must be throttled out of the human species—for our own good.

As the progressive movement has become more beholden to the idea that the accidents of America's birth render this nation morally tarnished, the movement has become equally convinced that many of the country's traditions are similarly tainted. To partake in and enjoy those customs is, at best, an expression of ignorance. At worst, it is an act of collaboration with systems of oppression.

These conventions, today's progressives say, are steeped in the same classism, racism, and sexism that pervades every other American institution. To engage in an uncritical veneration of even commonplace amusements is to blind yourself to the evil that lurks beneath their surface. A failure to critically deconstruct recreational activities as enthusiastically as one would a piece of legislation or a bureaucratic initiative isn't just a display of willful obliviousness. It is a sin.

Even the most banal episodes that typify the human experience are under attack, in part, because you might enjoy them. As you could expect from such a severe conception of what an idealized life should be, the New Puritan's approach to popularizing its ideas has a fatal flaw: It is making its followers into miserable people.

It is important to evaluate these trends with the understanding that the modern progressive project is, in the abstract, devoted to promoting goals and ideals to which few would object.

Progressives are committed to inclusivity and acceptance on one's own terms—breaking down the stigmas around identity and eliminating taboos associated with affiliations of choice that are deeply personal.

They are dedicated to the cause of environmental conservationism and the preservation of our ecological inheritance for future generations.

They are devoted to the communitarian ideal and believe that your comfort, security, and freedom are only as assured as your neighbor's. After all, a society's goodness is ultimately a function of how it provides for its most vulnerable members.

They are zealous advocates for democratization, even at the risk of inviting the worst abuses of the Athenian mob. The excesses of the crowd are a source of concern, but the risk of disenfranchising and disempowering the general public is, to them, a greater threat.

What unites these disparate causes and values is that they are, as an abstract philosophy, manifestly *virtuous*.

Antidiscrimination and the rooting out of base prejudices; a distaste for wanton ecological destruction fueled by conspicuous consumption; a detestation for suffering and the provision of charity; the benevolent grace of neighborliness: These principles make for a righteous moral code.

The level of commitment a particular kind of progressive devotes to these priorities verges on the spiritual. In fact, many observers have concluded that the exaltation on display mimics a secular faith.

Columbia University's iconoclastic professor of English and comparative literature, John McWhorter, observed something distinctly ecclesiastical in the practice of what he called "Third Wave Antiracism," in part because the philosophy is rife with contradictions.

White silence in the face of racism constitutes the acceptance of racism, but whites are also supposed to subordinate their voices to people of color. The black experience in America is unknowable to anyone not born into that condition, but you are obliged to devote yourself to the unattainable pursuit of that knowledge. African Americans must have access to segregated spaces in society, and you're not at liberty to invade them. But if you don't have any close black associates, you're probably harboring racial hatreds. And so on.[17]

The illogic of these contradictions is, McWhorter contends, the whole point. They represent a test of faith, which its most committed devotees strenuously avoid reconciling. "The problem is that on matters of societal procedure and priorities, the adherents of this religion—true to the very nature of religion—cannot be reasoned with," McWhorter wrote. "They are, in this, medievals with lattes."

The columnist and former editor of *The New Republic*, Andrew Sullivan, agrees. Social justice and its prescriptions for powerful institutions tasked with redistributing both economic *and* social goods "does everything a religion should," he wrote. It establishes a simple historical narrative that sorts past, present, and future generations into oppressed and oppressor camps—good and evil—and it prescribes manners of public and private methods by which the faithful can receive penance.

Like McWhorter, Sullivan sees religious parallels in how hostile the believers are toward sweet reason. "You cannot argue logically with a religion," he wrote, "which is why you cannot really argue with social-justice activists either."[18]

The late science-fiction writer Michael Crichton might be the earliest skeptic of the new creed. His 2003 speech outlining how modern environmental activism "remaps" precepts of Judeo-Christian theology is as relevant today as it was on the day it was delivered. The environmentalist's Genesis is an eerily familiar story: There was an "Eden," a "state of grace and unity within nature," with which we've become estranged after heedlessly consuming the fruit from the tree of knowledge. And the result of our sin is that "a judgment day is coming for us all."[19]

If this is a faith, it's an unforgiving one. We cannot seek salvation through incremental legislative reforms like efficient energy standards, reparative racial initiatives, or redistributive economic policies. Redemption is a very personal project. It involves rites, rituals, and the provision of indulgences by a priestly caste. Like Sullivan and McWhorter, Crichton notes that there is no rationalizing a believer out of this dogma, "because the tenets of environmentalism are all about belief."

If what we are witnessing were only the practice of a secular faith in which meaning and identity were derived from political activism, it would not be a unique occurrence. The periodic rise and fall of similar phenomena pepper American history books. Moreover, to call this a religion is ultimately unsatisfying, because it is without the deism that typically accompanies spirituality. Rather, what we are seeing is the rehabilitation of an all-encompassing code of social conduct that transcends politics and religious practice.

That, too, is familiar to students of transatlantic history. "Puritanism was not merely a religious creed and a theology," the historian and intellectual Perry Miller wrote, "it was also a program for society."[20] What New England's colonists established wasn't just a church or a set of moral codes by which the righteous should be guided as an example to their neighbors. Theirs was a way of life.

The Puritan lifestyle orbited around their church, but the constellation of ideas to which the faithful were beholden was not solely theological. Their communal covenant involved the strict management of social and familial relations. It was accompanied by codes of conduct designed to set individuals on a course toward a moral life. The Puritan compact established aesthetic and pedagogic standards that almost every vocation was expected to observe. All this was overseen by authorities empowered to preserve Puritanism's preferred social milieu, but only for the greater common good.

The New Puritans also follow a totalistic moral code. They, too, would see it enforced by powerful institutions unresponsive to democratic contrivances or public opinion. They, too, would impose on the public mechanisms ostensibly designed to promote earnestness and decorum, but that eventually become tools the powerful use to preserve class and status distinctions.

The advocates of this new value system discourage humility and toleration in its practice. They do not allow for acceptance of alternative ethics because to make room for such a thing is to countenance depravity. Moderation in the observance of this ideology's tenets tacitly condones a wholly immoral status quo. Given the broad array of threats to social probity, practitioners of this unrelenting creed have no time for patience, leniency, or kindness.

Untethered to community-level moderating institutions and exposed to the intoxicating psychological accelerants on social media, the practice of the New Puritans' virtues doesn't seem so very virtuous at all. They more closely resemble passions—appetites that can never be sated. Just look at the tools the advocates of this new dogma wield to enforce their preferences: shaming and humiliation, transparently forced confessions, obsequious petitions for relief from the mob's judgment, and public displays of labor in pursuit of atonement.

This is not a religion, per se, but its customs are *aesthetically* religious. That is no accident.

What we are witness to in the stories of Holy Land, Aleksandar Katai, the Poetry Foundation, and countless other similar episodes is not just more evidence of a trend toward the censorious and reactionary politics that fits within the rubric of "cancel culture." These incidents are notable because they demonstrate how no person or profession can exist outside politics anymore.

It is not particularly anomalous that the mob's targets were dragged into the conduct of politics even though their respective professions were—or, at least, should have been—apolitical. Today, everything is a cultural signifier. Everything could conceivably have a broader social impact that affects the lives of others. Everything, therefore, is fair game. Those on the left who are prosecuting this campaign have made it clear that their intention is to force even depoliticized aspects of life to serve what they think is a civically useful purpose. And as this movement's objectives have ballooned in scope, so have its targets.

No longer is this ideology satisfied with imposing its values on life's public-facing aspects alone. The distinctions between public life and private, personal conduct are no longer so clearly defined.

There can be no happy pastimes or casual diversions that distract from the seriousness of this moment. Frivolities for their own sake are a luxury we cannot afford.

This is progressive-on-progressive savagery, a form of intracommunity policing. The instinct to enforce cultural homogeneity is a human trait. After all, conservatives encourage cultural uniformity, too. What's notable, however, is that the brutality meted out by far-left activists to those who trespass against their value system—even their own—reveals how fully the arbiters of progressive discourse have turned against heterodoxy. Once celebrated virtues, diversity and dissent are today regarded with suspicion.

In the same way the religious right could once be counted on to inveigh against all pursuits that did not contribute to the saving of souls, the progressive activist class regards activities that are not useful to their cause with contempt.

There seems to be something special about America that encourages this kind of zealotry.

At the dawn of the American experiment, the unadulterated Puritanism that put down roots in colonial New England lacked the natural predators that had hounded it in Europe. As such, the puritanical thought that emerged over the course of the seventeenth and early eighteenth centuries was as uniquely American as it was uniquely uncompromising.

The litany of wicked activities that were deemed sinful, or that could eventually inspire sinful conduct, exploded as England's Puritans fled their persecution in Europe for the relative safety of the New World. A late seventeenth-century synod of the Massachusetts church established a uniform set of proscriptions on recreational practices, in which even trivial diversions were prohibited. Among them, "walking abroad and traveling on the Sabbath," "having unsuitable discourses," "sinful drinking," abusing the "days of training and other public solemnities," "mixed dancing, light behavior or expressions," "unlawful gaming," and, most wickedly, "an abundance of idleness." That which was not an instrumental contribution to Puritan philosophy was regarded as an assault on it.[21]

As American puritanism blended with religious populism, American moralists emphasized individual conversion experiences and political activism as evidence of high-mindedness. "Individual piety was not enough," wrote George McKenna in the most comprehensive exploration of puritanical thought's impact on American politics, *The Puritan Origins of American Patriotism*. "To be active in one's salvation meant also to be active in the world."

Initially, this took the form of determined abolitionism—an antipathy toward the practice of slavery so absolute that it compelled those with puritanical leanings to back Mexico in the Mexican-American War. To take any other stand was to be complicit in an action designed to add more slaveholding states to the Union.[22] You can see why puritanical enthusiasm quickly wore out its welcome in mixed company.

With the Union's victory in the Civil War in 1865, the puritanical project evolved from the cause of antislavery to creating a brotherhood of man overseen by an activist state. "The Puritans' ethic of self-discipline and austerity was reflected in the numerous paintings and sculptures of Puritans that appeared during this period," McKenna wrote.[23] Indeed, it was in the Gilded Age that puritanical progressivism took a form that looks recognizable to modern observers of American politics.

From crusades against the influence of moneyed interests and for the rights of laborers, to the development of institutions dedicated to providing destitute children with religious instruction, to the Temperance movement and the prohibition of alcohol, progressivism's most famous political causes owe their origins to puritanical sensibilities.

The legacy of puritanical thought is apparent even in the rhetorical flourishes to which so many admired American politicians on the political left appealed. John F. Kennedy declared the United

States the fruition of a providential design in a 1961 address to the Massachusetts state legislature, taking directly from the Puritan minister and third governor of Massachusetts Bay Colony, John Winthrop. "We must always consider," Kennedy averred, "that we shall be as a city upon a hill."[24] This is the distilled essence of puritanical utopianism.

In the speech Kennedy quoted, Winthrop insisted that "the eyes of all people are upon us"—a reflection on the catastrophic blow to the Puritan cause that would be dealt if the Massachusetts colony failed. Woodrow Wilson, who habitually adopted the preacher's cadence he learned from his Presbyterian minister father, was not shy about invoking God's will. "The eyes of the world will be upon you," the twenty-eighth president told the soldiers departing for Europe's battlefields on the eve of America's intervention in the First World War, "because you are in some special sense the soldiers of freedom."[25] Wilson echoed these providential themes in his 1917 State of the Union Address. "The hand of God is laid upon the nations," he said. "He will show them favor, I devoutly believe, only if they rise to the clear heights of His own justice and mercy."[26]

The "rendezvous with destiny" that Franklin D. Roosevelt said was soon to be upon Americans in a speech before Democratic delegates to the 1936 nominating convention evoked a brand of puritanism to which his Congregationalist mother, Sara Delano, was partial. Even the misbegotten expression coined in 1910 by William James—the "moral equivalent of war," which was cited favorably by Democratic presidents from Lyndon Johnson to Jimmy Carter—has a puritanical flare to it. "It was puritanism brought up to date," George McKenna wrote of James's call to action and the progressive era ideals it captured. The phrase combined "the optimistic postmillennialism of the Second Great Awakening with the more liberal, secular Protestantism that emerged in the post–Civil War period."[27]

So, why do we associate the uptight and the self-righteous only with the political right? The answer to that question is buried beneath the rubble of an intergenerational cultural conflict waged and won by the baby boomers.

McKenna's exhaustive study of puritanism's legacy exposes a common misunderstanding about who the real inheritors of the Puritan tradition are. Though we are all a product of our shared history, progressivism's penchant for moral crusades coupled with the right's more practical concessions to American political realities contributed to a great role reversal.

Puritanism, with its utopianism and messianic mission, was comfortable as part of the coalition that gravitated toward the Republican Party in the days when the GOP was more inclined toward Whiggish idealism (their understanding that the arc of history flows inexorably toward the betterment of the human condition) than conservatism. But as the Republicans adopted a more individualistic political philosophy and made explicit appeals to Southerners (and Southern segregationists), that affinity waned.

"The Puritans, who became Whigs in the 1830s, who became Republicans in the 1850s, who became Progressives in 1912, were now on their way to becoming Democrats," McKenna wrote. To emphasize the point, McKenna cited University of Texas professor of political science Walter Dean Burnham, who observed that "the counties in upstate New York that voted Democrat and supported civil rights in 1964 were the same ones that voted Republican and opposed slavery in the mid-nineteenth century."[28]

As the GOP was becoming more conservative, a countercultural revolution was under way, transforming the Democratic Party from the bottom up.

The libertine attitudes adopted by the countercultural New Left cut a swath through American popular culture before gradually overtaking respectable left-of-center politics. By the early 1990s, the convergence was complete. An oversimplified narrative that regards hippie counterculturalism as the wedge dividing left from right was best summarized by the epitome of the phenomenon, former president Bill Clinton.

"If you look back on the '60s and on balance you think the '60s did more good than harm, you're probably a Democrat," the forty-second president said in 2003. "If you think that the '60s did more harm than good, you're probably a Republican."[29] That's a defensible statement on a superficial level, but it does not withstand scrutiny.

There were dissenters against libertinism on the left even during the countercultural revolution. Their objections to decadence, forbearance, and licentiousness were ahead of their time and would one day find a devoted audience. Foremost among them were the more radical theorists within the women's liberation movement.

"Pornography," the radical feminist Andrea Dworkin argued before a 1986 commission on the subject, "is used in rape—to plan it, to execute it, to choreograph it, to engender the excitement to commit the act." Dworkin was famously hostile toward heterosexual courtship rituals.[30] As we will explore in more detail in chapter 6, this message would find its niche a decade after Dworkin's death in 2005. But she was not without victories in her lifetime.

Beginning in 1983, Dworkin and her colleague, the feminist academic Catharine MacKinnon, coauthored various antipornography ordinances that treated pornographic material as a violation of women's civil rights and allowed its victims, such as they were, to seek damages in U.S. civil courts. Though these laws did not survive constitutional challenges in the United States, Dworkin won her share of fights. In 1992, the Supreme Court of Canada upheld the legality of a Canadian obscenity law that incorporated Dworkin's theories elevating legal guarantees around sexual equality above those protecting free expression within "reasonable" limits.[31]

The New Left's live-and-let-live philosophy was quietly rejected by another critical member of the coalition, the movement's preeminent philosopher, Herbert Marcuse.

Marcuse lamented that capitalism was just too comfy to produce the necessary friction between classes. Even the unworthy can "have the fine arts at his fingertips, by just turning a knob on his set," he mourned.

What might be Marcuse's most famous essay—1965's "Repressive Tolerance"—is an argument against a laissez-faire culture of free inquiry. That argument quickly leads to a variety of paradoxical conclusions: Among them, that liberty is tyranny because an unconstrained intellectual environment provides fertile soil in which fascism can take root.

Marcuse advocated "the withdrawal of toleration of speech and assembly from groups and movements which promote aggressive policies, armament, chauvinism, discrimination on the grounds of race and religion, or which oppose the extension of public services, social security, medical care, etc." In his time, these ideals were antithetical to liberalism's first principles. But like Dworkin, his domineering philosophy would find its audience.[32]

America's complicated relationship with the liberties associated with sexual relations and provocative speech—what the Puritans called "unsuitable discourses"—is perhaps where the Puritan restoration begins, but not where it ends.

In the decades that followed the late 1960s and early 1970s, those on the countercultural left who wanted to drop out of society did just that. Meanwhile, its sympathizers who declined to retire to the hillsides to grow cannabis and live off the grid integrated into society. The Democratic Party to which this movement was predisposed, though by no means affectionate toward, spent the final two decades of the twentieth century assimilating these countercultural revolutionaries into its generally liberal majority.

As such, the New Left's illiberal iconoclasts—its heterodox agitators against liberty and libertinism—remained outside the coalition. They were still pure, unsullied by the compromises demanded of those who participate in mainstream politics. And they are now being rediscovered by a generation inclined toward purity.

In the second decade of the twenty-first century, a new intergenerational struggle would take shape. It would pit the forces of liberty against those devoted to, above all else, security. It would set an indulgent social contract against a rigid moral code. And it would prove once again that history repeats.

The tension that we see on display today in the streets and on American college campuses—a conflict between the live-and-let-live generation and their austere progeny—affirms the central premise of this book: In the abstract, we are witnessing a war of competing virtues.

Because what the New Puritans have dedicated themselves to are, in theory, virtues, this book is organized around a set of unimpeachable puritanical values: piety, prudence, austerity, the fear of God, temperance, and order.

Just as it was four centuries ago, these are essential moral precepts. But in the hands of zealots dedicated to cultural hegemony, they are being wielded like weapons to enforce a particular political dogma. As an unintended consequence, the New Puritans are draining life of its spontaneity, authenticity, and fun.

No longer is the American left comfortable with hedonistic pursuits—not those, at least, that are not tempered by a grand social purpose. To the New Puritan, all society's engines must be harnessed to restore a lost paradise—a moral conviction if there ever was one. Enchanting diversions and happy frivolities are distractions to be avoided or even forbidden.

Puritanical ideals produced some of the greatest achievements in human history. The ideas bequeathed to the children of the Pilgrims brought into existence our experiment in self-government, the abolition of slavery, and a social contract that ensures society's most vulnerable are not dependent upon charity alone in their darkest hours. This book is not an attack on puritanism, per se. Rather, this is a study of an all-encompassing ideology that failed and an analysis of why that experiment seems destined to be repeated throughout our history.

Though it has liberalized and secularized through the centuries, the progressive political outlook has retained its puritanical fondness for the Manichean binary. In life, there are good guys and bad guys. Existence is without meaning if it is also without struggle. Social malaise results from insufficient collective sacrifice, the hardships of which must be equally and evenly endured.

The fatal flaw in the practice of new puritanism is that it immiserates its adherents, and misery is unsustainable in the absence of a coercive mechanism. For now, that mechanism is, as it was centuries ago, the guilt and shame imposed upon transgressors by the public square. With the advent of social media, the public square now resides in your pocket. It is in your bed when you wake up in the morning. It's right there on your commute to and from work and on your couch as you wind down for the night. It is with you, judging you, always.

But shame is not an adequate inducement unless you voluntarily participate in being shamed. *You* have to take yourself far too seriously. *You* must become hypersensitive toward the conduct of your neighbors. *You* must be thin-skinned, self-conscious, and consumed with that which is beyond your immediate control. *You* must be miserable—or, at least, miserable to be around. For most of us, that is not a tenable condition.

H. L. Mencken famously defined puritanism as "the haunting fear that someone, somewhere may be happy." It's a contemptuous line, but one that contains a grain of truth about any philosophy with utopian designs. The perfect is often the enemy of the good, as the saying goes. It should be added that the pursuit of the perfect is also the enemy of joy.

2

PIETY

THE WORK IS ITS OWN REWARD

The rigorous pieties to which practitioners of progressive puritanism demand you submit rarely advance their stated objectives. Indeed, achieving one narrowly defined goal is often beside the point. Struggle in its pursuit is its own reward.

In its seventeenth-century conception, genuine piety involved the understanding that you were utterly powerless to achieve your own salvation in the absence of a grueling labor through which you might one day approach, though never truly attain, enlightenment. Today's version of piety operates in much the same fashion. It manifests in the progressive admonition to "do the work," usually in the pursuit of a heightened racial consciousness. That tendency is especially pronounced in the arts. The New Puritans are committed to transforming artistic endeavors and entertainment—both the high and low varieties—into vehicles through which your unending reeducation will continue, interminably, until the day you mercifully die.

Can that purified entertainment ever be any good? And is being "good" really a worthy goal?

• • •

In the summer of 2020, mired in the depths of a pandemic, the Western world was rocked by a spontaneous expression of outrage following what a court later determined was the murder of George Floyd at the hands of a Minneapolis police officer. In response to this outpouring, virtually every major American industry committed to the pursuit of racial equality. In some unfortunate cases, that venerable goal took the form of a moral panic. That is illustrated best by the bizarre backlash against cop shows.[1]

"As the protests against racist police violence enter their third week, the charges are mounting against fictional cops, too," *The New York Times* reported. "The effort to publicize police brutality also means banishing the good-cop archetype, which reigns on both television and in viral videos of the protests themselves."[2] With remarkable speed, programs that depicted police—unscripted and scripted alike—met the chopping block.

The show *Cops* was abruptly canceled after a thirty-three-year run. A+E Networks scrubbed its most popular program, *Live PD*, from the airwaves. The comedy series *Brooklyn Nine-Nine* publicly struggled to reimagine how police should be portrayed—if they are portrayed at all. Warren Leight, the showrunner of *Law & Order: SVU*, professed agreement with the notion that his program portrayed police "too positively" and affirmed that "collectively" such programs are "miscontributing [*sic*] to society."

"With such a volume of crime series on air, one wonders what messages they're disseminating," wrote *The Washington Post*'s Sonia Rao. The *Los Angeles Times* singled out *Law & Order* executive producer Dick Wolf for producing a show that critics allege "contributes to all the things that are killing us." No concern was shown for the artists, creatives, and production staffers who put these shows on the air. Even less consideration was given to the good some of these programs had done beyond the enjoyment and satisfaction they provided millions of viewers. A+E's *Live PD*, for example, was credited with helping solve missing children's cases and helping law enforcement to apprehend suspects at large.

The good this show had done was empirical and tangible; the harm it causes almost entirely theoretical. But the theory won out over the facts.

This panic's magnetism was so powerful that even the Nickelodeon kids' show *Paw Patrol* was pulled into it. Future generations will marvel over why an animated program portraying cartoon dogs as first responders felt the need to issue a tweet demanding "Black voices to be heard." Those generations will also ponder why this anodyne expression of inclusivity produced such a venomous response. "Euthanize the police dog," the mob shouted back. "Defund the paw patrol!" "All dogs go to heaven, except the class traitors in the Paw Patrol."[3]

"It's a joke," *New York Times* reporter Amanda Hess wrote, "but it's also not."

No. It isn't.

This was, in part, a desperate, groping attempt to exercise personal agency at a time when events seemed to have spiraled out of anyone's control. That's a deeply human impulse. And yet, this episode tells us more than that the New Puritans are flesh and blood. This fleeting moral panic is also attributable to the misguided application of an important principle—a standard that maintains law enforcement must be subordinate to the publics they serve. But that unobjectionable principle was not what these advocates of a heightened social consciousness emphasized. Rather, they stressed the exertion and sacrifice demanded of those who would defend this principle over the principle itself.

How banishing the "good-cop archetype" from media would advance the progressive project was neither asked nor answered. It was just another float in a big, booming parade of performative sanctimony. The pursuit of racial justice, while desirable, was less important than a showy, zealous pageant. The piety was the point.

We've seen this sort of thing before.

In the late sixteenth century, the famously austere English minister John Dod began to amass a devoted following, in part because his sermons struck a sterner note than his ministerial competitors. Dod was among the earliest Protestant reformers to identify and satisfy an emerging demand among churchgoers for much stronger medicine than what was on offer.

As Puritanism scholar Michael Winship notes, Dod and his puritanical followers sought to communicate to their congregants "the full, bone-breaking weight of God's law," so as to "trigger in them a horrified realization of how entirely incapable they were of getting to heaven except through Jesus."

"It was only when sinners realized through protracted, anguished self-examination how completely lost they were that they could truly understand how completely they needed Jesus," Winship continued. "That realization was the first step to real faith." But realization alone was not enough. After all, how would your neighbors be made aware of your transformation so they might be shamed or coerced into their own?

Winship observed that what Dod and his congregants wanted to see were garish displays of fealty to Puritanism. And that could only be the result of a "wrenching, protracted confrontation with your own wicked heart." Salvation, then, was the fruition of an emotional process culminating in acceptance of the incontestable fact that "you had not the slightest power to save yourself."[4]

These onerous theological mandates had practical utility. Performative guilt was not just a prescription for despondency, though depression was probably an unavoidable by-product. Rather, their severity allowed individuals to seek redemption and deliverance while also exhibiting obedience to the religious powers that be. Salvation could be yours so long as you were willing to work toward it—the operative word being "work."

America's puritanical heritage has left many durable marks on the country's culture, but few are as pervasive as the so-called Protestant work ethic—a close cousin of the Puritans' dramatic piety.

According to John Calvin's theology, to which many early Puritans were predisposed, God determined the fate of your eternal soul long before your birth. There was nothing that could be done by human agency in this life to alter the destinies of the elect and nonelect. "Predestination" was a stern philosophy, and most Puritan theologians eventually discarded it in favor of narratives around personal conversion and redemption.

While Calvinism maintained that your prospects for salvation or damnation were unknowable, there were certain "outward signs" that might indicate your fate. And what easier way to identify the elect in the here and now than the sweat on their brows or the great works they left behind? The Puritans regarded labor as one of the most powerful ways in which they could glorify God—and, though it was left unsaid, themselves.

Surprisingly enough, the Protestant work ethic is a measurable phenomenon. In 2013, Dutch researchers André van Hoorn and Robbert Maseland found that the links between work and personal fulfillment were more pronounced in Protestant-dominated countries than elsewhere. "Analyzing a sample of 150,000 individuals from 82 societies, we find strong support for a Protestant work ethic: unemployment hurts Protestants more and hurts more in Protestant societies," the researchers concluded. "Whilst the results shed new light on the Protestant work ethic debate, the method has wider applicability in the analysis of attitudinal differences."[5]

The authors determined that their findings comport with a thesis advanced by German sociologist Max Weber, the author of 1905's *The Protestant Ethic and the Spirit of Capitalism*. Weber argued that the most devoted observers adhere to the "idea of the necessity of proving one's faith in worldly activity."

"Therein," Weber continued, "it gave broader groups of religiously inclined people a positive incentive to asceticism." That ascetic was often on display in Puritan societies, and it was frequently accompanied by physical and intellectual as well as spiritual labor.[6]

In Massachusetts Bay Colony, asceticism was demanded of

would-be church members in that they were required to behave in ways befitting their status as "visible saints." These were congregants whose behavior exemplified the virtuous life. They were empirically devout, repentant for their sins, and studious practitioners of the doctrine. Once "visible saintliness" had been sufficiently demonstrated, the congregant ascended to church membership and enjoyed full voting rights. But as the Calvinist doctrine of predestination fell out of favor, proving your sainthood became a more involved affair.

"By 1636," Winship wrote, "it was not enough to act like a visible saint, you had to explain how God transformed you into one."[7] It was crucial both for the sake of your eternal soul and the preservation of a desirable level of social conformity that you prove your sainthood with a convincing tale of your own religious transformation. And, of course, maintaining and preserving your saintly status was a project without end.

Thus, we begin to see the outlines of what has become the modern progressive activist's primary demand of those who would seek enlightenment. It's not going to be fun. It's not supposed to be fun. It will be *a struggle*. This is a secular evolution of the old Puritan guilt crossed with a Protestant work ethic. It's what the New Puritan calls "doing the work."

"To effectively defeat systemic racism—racism embedded as normal practice in institutions like education and law enforcement—you've got to be continually working toward equality for all races, striving to undo racism in your mind, your personal environment, and the wider world," National Public Radio's television critic Eric Deggans wrote in a 2020 article on the philosophy of "antiracism."

At the heart of this doctrine is the idea that "systemic" and "institutional" discrimination are outgrowths of discriminatory behavior patterns in individuals. Systematic discrimination is only a result of the racial antipathies that were long ago encoded into the genomes of institutions forged in environments rife with ambient racism. Systems and institutions, therefore, cannot be reformed before American hearts and minds are reformed first.

In the pursuit of that objective, Deggans and NPR's *Life Kit* teamed up to produce a curriculum for the aspiring antiracist's continuing education. It involves consuming antiracist literature— primarily, bestselling works like Ibram X. Kendi's *How to Be an Antiracist* and Robin DiAngelo's *White Fragility*. It advocates a process of deep personal introspection and self-criticism, to which aspirants may react by going "through a process similar to the stages of grief." Most relevant from a television critic's perspective, it requires you to "seek out films and TV shows which will challenge your notions of race and culture."

As it relates to combating discrimination, antiracism posits that the internalization of racist ideas is not just a personal moral failure. It is an inescapable result of the conditions into which you were born—a fall from grace that influences nearly every aspect of the community to which you belong. Racial discrimination "is woven deeply into our systems of education, criminal justice, housing, health care, and economic function," E. C. Salibian wrote for the *Rochester Beacon*. "The work is to dismantle it both inside ourselves and out in the world."[8] This phraseology would not be out of place in a seventeenth-century Puritan text describing the total depravity of man. All it lacks is the off-ramp of a divinity that might forgive us our sins.

"What's also true is that anti-racist work, learning about racism, understanding how racism has shaped this country (or however you decide to frame it) is never done," the author and *The Atlantic* contributor Clint Smith clarified. "It's not some threshold you cross, and then you're done. It's ongoing. Always."[9]

Of course, no education on any subject worthy of study ever definitively ends. To examine anything in detail is to risk an encounter with the knowledge paradox—that is, the more you know about a subject and the more its complexities are revealed to you, the more difficulty you will experience in the effort to fully comprehend it.

Indeed, at a certain level of understanding, the subject, whatever it might be, becomes enigmatic and all but impenetrable.

But real scholarship is also the exercise of informed discretion. A student should be empowered to compartmentalize, separating the pertinent from that which is relevant but ancillary. In that regard, "the work" is not academic. "The work" is actively disempowering because its advocates discourage that kind of scholarly discretion. It more closely resembles theological indoctrination insofar as it requires its pupils to understand that their goal—wisdom—is unattainable.

"The work" is not toward increasing the sum of human knowledge and advancing toward mutual understanding. Your contributions to that sum are neither solicited nor particularly desirable, and mutual understanding is impossible. The goal for students of this school is quiet reverence and submission. From the outside looking in, "the work" looks less like scholarship and more like arduous sacraments.

"It's called 'the work' because it's not something that happens overnight," wrote the blogger for the artists' collective Fractured Atlas, Nina Berman, "and while we can approach it with joy and optimism, it is frequently difficult and painful."

In an exploration of what this oft-deployed phrase really means, Berman and her colleagues discuss the many forms "the work" can take. It can be posting on social media. It can be *not* posting on social media, so long as your silence is perceived as deference to people with a marginalized identity. It can be educating your peers and colleagues on the tenets of antiracism. It can be flamboyantly *refusing* to educate them because they should be expected to familiarize themselves with the dogma on their own.

"The work" is everywhere, particularly in the entertainment business. "I do worry because white supremacy demands that we come away from things with a checklist or a clear pathway," Fractured Atlas's chief external relations officer, Lauren Ruffin, opined. She added that "in the art sector," the goal is to provide aspirants with "a smorgasbord of options with an approach that you can pick and choose to find your own way forward."

In Berman's estimation, one place "the work" is not is in "the framework of capitalism, which is built on the exploitation of Black and Indigenous people." Another word that accurately describes "the framework of capitalism" is a "job." Thus, the very concept of commercial success, particularly in the arts, is often seen as an obstacle to "the work" or even a betrayal of that mission.[10]

"The work" is a spiritual quest. The labor is both the means to an end and the end itself. If there is any joy in it, it is derived from exalting your own deficiencies and accepting that you cannot achieve salvation on your own.

As we shall see, doing only some of the work can be judged more harshly than not doing the work at all.

In Puritan society, arts and aesthetics had to adhere to the same utilitarian principle that was applied to virtually every other aspect of the human condition. For Protestant reformers in this period, much of what constitutes the arts today was regarded with some mistrust.

"Puritan ideology also condemned music, art, and dancing as illegitimate recreational or leisure activities," observed University of Connecticut history professor Bruce C. Daniels. Most of the performing arts were all but forbidden. Music, save for church choirs, led to "ribaldry," which could, in turn, lead to dancing. From there, every manner of debauchery would follow.

Artistic endeavors on canvas were rare. Puritans "opposed almost all iconography as part of the Catholic apostasy and, in as much as most European art reflected religious symbols, Puritans opposed it as part of their warfare with Rome," Daniels wrote. Rejecting these images "joined with the Puritan contempt of beauty for beauty's sake—which they regarded as a form of idleness."

The exception to this rule was portraiture. New England's portrait-painting industry was quite active, and its artisans were skilled at applying systems of perspective that dated back to

Elizabethan England. But this was considered less an artistic endeavor than the work of a skilled craftsman. Just as elaborate headstone decorations earned an exemption from Puritanism's moral proscriptions, portraiture got a pass only because it was less a display of idolatry than a record for posterity.[11]

Puritanism's artistic standards were relatively well defined. Art was just another craft, like shoemaking or furniture design. To the extent that the finished product was aesthetically pleasing, that was the result of the tradesman's expertise. Whatever the endeavor, it should reflect its time and place to communicate to future generations the conditions in which the artisan labored.

In this, we see a reflection of the ploddingly didactic artistic philosophy that guides the art world of today, the dawn of the age of new puritanism. Art *must* reflect the now; it must comment on current events. In the Puritan imagination, beauty for its own sake gave conceptual license to idleness—among the gravest of sins. That which had no purpose was an empty vessel, and that vessel would invariably be filled up by the Devil's influence. That which isn't useful to you will surely one day be used against you.

By the end of May 2020, almost every major American city was rocked by a profound outpouring of grief and outrage over George Floyd's killing during a fatal encounter with Minneapolis police. San Francisco was no exception. Like so many other left-leaning institutions at the time, San Francisco's Museum of Modern Art sought to express solidarity with the demonstrators.

The museum's staff chose to convey their sadness and resolve to seek change with an image posted on their social media accounts. It was a silkscreen on canvas by the artist Glenn Ligon featuring a crowd of black demonstrators holding up their fists in front of a white banner. The print was "a nuanced work that critically approaches the 1995 Million Man March, led by Louis Farrakhan of the Nation of Islam," which, according to Hyperallergic contributor Hakim Bishara, was controversial only because it excluded women—not for its association with a rather forthright anti-Semite.[12]

Nevertheless, the image was clearly intended to convey the museum's support for the cause, as the quote from Ligon that accompanied it made clear: "Why do we need to raise our hands in that symbolic space again and again and again to be present in this country?"

It wasn't long before the museum was singled out for unrelenting criticism by the very people with whom it had tried to ingratiate itself. "This is a cop-out," said former SFMOMA employee Taylor Brandon. "Using black artist/art to make a statement that needs to come from the institution. You don't only get to amplify black artists during a surge of black mourning and pain. Having black people on your homepage/feed is not enough." She went on to attack her former employers for "weaponizing their own black employees" and acting as "profiteers of racism."

That high-strung reaction to SFMOMA's perfectly anodyne statement generated a modest display of agreement from the community of internet-based antiracism devotees, and the museum reacted swiftly in response to their concerns. SFMOMA took down the image, deleting comments on it—including Brandon's—and disabling further responses to the post. Brandon responded to this act of contrition by deeming it "total censorship," and the museum's union agreed. "Censorship is racist!" the union declared.

The following day, SFMOMA lurched into a familiar defensive crouch. "We apologize," a hastily produced statement read. "Our social media post on Saturday should have more directly expressed our sadness and outrage as an institution at the ongoing trauma and violence that continues to disproportionately affect Black lives." That wasn't the end of the affair.

Local artists and collectives demanded space on the museum's digital properties to make their own statements attacking that very museum before they would countenance working with the institution again.[13] One outraged open letter accused the museum of being "complicit with" the "systemized violence against Black individuals."

The scandal did not die down in the ensuing weeks. Scalps were demanded. SFMOMA tried to make amends by promising to create a variety of new, well-compensated positions dedicated to "inclusion and belonging" and "employee experience," but it was not enough.

In July, the museum's senior curator of painting and sculpture, Gary Garrels, was made to account for a comment attributed to him involving the diversification of the museum's collection during a staff meeting. "Don't worry," he was said to have told museum patrons during a question-and-answer session, "we will definitely still continue to collect white artists." Garrels insisted that his comments were being misconstrued, and he defended their spirit. "I'm certainly not a believer in any kind of discrimination," he said. "And there are many white artists, many men who are making wonderful, wonderful work."

Some staff didn't believe Garrels's repentance was genuine. One contended that his statement was equivalent to saying, "All lives matter," which activists regard as an effort to dilute the sentiments that underly the expression "Black lives matter."

"I'm sorry, I don't agree," he replied. "I think reverse discrimination—" Before Garrels could finish his sentence, gasps erupted throughout the hall. "He didn't say that!" one horrified staffer shouted. The art community was appalled by the invocation of a phrase one University of California, Berkeley professor likened to "the hollow cry of the privileged when they find themselves challenged to share power."

Within five days, Garrels, who had served as the museum's curator off and on since 1993, was forced to resign.[14] But he was only the latest casualty. By mid-July, Garrels had become the fifth high-ranking SFMOMA employee to lose his job over the scandal that followed this one well-intentioned gesture.[15]

Racial tensions in the world of fine art are nothing new. Nor, for that matter, is the claim that museums promote racialist narratives, consciously or otherwise.

"Are art museums racist?" asked the late curator and art critic

Maurice Berger in a landmark 1990 essay. The question arose at a time when the industry, which was and remains dominated by white curators and financed by equally monochromatic interests, was trying to diversify its holdings and employees. Berger alleged that the effort only produced mere tokenism. "Not until white people who now hold power in the art world scrutinize their own motives and attitudes toward people of color will it be possible to unlearn racism," Berger insisted. When it comes "to race, art museums have for the most part behaved like many other businesses in this country—they have sought to preserve the narrow interests of their upper-class patrons and clientele."

The museum industry has been seeking to rectify its own inequities ever since. But, in the thirty years since the publication of Berger's essay, the consensus view among consumers of high culture is that little to no progress has been made. Indeed, according to *Los Angeles Times* columnist Carolina Miranda, museums have *only recently* taken steps to include artists of color. And those are, at best, "baby steps."[16]

What constitutes "equity" in the world of fine art is a moving target. In Miranda's telling, it involves paying higher wages to house staff and security guards whose job it is to preserve and protect priceless works. It includes the extirpation of what Miranda deemed "unsavory sources of museum patron wealth," by which she means benefactors whose largesse is derived from the ever-expanding list of industries that are in bad odor with the progressive left. And it requires the creation of high-paying positions at galleries and museums devoted to inclusivity and diversity.

All of this puts enormous financial strain on an enterprise that operates on relatively thin margins in the best of times. In the terrible year 2020, when in-person viewings became impossible, museums around the country were feeling the pain.

A June 2020 survey sponsored by the American Alliance of Museums found that a full third of museum directors confessed that there was a "significant risk" they would have to close their doors forever if the pandemic-related conditions that prevailed that summer lasted into the following year—which, of course, they did.[17] "It's a blow to our culture," said Sadie Thayer, president of the Washington Museum Association, following the announcement that three of the state's museums would have to fold.

By the end of the year, the average American museum had lost approximately $850,000 in revenue, but that figure obscures the parlous state in which America's premier art museums find themselves. "The Museum of Fine Arts, Boston expected a $14 million loss through July alone, and New York's Metropolitan Museum of Art has projected a $150 million shortfall," Artnet News reported.[18] Make no mistake: This condition has been exacerbated by the puritanical requirements imposed on curators.

"Museums find themselves in an intense battle against a double pandemic: trying to manage the financial stresses of a coronavirus landscape while responding to accusations from inside and out that they are bastions of white supremacy," *The Washington Post* reported. The director of New York City's Metropolitan Museum of Art, Max Hollein, confessed that "there are mechanisms embedded in our institutions that basically, yes, support and foster [white supremacy]." It is a struggle even to see those mechanisms, much less dismantle them.

For some of the more radical elements of this movement, reforming these institutions is a worthless half measure. "This is not a call to reform historically white and white-dominant museums," read an open letter by the organization Boston Arts for Black Lives, "this is a call to unmake them."[19] A similar letter authored by former employees of the National Gallery of Art described the place as the "last plantation on the National Mall" and wondered aloud whether it could, or even should, continue to exist.[20]

We must ask ourselves: What is the point of artistic exhibitions? The museum's purpose is to preserve our histories and provide its community with an uplifting, enlightening, and inspiring experience. The works they curate are often provocative, sometimes alluring or discomfiting, but always stimulating. They preserve posterity, sure. But often, they house exhibitions of beauty for nothing more than beauty's sake. The museum has many purposes, but foremost among them is your enjoyment of them. The Puritans of the seventeenth century could not abide such diversions. Nor can this new breed of puritanical moralizers.

The museum-going experience should, in their minds, be laden with historical baggage. You should be burdened with the understanding that the halls through which you're wandering are built on a foundation of lies and abuses. If these artistic institutions cannot meet the measure of the moment—however the arbiters of such things define both "measure" and "moment" at any given time—perhaps they shouldn't exist at all.

This kind of piety doesn't just ruin the enjoyment of culture. It destroys culture.

For a people who were so ambivalent toward conventional forms of high culture, it's a wonder that Puritanism left such an indelible imprint on the American cultural landscape. Beyond portraiture, they did not leave behind many moving works of art. They did not incubate great playwrights or produce an oeuvre of stirring musical compositions. We know so much about Puritan culture because its members were unusually literate for their time, and they were prolific writers.

"Puritan society espoused an intellectuality that made reading and writing its ideal form of quiet leisure," Daniels wrote.[21] Literature, he added, had the "ideological advantage" of posing a limited risk to the puritanical ethic partly because intellectual pursuits were not believed to present many temptations toward sinful behavior. "Puritans perceived fewer potential problems in literature than in almost all other ways of having fun," he noted.

Like so much of what Americans believe Puritanism to be, modern conceptions of the puritanical ethos have been confused over the years with Victorian sensibilities. The blurring of the distinctions between Puritan and Victorian ethics was complete by the time progressive-led moral reformation movements rose to the fore in the second half of the nineteenth century. Among moral reformers in the Gilded Age, "the promotion of public piety and virtue," the historian Gertrude Himmelfarb observed, necessitated the creation of educational institutions for the orphaned and destitute. This wasn't an act of pure altruism on the reformers' parts, but an effort to head off criminality and degeneracy in adulthood at the pass.

This initiative had the "incidental effect of teaching the children to read," Himmelfarb wryly noted. And it produced "a remarkably high degree of literacy among the poor" well before the creation of a public school system in the United States.[22] But the literature on offer from progressive moral reformers wasn't the debauched dime novels or tabloid journalism that people actually wanted to read. For the most part, it was religious instruction. The progressive mission wasn't to teach the frighteningly ungoverned children of Jacob Riis's "other half" merely how to read—it was to teach them what to think.

Reading and writing might not be everyone's idea of a good time, but we can assume that you find a measure of enjoyment in the consumption of literature. After all, you're doing that right now.

For the New Puritan, though, literature has all the immoral allure of any other depraved aspect of Anglo-American culture. Because the standards to which the modern left holds culture are so fluid, an author is likely to have violated one of its prevailing tenets within only a few years of a work's publication. But at least contemporary authors can protest their treatment at the hands of the New Puritans. The long-departed composers of classic literary works have no such recourse.

"What to do with 'classic' books that are also racist and hurtful to students?" pondered *School Library Journal*'s Marva Hinton. "Students have been reading *To Kill a Mockingbird, Adventures of*

Huckleberry Finn, and the 'Little House' series for generations," she noted. "But today, some media specialists are questioning the proper place for these and other novels."[23]

The American Library Association advised educators to inform consumers about the "dated cultural attitudes" on display in, for example, Laura Ingalls Wilder's books—as though this would not be obvious to a sentient reader of almost any age who encounters one of Wilder's characters insisting that "the only good Indian is a dead Indian." That recommendation followed the ALA's decision to strip Wilder's name from a major children's literary award, noting that her legacy "may no longer be consistent with the intention of the award named for her."[24]

This organization took pains to insist that theirs was not an attempt to "censor, limit, or deter access" to these books. But if you were taking your cues from the ALA, you might get the impression that restricting access to her dangerous books is precisely the right idea.

"We do harm if we don't teach that text in ways that are antiracist," said the assistant director of a teacher-training program in Massachusetts. The "intellectual freedom chair" for the Oregon Association of School Libraries, Miranda Doyle, seemed to agree with this mission statement. She determined that it is a literary teacher's job to ensure "that we are choosing books that are not problematic."[25]

Most of the librarians who are tackling this imperative are sensitive toward the accusation that they're engaged in censorship. And it's true that what they're doing is not that. But even though these concerned custodians aren't censoring anything themselves, they are establishing the predicate on which the suppression of these and other works is based.

In 2017, Minnesota's Duluth Public Schools put the kibosh on classic American works including Harper Lee's *To Kill a Mockingbird* and Mark Twain's *The Adventures of Huckleberry Finn.* Three years later, the Burbank Unified School District in California followed suit, adding John Steinbeck's *Of Mice and Men* and Theodore Taylor's *The Cay* to the forbidden list.[26] One Massachusetts school made the most of this momentary hysteria by removing Homer's epic poem *The Odyssey* from its syllabus. "Be like Odysseus and embrace the long haul to liberation (and then take the Odyssey out of your curriculum because it's trash)," one activist declared. Heather Levine, a ninth-grade English teacher at Massachusetts's Lawrence High School agreed: "Very proud to say we got the Odyssey removed from the curriculum this year!"[27] Quite the achievement.

No doubt, all these works include dated and offensive cultural references. Indeed, the protagonist's journey in many of these works involves navigating their society's nagging inequities. That virtue can be difficult to defend when it is buried beneath an avalanche of noxious stereotypes and racial slurs.

As my colleague, *Commentary*'s senior editor Abe Greenwald, observed, Jewish-American consumers of literature are frequently confronted with discomfiting portrayals of their coreligionists in history's greatest works. "If you have any love for Shakespeare, Dickens, Edmund Burke, Dostoyevsky, whoever, it's endless," he said of the anti-Semitic stereotypes in history's most celebrated works. "It's in the pages. It's woven through all of it." Yet, we "would be so much poorer for throwing it all out because of the bigotry of the authors involved," Greenwald added. "That is part of the history of being Jewish, having to come up against those portrayals and those ideas. Who would want that erased? That's something that was overcome."[28]

Not only would withholding access to the classics rob us of a proper historical education, we would also be complicit in creating a taboo around literature that will lead to its consumption for the wrong reasons—because it's naughty and transgressive rather than enlightening. And there will be no one left to correct that misapprehension. Moral ambiguity is a part of life that children will encounter eventually—whether they are taught that lesson or not.

Some more ideologically committed instructors of literature are walking right up to the line of dismantling their own professions in favor of some reconceptualized version of what teaching the classics *should be*. In a flattering February 2021 *New York Times Magazine* profile, Princeton University associate professor of classics, Dan-el Padilla Peralta, took the group #DisruptText's mission statement to its logical conclusion: If the study of classic literature is to be saved, the field must be destroyed.

The *Times* tells the inspiring story of Padilla Peralta's life and his complicated relationship with his chosen academic profession. He came to the United States as a young child, an impoverished immigrant from the Dominican Republic. He soon became enamored of ancient Rome, and his scholarship took him to Princeton University and on to graduate work at Oxford and Stanford universities. He eventually returned to his alma mater to teach the classics, only to become convinced that his life's work was a toxic sham.

The classics, *The New York Times* profile of this accomplished scholar contended, have "been instrumental to the invention of 'whiteness' and its continued domination." The only socially responsible course would be to break down "structures of power that have been shored up by the classical tradition." After all, Padilla Peralta added, "systemic racism is foundational to those institutions that incubate classics and classics as a field itself."[29]

Even Shakespeare has found himself in the censors' crosshairs. "We cannot teach Shakespeare responsibly and not disrupt the ways people are characterized and developed," wrote one of the teachers who helped form #DisruptTexts. Their quest to limit access to Shakespeare "is about White supremacy and colonization." As *School Library Journal's* Amanda MacGregor observed, this isn't the eccentric preoccupation of a handful of myopic teachers. It is an industry-wide phenomenon.

"A growing number of educators are asking this about Shakespeare, along with other pillars of the canon, coming to the conclusion that it's time for Shakespeare to be set aside or deemphasized to make room for modern, diverse, and inclusive voices," MacGregor noted. "There is nothing to be gained from Shakespeare that couldn't be gotten from exploring the works of other authors," insisted Jeffrey Austin, the chair of the English Language Arts department at an Ann Arbor, Michigan–based high school.[30]

This may sound like a frighteningly new psychological aversion to encountering dangerous ideas in literature, but it isn't new at all.

In 1804, the first volume of Dr. Thomas Bowdler's *Family Shakespeare* appeared in bookstores. The new compendium of the Bard's works had been purged of their raunchier aspects. References to sexual indiscretions, "God," allusions to Roman Catholic tradition, and half a dozen other offenses against prevailing Protestant propriety were rewritten. Bowdler's revisions proved so popular that he soon turned his attention to the classics, stripping the histories of Rome and even the Old Testament of their eroticism and impieties.

From Bowdler's work, we get the term "bowdlerization"—the rewriting or striking offensive passages from literature. Nearly two centuries on from Dr. Bowdler's death, the term has become insulting shorthand for preachy censorship. But Bowdler's works were considered a great public service in his time.

A similar effort is under way today, and the caretakers of modern literature are just as sympathetic to the cause of bowdlerization as they were in the early nineteenth century. Hopefully, it won't be another two hundred years before this intellectually stultifying impulse is disgraced once more.

The soul-sucking instinct to burden every work of art with some agonizing moral about the horrors and temptations that surround us was very much a feature of Puritan society. This was not, however, an unspoken code that was so universally understood it didn't need to be articulated. The Puritans who were starved for entertaining media didn't lack for instruction manuals informing them how to seek out enjoyment without offending God in the process.

In 1698, Thomas Brattle, a merchant and a wealthy colonist's son, completed work on Boston's fourth Congregationalist church. At the time, competition for congregants in colonial Boston was stiff. But Brattle's church wasn't happy to float along with the intellectual currents of the time—it would challenge them.

The Brattle Street Church is gone now, and the street on which it was situated was long ago renamed. But Thomas Brattle is not forgotten by history. His enduring legacy is owed, in part, to his convincing condemnations of the moral panic that culminated in the Salem witch trials.

"I am afraid," he wrote, "that ages will not wear off that reproach and those stains which these things will leave behind them upon our land."[31] His objections to Puritanism's excesses did not end with his contempt for the tyrannical maltreatment of his fellow colonists. The Brattle Street Church would distinguish itself by advancing a more even-tempered interpretation of Puritanism's social covenants. Toward that end, in 1699, the church extended an invitation to Benjamin Colman to serve as minister.

Colman's similarly relaxed standards were reflected in his sermons. In 1707, he wrote at length on "the Government and Improvement of Mirth," which remains the most comprehensive exploration of Puritanism's views on proper fun. Like so many of his forebearers, Colman looked fondly upon amusement and levity—but mostly in concept. A reflection on his views leaves the modern reader with the impression that Colman's definition of what merriment *should be* is so constrained that it leaves little room for genuinely satisfying recreation.

"I am far from inveighing against sober mirth," one illuminating passage from Colman's work read. "On the contrary," he continued,

"I justify, applaud, and recommend it." But as the qualification "sober" would suggest, the "mirth" Colman commended was not the trifling sort. "Let it be pure and grave, serious and devout, all which it may be and yet free and cheerful," he instructed. Not exactly the life of the party.

Though Colman's views on suitably straightlaced fun were relatively uninhibited for their time, the minister still adhered to the belief that amusements were a source of wickedness and temptation. After all, he wrote, "mirth may and generally does degenerate into sin."

Lightheartedness that was not "graceful and charming so far as it is innocent" remained "the froth and noxious blast of a corrupt heart." His endorsement of "virtuous mirth" was buried under a heap of admonitions against what he considered the bad mirths: "carnal and vicious mirth," "mirth ill-timed," and "idle or impertinent mirth."

In one sermon, the Brattle Street minister warned that once "licentious manner of expressing our mirth takes over, all possibilities of innocence, neighborly love, or sobriety vanish." That "wanton man" has succumbed to bold and immodest levity. He abandons "the gravity of reason and acts the part of a frolic colt," Colman insisted. "He roars and frisks and leaps."[32]

Few vocations encourage roaring and frisking and leaping as much as the performing arts. There were, therefore, few callings the Puritans despised more than acting.

"Hostility to the theater is as old as the theater itself," Yale University historian Edmund Morgan observed. "The longest, most bitter, and most effective attacks on the theater came from the English Puritans, or at least from the Englishmen living in the age of Puritanism."[33] The strain of strict reverence that overtook the British Isles in the late sixteenth and seventeenth centuries recoiled from anything that could end in carousing. And as anyone who has spent a considerable amount of time with performers will tell you, they do a lot of carousing.

England's Puritans managed to purge the landscape of theaters for a time, though this was to be as short-lived as Puritanism's dominance. King Charles I, a Stuart and husband to a French Catholic wife, revivified the practice in the most insulting of ways, from the Protestant reformer's perspective, by staging elaborate plays celebrating their own ascension to the throne.

In 1634, an austere Puritan lawyer, William Prynne, put his objections to the practice of acting in writing with his uncompromising tract, *Histrio-mastix*. Prynne paid for his insolence with his ears. They were severed from his head by a hangman's knife while he writhed in a pillory on a London street, watching as the copies of his book were ceremonially torched.[34] But Prynne's objections to the performing arts are illustrative both of how Protestant reformers viewed the practice as well as how today's New Puritans think about the performing arts.

"It is again a most abominable thing for women to become men," Prynne averred, "and to wear that apparel of a man." The act of cross-dressing transformed men into effeminate reflections of their former selves, robbing them of that which made them men to begin with. Of course, women could not perform theatrically either, lest their lascivious portrayals lead the audience into "whoredom." Logically, then, there can be no theater at all. There are simply too many "temptations to adultery" in performance art.

We might call this paranoia, but the Puritans' fears betrayed an unarticulated concern that gender and sexual identity might be terrifyingly mercurial things unless they were constantly reenforced by cultural stimuli. Prynne's manifesto "shows that there was an underlying fear that the self was unstable and could be altered (but only negatively) by the slightest suggestion," the scholar Sarah MacLeod wrote.[35] Identity might be nothing more than a social contract. If so, watching someone engaged in seductive mimicry could expose the instability of our most basic identifying characteristics.

We see something similar in how the modern Puritan views transgenderism not as a choice but a revelation—the fruition of a destiny conferred at birth. Any deviation from that belief, and any failure to reinforce it, is often treated as something quite dangerous.

We see this in the hostility with which a certain type of progressive regards the act of "de-transitioning" back into one's birth gender. Even writing about the phenomena elicits white-hot denouncements, like the one written by Jezebel's Harron Walker after reading the author and journalist Jesse Singal's account of adolescents whose experimentation with a different gender identity has come to an end. Singal is a "reactionary" who has succumbed to "cultural anxiety" over trans issues, Walker wrote. Worse, his prominence somehow robs trans journalists of the opportunities his "success" has brought him, as though journalistic achievement were a zero-sum game.[36]

The research suggests that most people who transition do not regret their choice, but some do. And yet, to even make mention of this very real occurrence is to question "the existence of trans identities," NBC News reported, citing the work of a U.K.-based LGBTQ legal advocate. Promoting these inconvenient facts "can be particularly harmful to trans youth."[37]

This ethos was on display in 2018, when the actress Scarlett Johansson found herself at the center of a firestorm of controversy after she agreed to portray a transgender man in a film based on the life of Dante "Tex" Gill, a gangster and massage parlor owner in the 1970s and '80s.

"As an actor, I should be allowed to play any person, or any tree, or any animal because that is my job and the requirements of my job," Johansson wrote after she was accused of "whitewashing" the Japanese anime *Ghost in the Shell* by playing the lead role in that 2017 feature film. "There are times it does get uncomfortable when it affects the art because I feel art should be free of restrictions," she continued. Similarly, Johansson was savaged for taking "opportunities from members of marginalized communities, namely transgender actors" when she took the lead role in the biopic *Rub & Tug*.[38]

In a denunciation reminiscent of William Prynne, the playwright

and trans activist Phaylen Fairchild accused Johansson of participating in "actual excision of trans individuals" from her industry.
"Johansson and those like her are determined to perpetuate the ongoing, damaging myth that we only exist in their form," Fairchild
insisted, "and not only should our actuality be portrayed on cellu-
loid by cis actors, but we should never be, ourselves, allowed to play
a cis role."[39] Worse, *Entertainment Weekly*'s Nick Romano noted, the
portrayal of a trans character by a straight, white woman "could
wind up spreading misinformation" that makes life harder for all
trans people. "If the 84 percent of Americans only know trans people through what they see on screen, the fear is that real trans men
won't be seen as men, and trans women won't be seen as women."[40]

Johansson bowed to the pressure. She publicly apologized for
taking the role and thanked her critics for her reeducation. But the
film will probably never be made. It died on the vine after the star
attached to the project withdrew. This was, at best, a Pyrrhic victory for trans activists, who may never see Gill's story translated
into a drama for a mass audience and who most certainly won't get
any work as a result of its production.

Developing talent in whatever physical form it takes is a virtue.
Trans actors should have access to as much opportunity as their
individual aptitudes merit. But the activism Johansson's critics undertook killed the film, thereby resulting in fewer opportunities for
actors, artists, and filmmakers—not more. If Johansson's critics are
satisfied with that outcome, we must conclude that their true goals
aren't nearly as benign as they claim.

Two years after this affair, the actress Halle Berry announced
that she would "probably" take a role in an upcoming feature film
in which she was slated to play a woman who transitions into a
man. She, too, was accused of perpetuating "dangerous" stereotypes
and lending credence to the idea that "trans people are just playing
'dress up.'"[41] But the controversy around her decision was far more
muted, in part, because she figured out how to play the game. Berry
insisted that she was going to tell a "female" story—sidestepping

some ideological land mines by anchoring her portrayal of a trans person in her own preexisting gender identity.

Citing the work of former Shakespeare Association of American president Phyllis Racki, Sarah MacLeod observed that "the term 'gender roles' implies that 'gender is a kind of act for all women, not only for actresses and not only for boys pretending to be women.'" She added that Laura Levin, author of *Men in Women's Clothing: Anti-Theatricality and Effeminization, 1579–1642,* came to a similar conclusion. "Men are only men in the performance of their masculinity (or, put more frighteningly, that they are not men except in the performance, the constant re-enactment of their masculinity)," Levin wrote. Or "that they have no way of knowing they are men except in the re-enactment, the relentless re-enactment, of their own masculinity."[42]

Slowly but perceptibly, the intellectual currents that typified Puritanism are waking from their slumber. Armed with the assumption that gender identity is such a fragile thing that challenging portrayals of it on stage and screen can shatter it entirely, the New Puritan activist would sacrifice art to enforce and preserve their preferred social conventions.

Ultimately, if the belief that individual identity is such an inviolable thing that it cannot be toyed with by mere performers, we will end up with less art. Or, at least, we'll have to settle for the kind of soulless "art" that is the product of a standards-and-practices committee.

This trend toward demographic essentialism in performance art isn't limited to gender alone. In 2020, the entertainment industry was overtaken by a sentiment that compelled many longtime voice actors to resign from their jobs because they were portraying cartoon characters of a different race from their own. *Family Guy's* Mike Henry, *Central Park's* Kristen Bell, *Big Mouth's* Jenny Slate, and *The Simpsons'* actors Harry Shearer and Hank Azaria stepped away from voicing characters of color to provide these opportunities to actors of minority descent.

That's a noble impulse. Fostering an environment that rewards representation in media has a value that white consumers of entertainment products may overlook. But for some critics, this voluntary expurgation of white actors voicing black characters failed to address the real problem: the irreverent way in which these cartoon characters are written.

"The tradition of white actors voicing black animated characters has its roots in another insidious form of entertainment: blackface minstrelsy," Shadow and Act's Jordan Simon wrote. "Perhaps the first form of theatrical entertainment that originated in America, these shows falsely and egregiously characterized black people as buffoonish and dim-witted. In other words, Caucasian actors impersonating how they believe black people speak and behave. Sound familiar?"[43]

That's an interesting claim that requires further exploration. Surely, if we were talking about live white actors exaggeratedly imitating black people, it would constitute minstrelsy. But do the same standards apply to voice-over acting when the character is innately caricatured—as all subjects are in a cartoon? And if so, does it only apply to animations depicting humans, as opposed to the many anthropomorphized animals, chimeras, or inanimate objects that occasionally come to life in illustrated art?

And if this isn't just about creating opportunities for black actors, would the same strict standards of representation apply to professional African American voice-over artists who occasionally voice white characters?[44] If so, talented actors like Phil LaMarr, Kevin Michael Richardson, Cree Summer, and even Samuel L. Jackson, all of whom have voiced white characters in their careers, would be artificially robbed of opportunities for work and we would be deprived of their talents.

This is sensitive subject matter. It would be impertinent to dismiss Simon's claims offhand, just as it would be to disregard the undesirable, albeit unintended, consequences of his preferences in practice. The restrictions he would prefer to see imposed on art would surely constrain creatives, forcing their imaginations to comport with the utilitarian demands of a particular political movement. And when those whose only intention is to be as inclusive as possible take these arguments to their logical conclusion, it exposes the fatal flaw in the logic.

"I'm watching the 'Boondocks' for the first time and I have feelings," said freelance columnist Cathy Reisenwitz of the adult animated series created by Aaron McGruder, which follows two young black kids navigating life in a white suburb. "I understand the viewer is supposed to laugh at some of these characters. But I must say it feels gross, as an exceedingly melanin-deficient person, to laugh at Black characters."[45]

That's a tragic thing to say about a genuinely funny and innovative program. Such a mind-set could have terrible consequences if it caught on. If enough well-intentioned white progressives decide a black comedy cannot be laughed at, networks that cater to younger, whiter audiences (like, for example, Cartoon Network's Adult Swim, which greenlit *The Boondocks* in the first place) aren't going to take on the financial risk of backing black comedies. We would all be worse off as a result.

Comedy as a craft becomes especially thorny when it is subjected to a critical racial analysis. And that may help explain why the feature-length comedy film is becoming an endangered species.

In 2019, *The Hollywood Reporter* ran the numbers, and they're not pretty. In 2008, comedies accounted for a full quarter of major motion picture offerings. A decade later, they made up just 8 percent of releases and accounted for a measly 8 percent of domestic revenue at the box office.[46] That drop-off cannot be blamed on the rise of streaming services and the proliferation of small-screen comedies alone. "It's becoming a little finicky," the actor Will Ferrell said of his industry. "I've recently come across things where I thought, 'Boy, what a great idea,' and went around town and everyone just went, 'Nope.'"[47]

Philadelphia Inquirer columnist Gary Thompson rightly noted that the reasons for comedy's retreat from the big screen are multifarious, but one of them is that the dominance of "call-out and outrage culture make it harder for comedies to pass muster with the vigilantes of social media."[48] The joke, he notes, is easily derided as a trite pleasure—particularly when it comes at the expense of a critical social cause. And all social causes are critical to someone.

It's not just comedies that are disappearing. The sexually charged blockbuster is similarly endangered.

"There's a huge opportunity for other kinds of movies, like those sexy date-night movies that have been left by the side of the road in the movie business," Amazon Studios chief Jennifer Salke told *The New York Times* in 2018, "like *No Way Out* and *Basic Instinct*."[49] She's not alone in sensing a gap in the market. "Sex is disappearing from the big screen, and it's making movies less pleasurable," a 2019 headline in *The Washington Post* read.[50] "Well-conceived sex scenes are capable of producing a spontaneous physical frisson just as cathartic—and gratifying—as a sudden belly-laugh or a good cry," wrote the *Post*'s film critic, Ann Hornaday. "And now, it's pretty much gone."

The same moral theory that imposed stigmas on classic American literature is busily scandalizing the film and television industry. But many of the caretakers of these works, who also profit handsomely from their broadcast, have chosen to thread the cultural needle by making them available while prefacing them with warning labels.

The streaming service Disney+ opted to broadcast a disclaimer before streamers could watch the unadulterated original versions of animated classics like *Aladdin, Dumbo, Peter Pan*, and *The Aristocats*, among others, because they traffic in the depiction of racial stereotypes. In 2021, Turner Classic Movies launched a series it called "Reframed Classics," in which "problematic" feature films from the 1920s to the '60s were played in their entirety, albeit with a warning, and then discussed at length by a panel of experts. Films like *Breakfast at Tiffany's*, which features Mickey Rooney playing an offensive Asian caricature; *Swing Time*, with Fred Astaire in blackface; and the many discomfiting aspects of *Gone with the Wind* were subjected to a critical examination.

"We're not saying this is how you should feel about 'Psycho,' or this is how you should feel about 'Gone with the Wind.'" TCM host Jacqueline Stewart told the *Canadian Press*. "We're just trying to model ways of having longer and deeper conversations and not just cutting it off to 'I love this movie. I hate this movie.' There's so much space in between."[51] If there is a right way to navigate the panic that has overtaken the entertainment industry, this is it. Only the most zealous cultural auditors could take issue with this approach. Unfortunately, our national discourse is arbitrated by zealous cultural auditors.

A cottage industry is built up around superficially intellectual critiques of art and entertainment from a critical race or gender theorist's perspective. And because the results of this activism are now self-evident, it is hard to avoid the conclusion that stigmatizing certain forms of art and driving them underground is the intended result.

This is a serious subject, and its consequences are profound. And yet, the shape this kind of activism takes is often more asinine than academic.

The film adaptation of the Broadway musical *Grease*, for example, was recently singled out as "homophobic," because the 1950s-era high school in which the play is set did not feature any LGBTQ students. What's more, the musical was simultaneously "rapey" and guilty of "slut-shaming."[52] Critics castigated the hit Netflix series *Cobra Kai* for leaning into its "whiteness" because its cast did not reflect the precise demographic breakdown of the San Fernando Valley according to U.S. Census data.[53] Yes, seriously.

There are real-world consequences for this sort of activism. The popular reality show *The Bachelor* found itself under attack in 2020 for being a bastion of racism because one of its contestants once wore "culturally appropriative costumes" at an "antebellum-themed party." And when the show's host asked the world to show grace and forgiveness toward this contestant, he was shamed to within an inch of his career and was forced to resign.[54]

We're regularly subjected to maximalism and moral preening at a decibel level that suggests a great historical crime is afoot. But when those crimes are examined in detail, they are often revealed to be unintentional trespasses against fluid standards of propriety—and only in an effort to provide the public with something they might enjoy.

So, why has the new progressive activist class leaned so heavily into "the work," emphasizing its least pleasurable aspects and the endurance required to persevere through it all? Perhaps because the perceptible displays of discomfort and offerings demanded of anyone reverent enough to engage in these labors signals not only one's tribal affinities but also an admirable level of commitment to the cause—a commitment so total it involves real sacrifice.

Maybe the devotion required of those who truly throw themselves into the drudgework of personal salvation cannot be measured in rhetoric alone? Maybe the obligations any upstanding person must observe are so sacred that the faithful cannot be trusted to perform these rituals as a matter of course? That commitment must be tangible, verifiable, and undeniable—a saintliness that is "visible" to us all.

3

PRUDENCE

HERESIES OF THE UNCONSCIOUS MIND

Increasingly, the food world has adopted the well-meant but misguided belief that the blending of cultural traditions in cuisine constitutes robbery, imperialism, and even ethnonationalism. For all the good the modern inquisitors think they're doing, the harm they've caused is difficult to overlook.

The Portland, Oregon–based taco truck Kooks Burritos is indicative of how success in the culinary industry can quickly attract a rapacious mob set on destroying something nice in service to karmic notions of fairness.

At first, Kooks was a smashing success, and its proprietors soon became local celebrities. In one interview with a Portland journalist, the truck's owners, Kali Wilgus and Liz Connelly, confessed that they had the idea for their little food truck following a trip to Mexico. There, they fell in love with the cuisine, asked local chefs to share their recipes and techniques, and brought them back to the Pacific Northwest. But the phenomenon's origin story soon attracted a horde of anti-appropriation enforcers.

The two women were accused of being "white cooks bragging about stealing recipes from Mexico." In 2017, the *Portland Mercury* placed their names on an ignoble list of "white-owned appropriative restaurants." "Because of Portland's underlying racism, the people who rightly owned these traditions and cultures that exist are already treated poorly," the *Mercury* exclaimed. Wilgus and Connelly were accused of "erasing and exploiting their already marginalized identities for the purpose of profit and praise." Kooks's online reviews went south and business dried up. The truck was soon forced to fold—not because the food these two women made was bad, but because it was good.[1]

In 2018, Abe Conlon won a James Beard Award for Best Chef in the Great Lakes Region for his work at the Chicago-based eatery Fat Rice. The restaurant had been a local favorite since it opened its doors in 2012. In 2015, it was proclaimed by *Chicago* magazine "the most universally beloved restaurant in Chicago." It specialized in cuisine from the Chinese autonomous region of Macau. Situated across the Pearl River Delta from Hong Kong, Macau was a Portuguese colony from 1783 until 1976. You can see where this is going.

In what has become a familiar story, the restaurant's proprietors sought to convey their support for the antipolice protests that erupted across the country in the summer of 2020 with some Instagram activism. So, the restaurant posted a few anodyne images of protests and a message: "We remain dedicated to our values, we oppose all forms of racism, and we stand with those fighting for justice and equality in our communities in Chicago and across the world." A former employee savaged the restaurant for what he deemed its insufficient gesture of support for racial justice. "You're not going to say #BlackLivesMatter, even though you take from Black culture ALL the time?" he wrote. With that, the dam burst.[2]

A handful of former restaurant employees took to social media to allege that Conlon was abusive and his business practices were racist. *The New York Times* described the chef as the "restaurant-business archetype: a tantrum-prone chef who rules by fear and bullying," and the outrage that was consuming his business a "growing intolerance for a type of verbal mistreatment that has long been accepted as routine in the industry." These are two explicit admissions that what Conlon was accused of was, in essence, standard practices. Perhaps they are standard practices that should not be tolerated as much as they are. But they are standard, nonetheless.

And none of this mattered much anyway. After all, it wasn't the claim that Conlon was a prima donna that did him in; it was the allegation of "cultural appropriation."

"They don't give any cultural context to the origins of their ingredients," wrote this former employee, who was outraged over Fat Rice's failure to namecheck "Black lives matter." "They hike up the prices and sell it back to people of color." Conlon apologized for his abusive conduct and for failing to accurately represent the culture his cuisine was *supposed* to reflect. But no one was looking for an apology; they wanted a sacrifice.

This social media uprising, layered on top of 2020's pandemic-related restrictions on commerce, proved too much to bear, and Fat Rice closed its doors forever. In an interview with Eater, the disgruntled employee who started it all took a victory lap: "I'm not surprised that he is not reopening Fat Rice," he said of Conlon. "I don't think people would have allowed him to. I know I wouldn't have."

In Toronto, Canada, the athletic apparel store Permission tried to set itself apart from the competition by offering its clients access to a chic "broth bar" while they shopped. In partnership with Ripe Nutrition, the store sold "superfood bone broth" along with other "wellness" products. Some enterprising agitators soon noticed that the shop's proprietor was white, and there was something unseemly about a white woman profiting off the sale of "bone broth" and "turtle pho."

"Also sexualizing 'jerk' sauce and pho hot sauce and making 'superfood dumplings' for profit?" *Toronto Star* columnist Evy Kwong contemptuously wrote of this "white-owned" business. "Y'all, I'm sick."[3] We can agree that sexualized jerk sauce does not sound at all appetizing. But transforming it and the revenue from its sale into a racial contretemps was innovative.

The "cultures they are taking from literally fight daily for legitimacy," Kwong added. Her outrage caught the local press's attention, and emulators soon began to mimic her aggravation on social media. Permission eventually agreed that its partnership with a purveyor of soups contributed to the pain endured by those of Asian descent. "We acknowledge the hurt this has caused and apologize sincerely," the apparel store's owner confessed in a statement. "Our pop-up was not in line with community values or our company ethos, and we have decided to part ways, effective immediately." Customers will have to be satisfied with bottled water from now on as they browse for athleisure wear.[4]

These episodes and others like them are revealing of some shared principles on the activist left. Inclusivity and cultural sensitivity, yes. But also, a level of judiciousness sufficient to establish boundaries for oneself and others. Those boundaries are designed to put you in your place and preserve social constancy as a result. And while this principle is ostensibly informed by the wisdom that comes with cultural competence, its practice is often accompanied by extravagant displays of self-denial.

What is it that the progressive left gets out of gratuitous demonstrations of their own capacity for self-deprivation? What satisfaction does any practitioner of a demanding doctrine derive from the rejection of baser temptations? In denying our own desires, we undertake a journey with a far-off goal, which should end—if it ever ends—in a fuller understanding of ourselves and our neighbors. By ignoring our own hungers, we can focus instead on our external conditions and maybe make some improvements. By abstaining from earthly pleasures, we practice restraint, good judgment, and discretion.

All of this is a form of prudence. It is also quite familiar.

It's reasonable to expect that many who adhere to the codes of conduct this book has singled out for criticism will regard the term

"Puritan" as an insult. They're not wrong. But that interpretation is owed as much to this author's intention as it is to the fact that the word "Puritan" was originally designed to be insulting.[5]

When the term first emerged in England in the mid-sixteenth century, it was used to lampoon an emerging religious zealotry. A new form of fanatically reverent Protestantism was on the rise. Its members didn't just hold themselves to unusually exacting standards—they held you to them, too.

It's hard to blame the Renaissance-era English who rolled their eyes at these strange new fundamentalists. The moral offenses they campaigned against ranged from drunkenness to theater, from merry dancing to the celebration of Christmas. The Puritans were, to say the least, exhausting.

As Michael Winship observed, that which invited "idleness, gambling, drinking, and 'wandering up and down from town to town'" was a cause of great concern among these devout Protestants. "They needed to demonstrate their faith by unceasing obedience to God's stern and demanding law." That obedience often manifested in public displays of self-imposed discomfort.[6]

"Fasting, a great ritualized drama of alienation and reconciliation with God," found its way into Puritanism's sixteenth-century instruction manuals. So, too, did humiliating exhibitions of "physical abasement." Swearing off earthly pleasures reinforced what Winship called "a deep sense of sinfulness and unworthiness" among the faithful. "For whom the Lord loveth," reads Hebrews 12:6, a passage favored by puritanical thought leaders, "he chasteneth."

God saves those who suffer for their faith. And few suffered quite like seventeenth-century Congregationalist minister Jeremiah Burroughs.

Burroughs was practically obsessed with unity. The well-known preacher dedicated his life to mending the bonds of religious kinship across Britain's fractious Protestant denominations. He proposed to achieve that through both spiritual exercise and politics, which he practiced as a member of the Westminster Assembly. Burroughs's prolific writings provide us with a window into the thought process of a figure who believed it was his mission to unite the faith.

One of his better-known works, *The Rare Jewel of Christian Contentment*, gives us some idea of what Burroughs believed would reunite quarreling puritanical factions: their own nauseating disgust with themselves.[7]

Burroughs reminds his reader that self-denial and a sense of helplessness before God's awesome might is the pathway to salvation. The acceptance of Christ's teachings demands nothing less than abject supplication. A handful of the maxims to which the aspiring must submit gives you some idea of the exacting nature of Burroughs's theology:

"I am nothing, and I deserve nothing."

"I can do nothing."

"I am so vile that I cannot of myself receive any good."

"I am not only an empty vessel but a corrupt and unclean vessel."

And "If we perish, we will be no loss."

This was not an uplifting read.

By wallowing in contempt for his own desires, though, Burroughs taught his congregants to find fulfillment in deprivation. "No-one ever denied himself as much as Jesus Christ did," Burroughs recalled. "And the nearer we come to learning to deny ourselves as Christ did, the more contented shall we be, and by knowing much of our own vileness, we shall learn to justify God."

Burroughs's sentiments crystalized a strain of puritanical thought that captured the imaginations of his coreligionists long after his untimely death in 1646. As one of America's most prolific Puritan philosophers, Cotton Mather, said: "By loathing of himself continually, and Being very sensible of his loathsome Circumstances, a Christian does what is very pleasing to God."[8]

Harsh as it was, submitting to this sort of merciless self-flagellation has its merits. Through abnegation, we might make ourselves aware of the needs of others that are going unmet. Through abstinence, we learn satisfaction with and gratitude for that with which we have already been blessed. Through self-restraint, we can take some small measure of God's plight. After all, as Burroughs wrote, "he has to deal with a most wretched creature"—namely, you.

What Burroughs describes is an extreme version of an otherwise valuable code of conduct. Circumspection, the skilled management of scarce resources, and governing one's appetites with discipline— these are prudent life skills. Prudence is something we expect from all functioning adults. In practice, the sort of discretion we demand from society's contributing members often involves self-denial—or, in the parlance of modern psychoanalytical discourse, delayed gratification.

Quite unlike their hedonistic predecessors on the left, the New Puritans are enthusiastic practitioners of self-denial. But we're not talking about something as quaint as the Marshmallow Test. The denials of the self toward which the modern progressive activist is inclined are not dissimilar from those that tested the faith of the seventeenth-century's Protestant reformers.

For modern progressive activists, what you should be revulsed by are the cravings and desires that arise from deep within the subconscious mind. Those visceral appetites of the body and the mechanical response they produce when satisfied are unbridled by reason. These pleasures generate involuntary reactions. The uncurbed sigh of contentment you exhale after a sinfully epicurean meal. The uninhibited laugh that bursts from your gut after a ribald joke. Your body betrays you when you succumb to these temptations.

Prudence requires that your every action be carefully curated to maximize virtue. Nowadays, that starts with what you eat.

In late 2018, the United Nations Intergovernmental Panel on Climate Change warned that humanity only had about a dozen years left to stave off a runaway greenhouse effect that could raise global temperatures by as much as 1.5 degrees Celsius. "There is increasing agreement that overall emissions from food systems could be reduced by targeting the demand for meat and other livestock products," the report read.[9] The solution to the problem would be to reduce the amount of meat consumed in the West by as much as 30 percent.

Nonsense! Thirty percent is for cowards and quislings, a study led by Oxford researcher Dr. Marco Springmann and published in the journal *Nature* concluded the following month. Real crusaders for the new nutritional paradigm know that only cajoling most of the planet into giving up at least *90 percent* of their meat-based diet will avert catastrophe.

Ideally, the globe would trade 75 percent of its beef, 90 percent of its pork, and at least half the eggs it consumes on a regular basis for beans, peas, lentils, nuts, and seeds. The restrictions on relatively well-off Westerners should be even more onerous. The industrialized world must all but eliminate beef and reduce milk consumption if the human species is to survive.[10]

By the time these studies and their draconian recommendations were published, a consensus around the need to curtail the developed world's protein intake had already become accepted dogma on the left. "Our changing climate is already making it more difficult to produce food," Barack Obama declared shortly after leaving office. He noted the obstacles before reformers were numerous and went beyond policymaking. "Because a lot of people don't just eat for health," Obama observed, "we eat because it tastes good, too."[11] We're left to wonder if that's a dispassionate statement of fact or an articulation of the problem nutritional reformers face.

If the environmentalist argument against eating meat doesn't move you, what about your health? "Consuming lots of meat is also making people in the United States and other affluent nations unwell," *New York Times* journalist Kendra Pierre-Louis claimed, citing research published in *The Lancet*.[12] And your wellness is not yours alone anymore. Given our increasingly collectivized conception of health care, your individual choices contribute to the overall risk pool. Your personal consumption habits are, therefore, a problem for us all.

"We are facing a growing epidemic of diet-related chronic diseases, and a climate change crisis, both of which are linked to high meat consumption," Harvard University's Nutrition Department chair Frank Hu insisted. Any "blanket recommendation that adults should continue their red meat consumption habits is highly irresponsible."[13]

A scratch at the surface of the facially compelling scientific arguments against eating meat soon exposes the philosophical and moral arguments at the movement's heart.

"We cannot go about our lives as if they were only ours," wrote *We Are the Weather* author Jonathan Safran Foer, who talked about his personal struggle against meat's temptations in almost revelatory terms. "I ate meat a number of times," he confessed. Worse, it "brought me comfort." Foer ached over his misdeed. "How could I argue for radical change, how could I raise my children as vegetarians, while eating meat for comfort?" he asked. "Confronting my hypocrisy has reminded me how difficult it is to even try to live my values."[14]

"Rational morality tugs at us with the slenderest of threads, while meat pulls with the thick-twined chords of culture, tradition, pleasure, the flow of the crowd, and physical yearning," the journalist Nathanael Johnson wrote, "and it pulls at us three times a day." He noted that the ethicist Paul Thompson recommends popularizing veganism "the way religious traditions treat virtues." Echoing Jeremiah Burroughs, Johnson concedes that "Jesus-level self-sacrifice" might be out of reach to us mere mortals. But that doesn't give us license to stop trying.

In 2021, *New York Times* opinion writer Frank Bruni sampled a variety of "fermentation-derived proteins made from microorganisms" marketed by an alternative meat company. He was apparently wowed by the reasonable facsimiles on which he dined. Bruni reported "ample flavor and appeal" in fungus repurposed as meatballs, sausage patties, and chocolate mousse. "Eating them," he wrote, "I felt I was doing good without sacrificing all that much."

The sacrifice of organic protein, he confesses, is measurable. But it is outweighed by the feeling of "doing good."[15]

"Consider a steak," the academics Jan Dutkiewicz and Gabriel N. Rosenberg pondered in *The New Republic*. "With the aroma, the texture, and the savory juices coating your tongue, you will be absorbed. This is what it feels like to eat a perfect steak," they admit. Moreover, "*it feels good*." And that's bad.

These researchers forecast a future in which animal protein is artificially grown in a lab, which will present consumers with a stark moral choice. "By uncoupling the pleasure of meat from suffering and death, cellular agriculture will force us to be more precise about the nature of the pleasures we crave," they contend. "Consumers need only opt for cellular meat over conventional meat: a choice between a moral right and a moral wrong that are otherwise indistinguishable. It is also an answer to the intransigence and passive cruelty of the everyday meat consumer."[16]

Thus, meat consumption is revealed to us as sin. It is an affront to the Eden into which we were conceived. It is a callous pleasure that makes you into a burden your family and neighbors must bear. It is a display of wanton cruelty toward animals, especially when there are alternatives. This is the language of morality.

What's more, it might all be wildly overblown. A Virginia Tech study published in early 2021 determined that the sudden disappearance of all dairy cattle from the United States would reduce greenhouse gas emissions by a whopping 0.7 percent, all while dramatically reducing the available supply of essential nutrients for human beings.[17] Indeed, the U.S. Environmental Protection Agency estimates that all greenhouse gases from meat and dairy production account for just 4 percent of domestic emissions.[18] If every man, woman, and child in America turned vegan tomorrow, estimates suggest the United States would produce just 3 percent fewer emissions than it does at present.[19]

Most global emissions are generated by burning fossil fuels, not the production and consumption of biomass. While livestock's global contribution to greenhouse gas emissions is not negligible, much of it is produced by livestock cultivators in the developing world. It's one thing to berate relatively well-off Westerners for their standards of living. It's quite another to lecture a herd owner in the developing world that his pathway out of subsistence living is killing the planet.

And what of those concerns about your health? In late 2019, researchers published a study in the *Annals of Internal Medicine* evaluating the claim that red meat consumption results in elevated risk of heart disease and cancer. Their research examined sixty-one past studies involving over four million participants, and they concluded that reduced red meat intake had little effect on your relative health risks, much less that someone else's diet will show up in your increased health insurance premiums.[20] "The certainty of evidence for these risk reductions was low to very low," Bradley Johnston, an epidemiologist at Dalhousie University in Canada, observed.[21]

Many advocates of a meat-free diet concede that not everyone will be enticed by the prospect of living on legumes alone. The more reasonable among them admit that animal protein is a dietary staple that cannot easily be replaced by vegetable matter. But they have a solution that they are eager to impose on you: eat more bugs.

There is nothing objectionable about adding (well-prepared) insects to the Western diet. Two billion people regularly consume creepy crawlies, and a minimally adventurous palate should at least be able to conceptualize appetizing insect cuisine. Yet, proponents of this sort of thing seem constitutionally incapable of arguing in favor of a bug-heavy diet because you might actually like it. Enjoyment seems to be beside the point. The point is, always and forever, the satisfaction you will get from the sense that you are contributing to a perceived social good.

"It is hoped that arguments such as the high nutritional value of insects and their low environmental impact, low-risk nature (from a disease standpoint) and palatability may contribute to a shift in perception," read a 2014 U.N. Food and Agriculture Organization report.[22] That hope springs eternal.

"We should be eating bugs to save the world," the entomologist Phil Torres told *The Atlantic* that same year. His arguments are familiar: Bug farming is less land-use intensive. It produces far fewer greenhouse gas emissions. They're better for you, though 100 grams of insects provides about half as much protein as the same amount of chicken, so you'll have to eat a ton of bugs. Finally, it's an exciting change of pace! Only in passing does Torres contend that they "taste good," though he qualified this aside by noting that you may occasionally "get a cricket leg in your tooth."[23]

A 2015 report in the Massachusetts Institute of Technology's *Angles* journal made many of these arguments with a bit more scholarly flair. Eating insects is an "experience," and experiences are nice. Westerners are terribly prejudiced against insect consumption, to their indelible shame. Additives in many of the food products you eat already contain insect derivatives or are a by-product of insect life (e.g., honey). And, of course, a bug-based diet is more sustainable than livestock production and, thus, represents "the last great hope to save the planet." Only once was the word "taste" mentioned—and then, only to describe hexapods as "yummy" and leave it at that.[24]

The almost fanatical way advocates for bug consumption discuss the issue ensures that taste is only an afterthought.

A 2016 interview with a roundtable of academics and experts hosted by *PBS NewsHour* journalist Lisa DesJardins is a case in point. The nearly hour-long discussion with professors, nonprofit directors, and insect-based food producers only briefly touched on palatability, and DesJardins's panelists seemed entirely unprepared to discuss flavor at any length.

"Quickly," the PBS host asked of University of California, Berkeley Graduate School of Journalism professor Michael Pollan, "what do insects taste like?" Pollan confessed to having eaten a few crickets before without elaborating on the subject. He had also once dined on a single ant in a four-star Mexican restaurant, which was "very lemony." Beyond that, "I have a feeling there's great variety in how insects taste." Later, DesJardins admitted that she once consumed a raw cicada and found "there wasn't much taste to it."[25]

At no point did the experts and journalists assembled consider the possibility that being unappetizing could be a bigger obstacle to the widespread adoption of insect consumption than, say, thoughtless Western bigotries or our addiction to resource consumption. That happens a lot.

"Apart from the quick energy boost and healthier lifestyle, eating insects could also provide an economically sensible and sustainable way of life," London's Natural History Museum insists. Also, you're "saving the world."[26]

"An overpopulated world is going to struggle to find enough protein unless people are willing to open their minds, and stomachs, to a much broader notion of food," professor of meat science Louwrens Hoffman told the BBC's *Science Focus* magazine. The invocation of overpopulation—a theory promulgated in 1968 by Paul Ehrlich, which has consistently proven inaccurate but has nevertheless justified almost every eugenicist abuse of the human species that has occurred since the end of the Second World War[27]—is a clue that what you're about to hear is not science.

Nevertheless, Professor Hoffman forged ahead: "There needs to be a better understanding of the difference between animal feed and human food, and a global reappraisal of what can constitute healthy, nutritional, and safe food for all."

If that doesn't sell you, the BBC averred, "Eating insects could help us save the planet."[28]

Even your dog should be eating bugs. "Animal agriculture is one of the biggest contributors to climate change," Mic contributor Susan Shain insisted. Already, we're off the rails. Still, she persevered: According to a 2017 study by University of California, Los

Angeles professor of environment and sustainability Gregory S. Okin, America's 163 million cats and dogs consume an inordinate amount of the world's meat supply and are, therefore, responsible for generating 64 million tons of carbon dioxide annually.

"So, what's an eco-conscious pet owner to do?" Shain asks. Well, PETA recommends feeding these carnivorous animals a vegan diet. While that would be eco-friendly, it has the unfortunate side effect of slowly torturing your pet until it dies an excruciating death. If that sounds unappealing, you can give your pet bug-based foods. It's markedly more expensive than the animal by-products that traditionally go into pet food production, and your dog or cat is unlikely to derive the same satisfaction from cricket protein. But it is "nutritious and bioavailable."

Most of all, "feeding your dog bugs" helps "save the planet."[29]

"I think it started as chicken little, thinking the sky is falling, if we don't all go vegetarian tomorrow the world will end," the culinary expert, chef, and television personality Andrew Zimmern told me. "The more reasoned approach with a more, I think, credible argument is for changing what is available to eat and why."

Zimmern is far from hostile to the arguments in favor of reducing the volume of energy-intensive foods on the market that might also be unhealthy in excessive quantities, like meats and sugars. What's more, he sees a role that governments can play in promoting healthier lifestyles. But Zimmern cautions against the dangers of "the community collective," the "movement from progressive to utopian" conceptions about the optimal relationship between individuals, their governments, and the food they consume to survive.

The conspicuous removal of taste from the equation is revealing of the social desirability biases informing the entomophagy movement. If feeling like you're "saving the world" was the only benefit you derived from eating a medium-rare filet mignon steak basted in butter and thyme, you'd see fewer filets on Western menus.

For the New Puritans, a smug sense of self-satisfaction is the most delicious dish of all.

• • •

Part of what makes dining an enjoyable experience is the educational opportunities afforded the adventurous eater. An ideologue might call the learning experiences savored by those with expansive palates "the work," but steeping yourself in the cultural, geographic, and historical heritage that contributes to unique cuisines is no burden.

There is joy in partaking of authentic, unadulterated, native cuisines. There is joy in the consumption of amalgamated plates that combine the best of many worlds—what is still sometimes called "fusion cuisine." There is joy in the artistry of a genius Michelin-awarded chef whose gastronomic mastery cannot be easily classified, just as there is joy in the simple but fulfilling fare produced by street vendors.

Cooking is an art, and the enjoyment you find in it is subjective. The only wrong way to judge a plate is to believe your assessment of it is objective, and all other interpretations are the flawed product of an uncultivated mind.

Somewhere along the way, the New Puritan has become obsessed with, well, purity. A certain class of activist treats creativity, composition, and synthesis in cuisine like it's an act of sabotage. Today, within certain circles, the distinction between cultural fusion and "cultural appropriation" has blurred beyond the point of recognition.

Food magazines like *Epicurious* and *Bon Appétit*—a venue whose commitment to woke progressivism is so total that it has taken to calling the cuisine native to the Philippines "Filipinx"[30] and confessed that its failure to condemn American sanctions against the Islamic Republic of Iran somehow "inadvertently delegitimized Iranian saffron"[31]—recently committed themselves to "archive repair." It's as Orwellian as it sounds. These publications are rewriting their own histories.

"The language that we use to talk about food has evolved so much from, sure, the 1960s but also the 1990s, and I think it is our duty as journalists, as people who work in food media, to make sure that we are reflecting that appropriately," said *Bon Appétit's* executive editor, Sonia Chopra.[32]

That mission is a work in progress, and progress cannot come soon enough for the activist class. In late 2020, one Twitter user stumbled across a recipe for the traditional Jewish cookie hamantaschen in an unadulterated section of *Bon Appétit's* archives. The offense becomes clear from the headline: "How to Make Hamantaschen Actually Good."

The recipe violated traditional kosher dietary guidelines, which prohibit, for example, mixing dairy and meat products like eggs and butter. The magazine's editors scrubbed it and apologized for their cultural insensitivities. But being "good" isn't something to which Jewish bakers are wholly allergic.

"One hundred years ago, the crunchiness and lack of taste was a source of pride for some Jews," the Takeout's Aimee Levitt observed. "Nowadays, kosher bakers, armed with regulated ingredients and ovens that hold temperature, have written reliable recipes. (Others of us who don't keep kosher just throw our hands up and say, the hell with it, I'm using butter. Or cream cheese.)"[33]

Being "good" isn't everything, but nor is it something to be ashamed of. And the existence of alternative preparations for a particular culture's favorites does not detract from that culture. It adds to it by expanding the number of people who wouldn't otherwise have been exposed to those dishes. Culture is not a zero-sum game.

"Authenticity" has, however, become an inviolable standard among anti-appropriation activists, to the detriment of talented chefs and those who would delight in their work.

Celebrity chef Gordon Ramsay's London restaurant, Lucky Cat, was savaged for marketing itself as an "authentic Asian Eating House," even though its head chef was not, in fact, Asian.[34] Cleverly, Ramsay put his critics on the defensive by noting that his restaurants "do not discriminate based on gender, race, or beliefs and we don't expect anyone else to," no matter how much anti-appropriation activists would appreciate it.[35]

It's probably no surprise that something as quintessentially American as apple pie is also tarnished in the New Puritan's imagination. *The Guardian*'s Raj Patel informs us that this comforting pastry is a moral atrocity. The recipe is "a variant on an English pumpkin pie recipe," thereby rendering the dessert both appropriative and sullied by the legacy of English colonialism. It is a symbol of "domesticity," harkening back to America's maltreatment of women with every tasty bite. It is a ruthless emblem of capitalist exploitation: Sugarcane is a by-product of the exploitation of black Caribbean laborers, and apples owe their origins to the Spanish colonists who brought this Central Asian fruit to North America in their quest to pilfer the continent's bounty. Every morsel is a sinful reminder of your place on the wrong side of the struggle for "food justice."[36]

Yogurt, too, is off-limits. "Using a transnational and comparative cultural studies approach, this essay investigates how yogurt, perceived as a strange and foreign food in the early to mid-twentieth-century United States, became localized through intersectional processes of feminization and de-exoticization," reads what I promise you is the very real abstract of a 2016 study published in the academic journal *Gastronomica*. The author, University of Notre Dame professor Perin Gürel, alleges that the yogurt's "connections to the Middle East" have led to Orientalist abuses of the product in the West.

Cultural appropriation in food is everywhere. Nutrition blogger Shana McCann noted that it can be found in "restaurants with a white [person as] front of house" or in "Asian-inspired" menu items. It is apparent when white bloggers post their "healthy soul food recipes," or in what critics of a particular ethnic background decide to label "refined" or "elevated" and what they don't.[37] In general, it is a theory that substitutes context, taste, and personal experience with race essentialism.

Not all scandalous episodes of alleged appropriation in the food world result in career-ending controversies. Most attacks like those above are intended as brushback pitches. It's a power play reserved almost exclusively for the successful.

Despite his Caucasian upbringing in Oklahoma, New York City–based chef Rick Bayless became one of America's most famous preparers of and experts on Mexican food. The successful restaurateur was even tapped by President Barack Obama in 2010 to cater a state dinner for Mexican president Felipe Calderón. His background has also landed him in hot water. "Just Google 'Rick Bayless' and 'appropriation' and you'll get plenty to feast on," NPR advised its readers. "Trust us."[38]

"I know that there have been a number of people out there that criticized me only—only—because of my race," Bayless said in his defense. "Because I'm white, I can't do anything with Mexican food. But we have to stop and say, 'Oh wait, is that plain racism then?'" For some self-appointed culture police, the very act of defending himself from accusations of racial bigotry was itself evidence of bigotry.[39] For others, it was simply "whiny."[40]

At least Bayless has had the strength and support structure to persevere through it all. Andy Ricker did not.

Ricker was an award-winning chef and bestselling cookbook author by the time he founded the popular Thai restaurant chain Pok Pok. He studied Thai cuisine for thirteen years, lived and worked in Southeast Asia for much of his adult life, and had become a recognized expert in his field. But Ricker is also white. For some, that's what mattered most.

In 2020, Ricker's restaurant group shut its doors permanently. In a statement, he blamed the pressures of the pandemic for the decision, but not entirely. "The ability to focus on the raison d'être of Pok Pok became more and more impossible," he said, "and it became more and more about logistics and putting out fires, less and less about hospitality and vision."[41] In an interview with *Mel* magazine, Ricker confessed that he would be taking his talents back to Thailand if only to escape the exhaustion of culinary politics in the United States.

"I knew before I opened the restaurant back in 2005 that what I was doing was potentially blasphemous," he confessed. "The best route for this would be to make the food as I learned it, try to do the best job I could, present it as it should be, and not take any credit for the recipe in any way. Or say I've discovered this shit." And just as he predicted, the mob did come for him.

"Some of the people who are really, really vocal with [criticism] you know, I've been alive and cooking this food since before they were born," Ricker said with disdain. He, too, is sympathetic toward the ideals of a movement that so drained him of enthusiasm for his life's work. But his ordeal appears to have shaken some of that conviction.[42]

"Everyone, not just my industry, is shying away from controversy for fear of being attacked," Andrew Zimmern continued in our conversation. "Social media has turned us into a gotcha society.

"When it comes to things like cultural appropriation," Zimmern added, "I thought of the phrase 'accountability before unity.' I think we do need to educate and hold each other accountable to a certain standard. Otherwise, we're going to increase the divide between us." While Zimmern is critical of the activists who have "used these things as an excuse to drive a wedge" or to "cancel someone," he maintains that there is utility in creating taboos around the outright theft of someone else's cultural heritage. "The argument made by these new culture warriors when it comes to food, in general, are mostly correct," he affirmed.

"Sometimes you're in the middle of a social-justice movement ocean and can't see the land behind you or in front of you," Zimmern concluded. "But you're not lost. The middle is where it seems really murky." That's a valuable perspective, but this policing action's mounting costs are tangible, while its benefits are mostly conjectural.

Gallons of ink have been spilled in the effort to define what constitutes "appropriation" and to help its opponents identify it when they see it. Most who commit to this course settle on the idea that there is a "fine line" between appropriation and appreciation. But what if it isn't a "fine line" at all? What if flippancy, mockery, and carelessness are not so subtle that you need a PhD to know what you're looking at (or, in this case, tasting)?

As we've now observed across multiple fields, there is a prominent strain of cultural criticism today that resents your enjoyment of anything that is not tempered by some grueling pedagogy. Those critics resent unalloyed enjoyment. But what if that internal torment is theirs, not yours? What if their torture is being imposed on you in ways that really *aren't* all that productive?

Ultimately, the logic of this ideological approach to reforming how Americans produce and consume food gives way to an unavoidable conclusion: Progress is the problem.

The Guardian's Damian Carrington summarized the matter succinctly: "The global food system is the biggest driver of destruction of the natural world," he wrote. A "vicious cycle" of "cheap food," which creates more competition, generates incentives to export food around the world and contributes to environmental degradation.[43]

A February 2021 *New York Times* profile of "activists working to remake the food system" echoed some of these sentiments. "In the blunt equation of capitalist production," *Times* contributor Ligaya Mishan wrote, we "treat food as a commodity rather than a necessity," which "is to accept that there will always be people who can't afford it and must go hungry."[44] That would be a moral atrocity if it were true. Fortunately, it is not.

Following the global triumph of capitalism after the collapse of the Soviet Union in 1991 (hidebound holdouts in places like Cuba and North Korea notwithstanding), undernourishment declined worldwide from 19 to 11 percent, according to the World Bank.[45] That happy condition coincided with the emergence of roughly 1 billion people out from the depths of extreme poverty (defined as surviving on less than $1.25 per day) over approximately the same time frame. This is attributable to the establishment in 1991 of the first real global marketplace since it collapsed in 1914 with the onset of World War I.

The capitalist enterprise has contributed to the development of heartier, disease-resistant produce and cereal grains. In the United States, production of cereal grains, soybeans, corn, and other aggregate crops has steadily increased while the price has declined.[46]

That trend—increased yields and reduced costs—is apparent all over the world. The exception to this rule is sub-Saharan Africa, where, as *National Geographic* reported in 2020, the "use of [genetically modified] crops is less common."[47]

"Since attitudes toward GM crops tend to correlate with education levels and access to information about the technology, there is a concern that sub-Saharan African farmers may be hesitant to adopt GM crops," the report continued. Not coincidentally, progress toward a hunger-free planet has not reached this region, where crop yields have failed to keep pace with the rest of the world, and child malnutrition remains persistently high.

Global inequalities are less a concern for the activists profiled in the *Times* than their chief focus: the "late-empire hedonism" apparent in Americans' love of food.

"It's no coincidence that as Americans have grown ever more estranged from the sources of their food and the largely unseen labor required to produce it, food itself has become a national obsession," the *Times* profile continued, "from televised cooking shows and the deification of chefs to Instagram #foodporn." Mishan laments how the modern "food movement" has rallied the public toward progressive activism with appeals to a "vaguely feel-good mantra" rather than calls to arms. But some activists are trying to fix that through, of all things, the selective application of racial discrimination.

For example, "a food stall where white customers are charged $30 for a plate of food that costs Black customers only $12, to reflect the disparity in median income between white and Black house-holds in New Orleans, or a church hall where the gentrification-themed dinner menu lists a half chicken for $50,000—again for white diners only, with Black diners eating for free."

The activists' goal, Mishan notes, is to promote a broader un-derstanding of racial disparities in various underexamined areas of American society. That's a laudable objective, but it is being pur-sued in the most unproductive way imaginable. This sort of activ-ism's practical (and likely desired) effect is to remove the possibility that you might forget even briefly the torment of existence.

As it happens, there is a broad marketplace for that kind of tor-ture. For all progressive activists' hostility toward capitalism's ani-mal spirits, they're not above exploiting that economic opportunity. Enter the organization "Race 2 Dinner."

"Our mission is simple," the organization asserts, "reveal the naked truth about RACISM in America and UNLEASH YOUR POWER as white women to dismantle it." How does this group propose to do that? Simple: by convincing wealthy white patrons to fork over upwards of twenty-five hundred dollars for the privilege of being lectured about their unconscious racism.

"If you did this in a conference room, they'd leave," Race 2 Din-ner cofounder Saira Rao told *The Guardian*. "But wealthy white women have been taught never to leave the dinner table." Presumably, Rao's casual ethnic stereotyping is the enlightened sort.

As *The Guardian* notes, the patrons for this sort of thing are unlikely to be those who would most benefit from the experi-ence. They are mostly "well-read and well-meaning" Democratic-voting women, some of whom have spouses of a different race or even adopted black children. Nevertheless, most don't need much prompting to "confess" their racial biases, acknowledge "wrongdo-ing," and be "willing to change."

"Before attending a dinner or seminar, there is required read-ing," NBC's *Today* observed. The ice is usually broken by the con-versation leaders, who bring up "a familiar topic," only to subject it to critical race theory–flavored dismemberment until it gives up its racist past. Take yoga, for instance.

"[The dinner] starts off, Saira says something about yoga and how yoga is cultural appropriation and yoga owners here in the U.S. do not hire black and brown Indian women to teach," Regina Jackson, the organization's other cofounder, recalled of one especially productive soiree.[48] In this way, the dinner party's attendees are guided toward a recognition of how they are "complicit in a system that hurts Black and brown people." Bon appétit!

The spirit of Jeremiah Burroughs is alive and well in the activism we see on display among the puritanical left. Only by understanding your own flawed and sinful nature can you learn to appreciate a gratuitous level of self-denial. The pleasures and comforts of eating good food around a table surrounded by friends might be gratifying, but not nearly as much as the spiritual rapture found in ruining that experience.

What do progressive activists get out of all this? Of course, the personal satisfaction derived from the practice of self-discipline, but also the sense that they're contributing not just to their own salvation but to the redemption of the entire world.

They satisfy themselves by making what they're certain are the right choices about what you should be allowed to eat, read, look at, and listen to, but the work doesn't end there. Perhaps nothing is as important to the promotion of a virtuous society as what you're allowed to laugh at.

Six years have now passed since some of stand-up's biggest names swore off college audiences. Comics like Jerry Seinfeld, Larry the Cable Guy, and Chris Rock loudly gave up on undergraduates, leaving a lot of money on the table in the process. "They're so PC," Seinfeld told ESPN's Colin Cowherd in 2015. "They just want to use these words: 'That's racist.' 'That's sexist.' 'That's prejudice.' . . . They don't know what the hell they're talking about."[49] The comics who continued to perform for those audiences have had to learn this lesson the hard way.

In a 2018 op-ed for *The New York Times*, the comic Nimesh Patel described the joke that got him removed from the stage mid-act:

> *I open by saying I live in Hell's Kitchen, a diverse area in New York populated by, among others, gay black men who are not shy about telling me they don't approve of what I'm wearing. I try to learn things from everyone I encounter, and one day I realize oh, this is how you know being gay can't be a choice—no one would choose to be gay if they're already black. No one is doubling down on hardship. Then I say, no black dude wakes up and thinks that being a black man in America is too easy. No black dude says, "I'm going to put on a Madonna halter top and some Jordans and make an Indian dude real uncomfortable." That's not a choice.*

The joke bombed. And maybe it should have, Patel confessed. By his own admission, it was a little dated. But it had worked in clubs and before diverse audiences before, so why shouldn't it sell with an audience full of college students?

Though he felt at the time like the entire audience had turned on him, Patel soon became convinced that his ordeal was imposed on him only by a few energetic activists. What's more, some of the students who objected to his mistreatment went out of their way to apologize to him in a more private setting. It turns out that they were only too afraid to speak up at the time lest they, too, become targets.

Patel found solace in that, but it is cold comfort.[50]

Much of the effort to impose a purity test on comedy relies on the retroactive application of artistic standards that either did not exist or were not rigidly enforced at the time of a work's composition. Comedians are as vulnerable to "archive repair" as anyone else.

Sarah Silverman, an outspoken liberal in good standing with her movement, found herself on the wrong end of one representative retroaction in late 2019.

"I recently was going to do a movie, a sweet part," she confessed during an appearance with podcast host Bill Simmons. "Then, at eleven p.m. the night before, they fired me because they saw a picture of me in blackface from that episode." The episode she's referring to was a 2007 segment on Comedy Central's *The Sarah Silverman Show*, in which the host painted her face in exaggeratedly stereotypical minstrel show makeup to satirically explore whether it was more difficult to be black or Jewish in America.

Silverman confessed that her judgment was flawed by any standard, but her intention was to be funny. A joke is a risky endeavor because the enterprise involves creating and releasing tension— often around social taboos. Generating that kind of tension produces anxiety and invites conflict. Nevertheless, Silverman acknowledged her mistake. "I'm horrified by it, and I can't erase it," she said of the offending sketch. "That was such liberal-bubble stuff, where I actually thought it was dealing with racism by using racism."[51]

Nonetheless, Silverman maintained that the effort to impose professional consequences on her for a bit that didn't even make a ripple in her industry at the time overturns the existing rules of engagement. "If you say the wrong thing," Silverman said, "everyone is, like, throwing the first stone. It's a perversion."[52]

Comic Shane Gillis found himself facing a similar set of circumstances. In September 2019, *Saturday Night Live* announced that Gillis was one of three new comics joining the cast for its 2020 season. Soon thereafter, journalists and activists alike applied a fine-tooth comb to Gillis's body of work.

One of those activists, freelance writer and comedy reporter Seth Simons, found that Gillis had used slurs when describing Asian Americans on one 2018 episode of a podcast he cohosted. "Why do the fucking ch**ks live there?" he asked of New York City's Chinatown. Later in the podcast, he adopted a mock Asian accent while describing his interactions with Asian migrants. Demonstrating some awareness of the buttons he was deliberately pressing, Gillis called out the bigotry in his own remarks. "Nice racism," he said of himself. "Good racism."[53]

Soon after this inorganic resurfacing, a familiar content engine revved to life. "It all raises the question," *Vulture*'s Megh Wright asked, "did *Saturday Night Live* vet its new cast members? It's 2019, so at this point, there's really no excuse for this kind of slip-up." Refinery 29's Tara Edwards reported that "many celebrities and comedians reacted to the clips by calling out both Gillis and SNL." She cited only one: actor, director, and producer Daniel Dae Kim.[54]

Gillis quickly penned an apology. "If you go through my ten years of comedy, most of it bad, you're going to find a lot of bad misses," he wrote. "My intention is never to hurt anyone, but I am trying to be the best comedian I can be and sometimes that requires risks." But the apology only drew more attention to the original offense, and *Saturday Night Live* was forced to act. "After talking with Shane Gillis, we have decided that he will not be joining *SNL*," the show's creator, Lorne Michaels, said in a statement. "The language he used is offensive, hurtful, and unacceptable. We are sorry that we did not see these clips earlier, and that our vetting process was not up to our standard."

"When I started," Gillis told me, "you could definitely get away with just about anything. I was in Philadelphia in 2016; that's when I noticed the big shift.

"It went from a group of these people that, like, we were all friends—like, everybody pretty much got along—and then it went from, I don't want to say overnight, but it really crept in where all of a sudden people got very, very political," he continued. "Every local scene has been experiencing this for the last five years. There's been a fracture in every comedy scene. Groups of people where we used to hang out—we used to go to parties together—they were doing interviews saying that I was a bad person as soon as they could."

Gillis recalled one episode in which an activist created a

spreadsheet of every local comedy show to inventory the gay people, minorities, or women performing at Philadelphia-based open mic nights. Unsurprisingly, she discovered that much of the talent pool on Philly stages were white and male. But that is more than likely a result of self-selection, not bigots keeping diverse comics down. "The people that were doing open mics were ninety percent weird white dudes," Gillis observed. Nevertheless, the sensitivities of the moment forced comedians to take a critical look at their own biases and turn on those who did not.

Gillis has apologized repeatedly for the failed attempt at humor that cost him his job on *SNL*. He "understood why some people were upset." And yet, of the activists' outrage, "I also understood that a lot of people were faking it." Gillis maintains that it takes a certain amount of effort and intellectual competence to "disregard intent" and "pretend" what they are hearing isn't designed to amuse but to foment hatred and division. "They have no problem disregarding what the absolute truth is," he insisted, "and I think a lot of them are intelligent enough to know what the truth is."

Like so many targets of this form of activism, Gillis says that his political affinities are not with the right. "When I got canceled, I could have gone on all these right-wing shows and become like a right-wing guy, which I'm not," he relayed. "I could have easily done that and got a huge fan base." But that would, in his view, be to surrender his convictions—professional, as well as political. "You do all these interviews where people are trying to get you to say, 'Fuck cancel culture,' and, 'Sorry, liberals. Are you triggered?' And I'm not going to do that."

Gillis isn't alone in expressing the concern that the effort to impose strict but evolving and unpredictable standards on performance art will have the unintended effect of thinning the progressive herd. Sarah Silverman has expressed similar concerns. "Without a path to redemption, when you take someone, you found a tweet they wrote seven years ago or a thing that they said, and you expose it and you say, this person should be no more, banish them forever," she worried. "They're going to find someplace where they are accepted, and it's not going to be with progressives."[55]

"Speaking into an echo chamber seems like the opposite of what stand-up is for," Gillis insisted during our interview. "I hate to ever talk seriously about comedy, because comedy is fun."

Ideally, yes. But not everyone agrees. Many of comedy's harshest critics contend that stand-up and comedic screenplays must, like everything else in society, not just be funny but *politically valuable*. Otherwise, comedy becomes a mere frivolity. Or, worse, a permission structure that allows you to shirk your responsibility to contribute to the making of a more just world.

"The biggest issue is that the intent is taken out of the equation," the comedian and author Judy Gold told me during a discussion about the censorious impulses overtaking her industry. "And that's where it all goes downhill. When intent and context and nuance are taken out of the equation, it's no longer a joke." For a particular sort of activist, "intent and context" are immaterial when the promotion of moral clarity is the goal.

The new puritanism is not a live-and-let-live movement. It is not tolerant of humor that may not appeal to its members, but that has its own audience. This is a movement that seeks to assimilate all things, even simple pleasures like laughter, into one central political project.

In one representative article on "the limits of liberal comedy" for the center-left journal *Current Affairs*, essayist Will Sloan skewers, of all people, former *Daily Show* host Jon Stewart for being a squish. Sloan marveled at Stewart's "false equivalence" in his appeals to national unity by equating "terrorists and racists" with "Stalinists and theocrats" (we are left to wonder which of these Sloan would presumably go to bat for). He marveled over how "clueless" Stewart sounds by the standards of today's "discourse on structural racism and microaggressions." But the meat of the author's indictment is that Stewart, who spent much of his television career attacking Republican politicians, is just not savage enough because he failed to consistently mete out "public humiliation" to the right targets.[56]

Sloan's critique of comedy that isn't politically useful isn't his innovation. In 2014, Thomas Frank, culture critic and author of *What's the Matter with Kansas,* took aim at Harold Ramis. The late comic actor and writer's ribald 1980s comedies tended to feature "prudish or strait-laced" antagonists. Those priggish heavies were routinely undone by a band of plucky upstarts, whose contempt for polite society's conventions was presented as a virtue.

In Frank's telling, Ramis was laying the ideological groundwork for social irresponsibility of the worst sort. His work advanced a paradigmatic shift in which "idealism" was regarded as "strictly for suckers." He established the goofy, misogynistic "frat boy" as a figure worthy of veneration. Worst of all, Frank seriously contends, Ramis's stylistic choices contributed to the 2008 meltdown of the mortgage market. "The dick joke is not always what it seems to be," Frank contended. "The dick joke is not always your friend."

"Jokes aren't your friend," laughed *National Lampoon* veteran and another target of Frank's ire, comedy writer P. J. O'Rourke, when we spoke. "Jokes are supposed to upset people." Structurally, anything resembling a joke must "upset people on moral or customary grounds" because "all jokes are a form of sprung logic. They're bad syllogisms."

The involuntary act of laughter is the result of setting an expectation and surprising the audience with an unanticipated conclusion. The joke is "two planes of meaning at an unexpected angle," O'Rourke explained. "All jokes offend the mind to one degree or another, just on the basis of rationality."

Judy Gold echoed O'Rourke's sentiments. "You'll make a joke about a subversive topic that is hilarious, and so many times the audience will laugh and then catch themselves, and switch over to 'ooh,'" she observed. "It's like their instincts are to laugh. And there's nothing wrong with that." The laugh is involuntary. The "ooh" is the conscious mind putting a stop to an unconscious response.

But evolving standards and tastes are a feature of the human condition, and stand-up is no exception. A student of humor for much of his influential career, O'Rourke observed that, like all things, "humor goes in and out of fashion." But just as it would be nonsensical to make everyone who ever wore a fur coat in the mid-twentieth-century account for their cruelty today, it is obtuse to judge artwork that is a product of its time by the standards that pertain now.

"There are shifting fashions in what is considered amusing," he continued. "Society shifts quite a lot on what is considered funny and acceptably funny."

"Acceptably funny." O'Rourke practically expectorates the phrase with deserved contempt. There have always been scolds for whom "these uncontrollable desires, these automatic responses" are dangerous. And there are few higher callings in life than to avoid being one of them.

"Serious people have always been opposed to pleasure for its own sake," O'Rourke concluded. "You've gotta be proud of yourself for something. And if you're not having any fun, you've gotta be proud of that."

In a "heartbreaking" twist that comedian Bill Burr likened to the "Red Scare," even working comics have begun to police the content of their fellow stand-ups to ensure that what they say isn't just funny but *politically valuable*.[57] Thus, the industry itself has begun to adopt and enforce standards imposed on it by its critics, and all with the singular aim of ensuring that there is value to stand-up beyond laughter for laughter's sake.

Just as the New Puritans care more about savoring righteousness than savory food, they would rather applaud comedians than laugh with them. Seth Simons, the freelancer whose reporting on Gillis led *SNL* to dissolve their relationship, wrote one of the more illustrative examples of this line of thought. As someone who has dedicated his career to covering the "inequality and extremism" that thrives in the stand-up "scene's transgressive edge," Simons wrote in an essay for *The New Republic*, he has unique insights into comedy's "right-wing politics."

The writer's particular focus is a form of the art that became popular in the early 2000s, and that fans and practitioners colloquially deemed "cringe." Transgressive is the right word for it. "Cringe" humor leverages racial antagonism, sexism, unspeakably tragic events, and even criminal activity for humor value. To read this clinical description of dark humor, anyone could be forgiven for assuming that the people who enjoy such jokes, much less tell them, must be pretty awful human beings. And yet, that is the essence of a lot of comedy to one degree or another—to satirize the terrible, to plumb the darkest depths of existence for levity, and to laugh your way up the gallows steps.

"The far-right did not come into being by chance. People shaped it," Simons averred. And many of those people, he insists, were humorists who did not know the kind of fire they were playing with. "They offered permission to revel in racism and sexism, in homophobia and transphobia, and they earned devoted followings in return," he concludes.

What Simons takes issue with isn't this style of humor so much as its valuelessness to the engineers of the virtuous society. No one expects any of the stand-ups he criticizes to act out the antisocial behaviors they're lampooning onstage. Simons is afraid that *you* might, impressionable sap that you are.

That sentiment is similar to what an earlier generation of puritanically inclined Americans said about comics like Lenny Bruce, George Carlin, and Richard Pryor. Bruce was arrested for violating the New York State penal code barring the "corruption of morals of youth and others."[58] The broadcast of Carlin's "seven dirty words" routine resulted in a complaint from a group named "Morality in Media," which found its way to the Supreme Court.[59] Pryor's eponymous 1977 show on NBC was routinely chopped up, censored, and bowdlerized by the network until it was canceled after just four episodes, in part because of its flippant attitude toward racial dynamics in the United States.[60]

To the extent that anything tethers these comics together across the generations it is their willingness to test and break taboos, and to do so from a perspective that offends aristocratic sensibilities. "This is why, as Constance Rourke has pointed out, the whole of the American comic tradition has been one of social criticism," read James McPherson's 1975 *New York Times* profile of Pryor and his critics. "And vernacular humorists, from Mark Twain and the great political cartoonists to the best stand-up comics, have depended on an earthy level of language to provide resonance to their criticisms."[61] That "earthy language" still offends those for whom challenges to social conventions are regarded as attacks on their very identities.

No matter how valuable they may be—and most conventions that discourage antisocial behavior are, indeed, valuable—stigmas invite iconoclasts to challenge them. That's the cost of living in a free society, and it's a low price to pay.

Comics whose shtick is to shock, offend, or confuse is as old as stand-up itself. But the New Puritan doesn't see all experimental forms of comedy as a threat to a wholesome society's good working order. At least, not so long as that experimentation comports with the new progressive virtues. One comic mind who has become a figure of veneration among the progressive activist clique is Australian anti-comic, Hannah Gadsby.

General American audiences got their first taste of Gadsby's act when her hit Netflix special *Nanette* exploded into the cultural zeitgeist in the spring of 2018. Most of her act is innovative and hilarious. At least, it is when she wants to make you laugh. But her most ardent fans do Gadsby a disservice. What they especially love about *Nanette* is when she is consciously, explicitly, and aggressively not funny.

Gadsby's style is unique. She makes you laugh, yes, but she will occasionally circle back to the punchline of that joke she told five minutes ago to dissect it, forcing you to critically examine your own sense of humor. She will critique her own joke structure to make you wonder if the trauma she experienced is really all that funny. And occasionally, she will build the tension that would otherwise lead to a laugh and ostentatiously refuse to allow you a release.

"I've made my story into a joke," Gadsby says at one particularly difficult point in her act. "And there's only so long I can pretend not to be serious." This, not the laugh, is what so enlivens the puritanical stylist for whom humor value is a trivial diversion we cannot afford.

The New Yorker's Cassie da Costa hailed the comic for abandoning the "neat package of setup and punchline" and replacing it with "her humility and her anger." Gadsby assaults the audience with the "revelation that pain has to be mined, manipulated, and stripped of context to make a good joke."[62] The same could be said of "cringe" humor, the subject matter of which is not at all funny at first blush. The primary distinction between these two approaches is that, while they build the same tension, "cringe" humorists allow you a laugh at the end.

"Gadsby wields her craft like a weapon, lancing out the trauma and forcing us to look at it," *The Guardian*'s Jane Howard wrote in what reads more like a threat than a review of a comedy special. "She looks at a world of people masking their trauma and gives permission for it to be seen."[63]

Throughout the performance, the comic "confronts" us, "challenges" us, and forces the audience to "interrogate its discomfort" with "her own humanity," *Vox*'s Aja Romano observed.[64] That's a bit overdone, but it gives you some insight into what the puritanical progressive revels in when it comes to comedy. It isn't the laugh; it's the labor. And Gadsby's act is laborious by design.

Contrary to the scolds, Gadsby's anticomedy and the anticomedy of the "cringe" humorists are more alike in their contempt for social conventions. The primary distinction between them is that fans of the former art form are beholden to an all-consuming integralism that doesn't allow for the existence of anything else.

"I think what Gadsby is getting at here is an overall allegiance to the idea of the joke, the setup, the punch line; a traditional stand-up ideology, as it were, that prizes familiar and reassuring rhythms that she's not loyal to anymore," entertainment writer Matt Zoller Seitz conjectured. "How we tell jokes and stories, and whether we decide to tell a joke or a story, expresses who we are and what we believe." Thus, the stand-up's act isn't an act at all. It's a reflection of your true self, and we can judge it just as we might judge you.

By contrast, Zoller Seitz found a special released around the same time by HBO host and comedian Bill Maher to be "listless, comedy-flavored grumbling" in part because it takes caustic aim at the priggishness Gadsby's fans embrace. It is particularly rich that Zoller Seitz seems to think he is singling out the forces of social conformity for criticism rather than enforcing social conformity himself.

"Maher's material is reactionary in the dictionary sense of the word," he insists, "opposing political or social liberalization or reform, or at least dramatically signaling his annoyance with the idea that there might be another way to live and think beyond whatever he's comfortable with." It's hard to square that assertion with Zoller Seitz's criticism of Maher's "libertarian posturing," or his palpable distaste for Dave Chappelle's "confused" (more accurately, nondogmatic) politics, and his claim that "Maher is the past" and "Gadsby is the future."[65]

What we are talking about are tastes, and tastes are personal. There is no wrong way to appeal to any one individual taste, just as there is also no right way to appeal to all tastes simultaneously. Only through the extirpation of taste entirely can we approximate the kind of cultural homogeneity that the New Puritan finds so comforting. And in that, we encounter a curious contradiction.

The modern progressive moralist prides himself on his embrace of diversity in all things but thought. She takes great pains to accommodate all forms of self-expression, just so long as they lead us toward a placid, governable consensus. They despise monoculturalism even as they devote their every waking moment to bringing that very condition about.

What this attack on imprudent humor amounts to is an assault on the immune system of our body politic. Satire forces us to confront our preconceptions, but it does so in a way that isn't so confrontational that your defenses are immediately raised. It is the antigen that stimulates an essential and strengthening intellectual response. We would be cerebrally infirmed without it.

Ultimately—and it may be inevitable now—the market pressures these trends are bringing about will give way to an atomized culture in which artists thrive not on mass appeal but small, committed audiences. That narrowness has its own benefits, foremost among them that a devoted band of supporters who are beholden to an artist—not an institution—render that artist un-cancelable. But this is not a wholly desirable condition.

Just as in the stigmatization of literature, that narrowness becomes harder to police. Prohibitions on impropriety and the taboos that render antisocial behaviors impolite thrive in environments dominated by like minds. Broad exposure to diverse audiences has a moderating effect on content. And if that moderation is what the aspiring censors want, their actions are making that outcome less likely.

There can be no doubt that social standards relating to comedy have shifted, but that is the result of agreed-upon cultural attitudes. No longer are Americans transfixed as they were at the turn of the twentieth century by minstrel shows. No longer would it be acceptable to produce a bit whose only humor value is found in satirizing ethnic stereotypes (like 1913's famously anti-Semitic "Cohen on the Telephone," which, incidentally, was the first record to sell more than one million copies).[66] Even the ribald fare that mainstream audiences flocked to just forty years ago, with their bullying protagonists and objectified heroines, only hold up today insofar as they are classic artifacts. Our evolving shared cultural standards beget a more universal set of values.

But common cultural standards require a common culture, which gives way to an intuitive understanding about what an artist's intention is. Without that commonality, the antisocial behaviors that the activist class wants to stigmatize will find a warm, dark space in which they can thrive just beneath the surface of polite society. And while the New Puritans are congratulating themselves on what a good job they've done sanitizing the culture, their worst fears will be metastasizing just out of sight and well beyond their reach.

"Neither the right nor the left had such a hair trigger in the old days," Noam Dworman, the owner of New York City's Comedy Cellar, told me. "It was also better because all the self-censorship that is going on now means that we're going to have inferior conclusions drawn in the public square. Garbage in, garbage out." Judy Gold agreed. "When you silence people, there's no discourse; there's no evolution. Without discourse, you don't evolve," she said. "You go backward."

Humor, like food, elicits involuntary responses. And just as we cannot evaluate those instinctual reactions without understanding that our impulses are innate, we cannot train ourselves to have a spontaneous reaction to boring stimuli. Not if we're honest with ourselves. Because the laugh is many things, but what it is not is an intellectual exercise.

And for the New Puritan, maybe that's no loss. These are serious times, after all. There's nothing funny about that.

4

AUSTERITY

AN UNADORNED LIFE

King Charles I dedicated much of his twenty-six-year reign to keeping the Protestant Reformation's heady passions from tearing his kingdom apart. Ultimately, he failed. But not before he'd shown his English subjects something they'd been missing: a good time.

From the start of his reign in 1626, Charles was hounded by the Puritan-led Parliament that resented his belief in the divine right of kings to rule their subjects however they saw fit. Although he lived a life of public probity and expected as much of his courtiers and nobles, Charles's naked antagonism toward the puritanical religious zeal overtaking his country contributed to the tensions that culminated in the English Civil War.

In 1642, following a series of protracted confrontations with Parliament, Charles joined an accompaniment of soldiers and personally sought the arrest of five of the assembly's more impertinent members. Charles's targets escaped, but the assault on Parliament's sovereignty catalyzed the formation of an antiroyalist army loyal to the legislature. The rest of Charles's life consisted of brutal warfare, ignominious surrender, imprisonment, exile, and, finally, execution for high treason in 1649. But the litany of offenses against Puritanism of which Charles was accused began long before the faith's adherents wielded that fatal axe.

Charles conspicuously rejected Puritanism's fervent religious antipathy toward the performing arts. That rejection led poor William Prynne to write his seditious book against the theater, costing that Puritan lawyer his freedom, his ears, and five thousand pounds. Charles sought to restore the monarchy's hegemony over the Anglican Church, forbidding bishops from residing anywhere outside their diocese. Levying taxes without parliamentary consent and making a Catholic Bourbon princess his wife enraged the public and the House of Commons alike. And when lawmakers objected to all this, Charles dissolved Parliament, popularizing the case against his rule.

King Charles seemed to know that making enemies of so many subjects was a risky proposition for any monarch. He needed *some* constituency. So, toward that end, he resolved to give his subjects back that which Puritanism had stolen from them. Specifically, their diversions.

In 1633, Charles reissued a declaration originally adopted by King James I, a Stuart, dubbed the Book of Sports. Initially applicable to only one city, Charles nationalized the decree, to the horror of the Puritans. The document proclaimed that games and dancing, which were strictly proscribed on the Sabbath, would now be legal once church services had concluded.[1]

Sports, such as they were in Caroline-era England, were not quite what we would recognize as professional athletics today. But what Puritans found offensive about them is still recognizable to us. Bruce Daniels observed that athletic competition in this period "involved injury-producing violence as an inherent part of the activity and engendered rowdy behavior among both participants and spectators." That's something of an understatement. "Sometimes their necks are broken," Philip Stubbes wrote in his 1583 reflections on *The Anatomy of Abuses* in Tudor football, "sometimes their backs, sometimes their legs, sometimes their arms, sometimes one part is thrust out of joint, sometimes the noses gush out with blood." Sixteenth- and seventeenth-century English clergy routinely inveighed against the "evil game," with its "beastly fury and extreme violence."[2]

In his day, Charles was representative of a populist gentry class who derived political power from the garish hedonism that offended patrician sensibilities. This was a recipe for political success; the general public was just not inclined toward the kind of austere simplicity preferred by a vocal minority of self-righteous moralizers. Today, this same phenomenon is apparent in the elites who roll their eyes at the unsophisticated amusements enjoyed by the riffraff.

In a February 2013 issue of *The New Republic*, then president Barack Obama was pressed to weigh in on the many ways in which American football sinned against the idealized American compact. The president said that the game was so violent that, if he had a son, Obama would not let him take the field. He went on to back changes to the game that might make it "a bit less exciting" but nonetheless safer.[3]

While some cultural arbiters blamed the National Football League and its owners for the violence on display, others blamed the fans. After all, it was their barbarous tastes that made football into the gory spectacle it had become. As Bleacher Report's Andrew Miller wrote three years prior, it's the fans who demand ever-larger athletes, more exciting and dangerous plays, and, subsequently, more catastrophic collisions between players. "Call it a desire to see blood sport, a strange kind of vicarious thrill," he wrote.

The controversy Obama inserted himself into didn't arise from thin air. In 2012, thousands of former players joined a class-action lawsuit against the league, seeking compensation for the serious medical conditions associated with the traumas they experienced on the field.[4] In 2014, the league settled that suit to the tune of $765 million—no admission of guilt, of course, but certainly an acknowledgment of the merits of the former players' claims. In the years that followed, the NFL introduced concussion protocols that prescribe measures designed to prevent potentially injured players from retaking the field.[5]

In the end, progressives succeeded; they and their allies made compelling arguments, persuaded skeptics, sought incremental reforms, and secured them. You'd think they'd be happy with victory. But a marginal reform like this could not satisfy the game's most vocal opponents.

In an interview with Bloomberg News, bestselling author and *New Yorker* columnist Malcolm Gladwell called the sport a "moral abomination" with "no real connection to American society." The NFL is "socializing young men into a culture of violence," he continued. Gladwell predicted that the natural evolution of American public ethics would lead the game of football into extinction. "I don't see how it doesn't," he speculated. "It'll start to shrivel up at the high school and college levels and then the pro game I think will eventually wither on the vine."[6]

Gladwell was not the first to indict football on moral grounds. "Considering all the morally problematic aspects surrounding football, it is worth asking," Penn State professor Francisco Javier López Frías and State University of New York, Brockport, professor Cesar R. Torres wrote in a joint 2018 op-ed. "Is this the kind of social practice around which Americans should imagine and build their national identity?"[7] It is not just that the sport is injurious to the young men who voluntarily play it, or that the league did not behave as responsibly as it should. The problem is that the sport contributes to the degradation of a virtuous society.

Why was it that this one game took on such an outsize place in the minds of these reformers? Beyond its violent delights, progressives were frustrated with the factionalism, jingoism, and consumerism football encourages. It is a pompous show of fate-tempting pride. It rejects humility and simplicity. It exposes our outrageous decadence—a manifestation of our innate corruption and selfishness. Maybe by pushing back against this depraved pastime, we might also hold our own debauched appetites in check.

Football's grudging effort to curb gratuitous violence on the field would prove only the first of many concessions it would make to its critics, some of whom seem hostile to the game's very existence. Eventually, the sport would be sucked into the whirling progressive vortex in which the New Puritan believes all society must be consumed.

Progressive reformers unfamiliar with their own ideology's history might be surprised to learn how directly they have channeled their puritanical ancestors' distaste for brutal athletic exhibitions.

Hypothetically, at least, the Puritans could admit that exercise and athletics were relatively wholesome activities that broke up the mundanity of daily life. "When I had some time abstained from such worldly delights as my heart most desired, I grew melancholic and uncomfortable," Massachusetts Bay Colony governor John Winthrop wrote wistfully. "I grew into a great dullness and discontent: which, being at last perceived, I examined my heart and finding it needful to recreate my mind with some outward recreation, I yielded unto it, and by moderate exercise herein was much refreshed."[8]

Like so many other pleasant diversions, however, the Puritan mind took issue with just about every aspect of athletics that was not an abstraction.

"Magistrates," the scholar Nancy Struna observed, "restricted sport, or more precisely the occasion for sport, when this distracted from the economic success of the colony and social order."[9] The zealous Protestant reformers of this age opposed (and, in New England, outlawed) "blood sports" involving animals.[10] They were suspicious of sports like football, in part because they were played on days of religious observance and involved teams, which "encouraged idleness" and "created bitter rivalries."

The practice of spectating often led enthusiasts to lose themselves in celebration, engage in ritual, and dress up in costume—a custom odiously similar to acting. "Still other games," Bruce Daniels continues, "such as tennis and handball had been the preserve of the English elite and the Puritans disdained them because of their association with the Established Church and the idle nobility."[11] Too often, sports were (and are today) accompanied by all sorts of degenerate temptations: gambling, drunkenness, cavorting, ribaldry, and overspending on trivial pursuits.

The Puritans did favor a few physically intensive competitive endeavors, including archery, marksmanship, running, and wrestling. But these all had a martial dimension and were usually practiced within militia companies. Sports could not be fun just for fun's sake; they had to be *useful*.

Once more, a theme emerges: Although the Puritan mind was open to athletics *in theory*, they were reliably repulsed by its practice. A far more engaging sight, to old and new Puritans alike, would be some performative piety to undercut the arrogance inherent in displays of athletic prowess.

"I am not going to stand up to show pride in a flag for a country that oppresses black people and people of color," former San Francisco 49ers quarterback Colin Kaepernick declared in 2016. "If they take football away, my endorsements from me, I know that I stood up for what is right."[12]

Kaepernick's grievances with the American status quo were omnidirectional. He was rebelling against America's culture of police violence targeting black Americans. He was raging against the nation's two political parties, which had that year produced a Republican presidential nominee who was "openly racist" and a Democratic nominee who "called black teens or black kids super-predators." He was angry over living in a nation built on a "foundation of slav-ery" and stained by "genocide of Native Americans." And he was dissenting against America's culture of "mass incarceration," which Kaepernick said contrasts unfavorably with the morally superior al-ternative offered by Communist Cuba.[13]

Kaepernick's stand took the form of a kneel—an act of pro-test he undertook during the playing of the American national anthem. The protest became a source of controversy for his team and the National Football League. While most of his teammates did not follow Kaepernick's lead, only a handful were vocally crit-ical of his decision. The same thing could not be said of the NFL's fans. When Kaepernick repeated his act of protest the following week, he was "booed throughout the game." While the breadth of Kaepernick's resentments—and the revered nature of the flag he rejected—probably meant fan motivations for booing were widely varied, *Rolling Stone* contributor Kenneth Arthur explained simply that the "fan reaction" to Kaepernick's kneeling was "about racism, not patriotism."[14]

That sequence of events—kneeling, booing, and elite condem-nation of football's fan base—was repeated throughout the 2016 season.[15] "Kaepernick wouldn't have to take a knee if Americans listened to black athletes before him," read the subhead of a *Vox* article that berated sports fans who fail to consistently "acknowl-edge racism," even in the diversions in which they partake to escape social conflict.[16]

The NFL eventually objected to the kneeling protests and took a stand against them, albeit timidly and without punishing the protesters. The league was summarily attacked by progressives for seeking to cocoon its fan base in a red-, white-, and blue-colored blanket of lies. But that was uncharitable. The NFL had a track rec-ord of avoiding political issues altogether, even those that appealed to the American right.

In July 2016, a lone gunman ambushed a group of Dallas, Texas, police officers, killing five. To honor their sacrifice, the Dallas

Cowboys asked the league to allow their players to wear decals commemorating the fallen and to pay tribute to local police. The request was denied. The denial became a cause célèbre among social conservatives, who detected a double standard at work. That was probably unfair. Later that year, the league would deny requests from players who wanted to wear regalia that drew awareness to breast cancer, and fined Denver Broncos receiver Brandon Marshall ten thousand dollars when he wore green shoes designed to bring attention to mental health issues.[17] For a time, the no-advocacy-on-the-field standard prevailed.

The stewards of football were trying to preserve the game as a source of escapism. But as the pressure on the league mounted, its commitment to consistency would not last.

By the end of 2016, much of the season had been overshadowed by Kaepernick's politics—even at the expense of his record on the field. In March 2017, following a year in which he led his team to a 2–14 record despite starting in eleven games that season, Kaepernick opted out of his contract in the hope that he would receive a better one somewhere else. But despite the league's efforts to showcase Kaepernick's talents, there wouldn't be a new contract.[18]

By 2018, the NFL's general distaste for the kneeling protests transformed into outright hostility. That spring, the owners adopted a rule that penalized players who protested the national anthem. Athletes who wanted to protest would now have to remain in their locker rooms for the duration of the song. But the protests continued in defiance of the rule. And in 2020, the league's resistance broke down entirely.

Just one week after protests against police violence erupted across the country that summer, the NFL reversed itself. "We were wrong for not listening to NFL players earlier, and encourage all to speak out and peacefully protest," NFL commissioner Roger Goodell repented. "Protests around the country are emblematic of the centuries of silence, inequality, and oppression of black players, coaches, fans, and staff."[19]

Practically overnight, kneeling evolved from a niche act of protest into an instrument of essential political hygiene, and there was little room for dissent.

Some, like New Orleans Saints quarterback Drew Brees (who was one of the few players to openly criticize Kaepernick in 2016) reiterated his distaste for "anybody disrespecting the flag of the United States of America." But the backlash against his remarks was swift, as was Brees's subsequent apology for them.

"I acknowledge that we as Americans, including myself, have not done enough to fight for that equality or to truly understand the struggles and plight of the black community," read the quarterback's chastened statement. Not good enough, Fox Sports host Shannon Sharpe contended. Brees's apology was "meaningless because the guys know he spoke his heart the very first time around," Sharpe asserted. "I don't know what Drew's going to do, but he probably should just go ahead and retire now."[20]

The NFL became so dedicated to wooing its critics that the league adopted *two national anthems*—the American national anthem and a "black national anthem," the early twentieth-century civil rights hymn "Lift Every Voice and Sing." Once again, the league's fans failed to appreciate this "moment of unity" cleverly disguised as an act of racial separatism, and they booed.[21] And once again, the fans were soundly admonished by the world of sports commentary.

"What they probably don't like is having to think about something that challenges their belief system," the Minneapolis *Star Tribune*'s Michael Rand wrote of the game's spectators.[22] "What in the world were the boo-birds thinking?" asked *Kansas City Star* columnist Michael Ryan. "As if the life-and-death matter of racial inequality and generational disadvantage and neglect can't be allowed to get in the way of our entertainment?"[23]

The sport could not be fun just for fun's sake; it had to be *useful*.

By September of the demonic year 2020, professional sports had found itself on the wrong end of public opinion. Gallup pollsters determined that professional sports were one of just three institutions, along with the pharmaceutical industry and the federal government, to see its image decline precipitously compared to the year before. But pro sports' reputation suffered the biggest drop by far, dipping by 15 points from 45 percent to just 30 percent approval.[24] And though the beatings continued, morale failed to improve.

In a year when most people had nothing better to do than stay home and watch sports, millions of Americans who would have otherwise done just that chose to tune out instead.

While football was being drained of entertainment value for political purposes, the same thing was happening to the so-called Entertainment and Sports Programming Network.

Like so many other entertainment venues, ESPN dedicated itself in 2020 to the noble pursuit of racial equality and extirpating the remnants of institutionalized discrimination from within its ranks. And like so many other entertainment venues, that project often took the form of hectoring its audience over their moral failings.

"This is what it means," ESPN contributing writer Tom Junod said in one representative video exploring the "many forms" that white privilege can take. "It means never having to acknowledge your power while always being able to wield it. It means telling yourself that Colin Kaepernick made a choice, and thirty-two NFL owners made a business decision.

"It means your power is all the more potent for being invisible to you," Junod continued. "It means never having to think of yourself as white while always seeing black. It means thinking 'they don't mean me.' . . . It means thinking the American ideal is color-blind and the American 'we' is universal. . . . It means confusing protesters and rioters, peacekeepers and instigators, the lawful and the lawless. It means hearing 'All Lives Matter' as an idealistic adage rather than a brutal rejoinder. . . . It means asking yourself anything but what you will give up."[25]

It means not asking what any of this has to do with last night's game.

This lecture was typical of 2020's offerings. So much so, in fact, that ESPN viewers could be forgiven for concluding that shoehorning racial politics into sports coverage became as much or more of an imperative as the sports coverage itself.

When the Brooklyn Nets hired Hall of Fame point guard Steve Nash as head coach, ESPN host Stephen A. Smith determined that the decision was entirely attributable to "white privilege." It was of no consequence to him that Nets guard Kyrie Irving and forward Kevin Durant, both of whom are black, "signed off" on and "supported" the hire. Perhaps they had not fully internalized the insidious workings of white privilege?[26]

"Go talk to your white friends, and your white families, and your white co-workers," said columnist Clayton Yates in a promotional spot for The Undefeated, an ESPN online venture dedicated to exploring the "intersections of race, sports, culture," and more. When white people are not forced to confront their race in the everyday aspects of modern life, Yates continued, "that's what privilege is called, and that's why it's a thing."[27] Thus, even succumbing to the desire for escapist entertainment is branded an act of racial hostility.

"Kentucky coach John Calipari said white privilege has helped him throughout his life and career," read an August 2020 ESPN feature. "I was still white, which means I had an advantage," the head coach of the Wildcats confessed. "I had one pair of tennis shoes. But that didn't matter."[28]

"The best analogy I've heard that explains white privilege is that it's like an invisible backpack that every white person wears," Los Angeles Lakers forward Kyle Kuzma wrote in an op-ed for *The Players' Tribune* that was heavily promoted by ESPN's anchors and commentators. "If you're white and you're ever in a situation where you might need help, you can take that backpack off, open it up, and pull out all sorts of shit. Get Out of Jail Free card. Job opportunities. Health benefits. Housing loans. Don't get me wrong. Black people can get those things, too, but it's a lot harder."[29]

"What I'm realizing is, no matter how passionately I commit to being an ally, and no matter how unwavering my support is for NBA and WNBA players of color," Utah Jazz guard Kyle Korver wrote in another article for the *Tribune* that received outsize coverage on the network, "I'm still in this conversation from the privileged perspective of opting into it."[30]

So total was ESPN's commitment to the idea that sports fans hate confronting their own whiteness that ESPN didn't seem to realize how much programming time they devoted to the subject.

Given the hours ESPN spent subjecting viewers to a critical audit of their own prejudices, a programming strategy had to inform the trend. There must be *some* audience for this sort of thing. And there was: ESPN's employees.

"ESPN is far from immune from the political fever that has afflicted so much of the country over the past year," the company's public editor and ombudsman, Jim Brady, wrote in November 2016. "Internally, there's a feeling among many staffers—both liberal and conservative—that the company's perceived move leftward has had a stifling effect on discourse inside the company and has affected its public-facing products. Consumers have sensed that same leftward movement, alienating some."

To his credit, Brady included a counternarrative in his dispatch on the quiet discomfort shared by the network employees with whom he spoke. Following his account of the self-censorship ESPN's staff felt they had to accept, Brady quoted Jemele Hill, who was at the time the cohost of ESPN 2's *His & Hers*. Hill essentially said their distress was a manifestation of their own well-deserved racial guilt. "I would challenge the people who feel suppressed," she said. "Do you fear backlash, or do you fear right and wrong?"[31]

Hill's self-confidence notwithstanding, the question before

ESPN wasn't the historical rectitude of the ideology to which the network's hosts and executives committed themselves. It was whether those political positions were finding their way on air, thus expanding the network's mission statement beyond its remit as an entertainment venue.

Hill never shied away from courting political controversy as an athletics reporter, and her employer was eventually dragged into one of those controversies. In September 2017, Hill tweeted that then president Donald Trump was "a white supremacist who has largely surrounded himself [with] other white supremacists." Her network initially stood by their embattled host, even as the White House leveraged Hill's comments for as much publicity as they were worth—thereby putting a human face on the Trump administration's ongoing feud with "the media."[32]

Despite the high-profile efforts by ESPN to protect their employee (including a supportive network statement and a prolonged defense of her views from none other than Disney CEO Bob Iger), Hill continued to produce political commentary and subsequently became a lightning rod for controversy. In late 2018, the network bought out the remainder of Hill's contract for $5 million, and she moved on to write about politics as a contributor to a more overtly political venue, *The Atlantic*.[33] And yet, for some prominent ESPN employees, the network's refusal to uncritically embrace Hill's politics represented a moral failure.

"Black ESPN employees repeatedly brought up the experience of Hill," read a *New York Times* report that alleged widespread "racism" within the organization. The allegations included the network's conspicuous failure to promote black employees to executive offices, "microaggressions and dog whistle words," and a host who was interrupted during a conference call "by a white male play-by-play announcer who apparently did not realize that his microphone was not muted." No one disagreed with the idea that this progressive network was plagued by racial biases, conscious or otherwise. All, however, insisted that ESPN's heart was in the right place. "I truly, truly believe ESPN wants to be on the right side of history," said *SportsCenter* anchor Elle Duncan.[34]

These internal tensions had been visible to the public for some time. In the summer of 2019, President Trump played host to a campaign-style rally in which he took aim at Somali-born Democratic representative Ilhan Omar, to which his supporters responded by chanting "Send her back." It was an ugly spectacle—one that few in the world of professional political commentary defended. The anger and discomfort this moment produced in those who were antagonized by it is entirely understandable. But ESPN radio host Dan Le Batard took that opportunity to castigate not just Trump and the xenophobia to which this rally's attendees appealed, but also his employer.

"There's a racial division in this country that's being instigated by the president, and we here at ESPN haven't had the stomach for that fight because Jemele did some things on Twitter," Le Batard said. "And then here, all of a sudden, nobody talks politics on anything unless we can use one of these sports figures as a meat shield in the most cowardly possible way."[35]

That lack of politics in ESPN's programming was, in fact, a relatively new development in the summer of 2019. That was a conscious choice, even if it proved short-lived. "Under the tenure of John Skipper," *Variety* reported, "ESPN personalities felt more empowered to take on topics outside the lines." But when the network's presidency changed hands in 2018, ESPN's new chief, Jimmy Pitaro, sought to rein in the talent. "We are not a political organization," Pitaro said. "We are a sports-media company. And our focus is on serving the sports fans."[36]

As we've seen in so many sectors of society, the perception that a meaningful life could be dedicated to something as insignificant as entertaining an audience does not sit well with the modern progressive activist class. "Black people, brown people, women. That's who we're going after now," Le Batard's prosecution of ESPN continued. "We don't talk about what is happening unless there's some kind of weak, cowardly sports angle that we can run it through.

"It is antithetical to what we should be," the radio host concluded. "If you're not calling it abhorrent, obviously racist, dangerous rhetoric, you're complicit." To hear his impassioned plea, it's hard not to sympathize with Le Batard's frustrations. Extraordinary events sometimes compel men and women of principle to deviate from the script. But to serve is not a lesser calling than to speak one's mind. And to serve sports fans involves covering sports, even at the expense of the occasional pang of conscience.

Washington Post sports reporter Ben Strauss summarized the fallout from this episode succinctly. "For those wondering about ESPN's politics data in the wake of Le Batard commentary," he wrote, "per the network, market research says 74 [percent] of fans don't want to hear about politics on ESPN." That figure included 85 percent of "avid fans," 84 percent of self-described Republicans, and nearly seven in ten self-identified Democrats.[37]

Like professional athletics, ESPN's ratings declined substantially in 2020.[38] And while the network is well positioned to succeed as a streaming service in the same way its parent company, Disney, has, the conditions forcing it to focus on the digital market must concern ESPN's financial stakeholders. In a note to clients in the summer of 2020, Morgan Stanley analyst Ben Swinburne estimated that ESPN's operating income will decline by between 10 and 15 percent per year through 2024. That "has brought the network and the entire ecosystem to this point," he wrote. "The risk of unbundling ESPN may finally be worth the potential reward."[39]

"ESPN also shared one anonymous comment that it collected from a focus group that the network feels best illustrates a common view: People come to ESPN to get a break from the political news cycle," Sports Business Daily subsequently reported.

"There are so many places where I get news about politics, and I don't need it on ESPN," that irritated focus group participant mourned. "When you introduce that element of broad politics, it ruins having a diversion."[40]

For the New Puritan, ruining your diversion is the whole point. Unnecessary recreations are a luxury you do not deserve.

If these advocates of what *should* constitute virtue in the world of athletics sound like they're dancing around the point they really want to make, it's because they may well be. Their problem with sports is that they just aren't important. Not compared with the urgency of the progressive project.

"With appalling regularity, our most disregarded sin keeps resurfacing in sports. Men mistreat women," wrote *Washington Post* sports columnist Jerry Brewer, citing the genuinely discomfiting number of high-profile cases in which professional athletic organizations played host to members accused of objectifying or abusing women. "The world of sports, often a cartoonish illustration of stereotypical masculinity, fosters an unending cycle of virulence," he continued. "Confrontation is a necessity of sport, but when are we, as men, going to get in the face of this problem?"[41]

Sports encourage the kind of "toxic masculinity" that makes the work of building a healthier society that much harder. And that's what's really important.

Athletics don't just inculcate the wrong values in men. They also distract impressionable youth from more objectively important and fulfilling uses of their time, like study.

To that end, author and *The Atlantic* contributor Amanda Ripley determined that we should consider eliminating high school athletics altogether. After all, the point of secondary education is scholarship. Though "sports can be bait for students who otherwise might not care about school," she wrote, "using sports to tempt kids into getting an education feels dangerously old-fashioned.[42]

"Imagine, for a moment, if Americans transferred our obsessive intensity about high-school sports—the rankings, the trophies, the ceremonies, the pride—to high-school academics," Ripley continued. Wouldn't our society more closely resemble overachieving East Asian societies, like Japan and South Korea? And wouldn't that be great?

Why stop with high school? "If colleges got rid of athletics, how many more students could they fund?" Urban Institute's senior research associate Erica Bloom queried. "Based on various assumptions, I calculate that colleges could fund at least an additional 200,000 scholarships." The abolition of college sports would probably eliminate the temptation to provide athletic scholarships and the substandard educational experiences associated with them. It would also go some way to addressing the "potential long-term health consequences of football," as well as "increased incidences of campus sexual assault" linked to hosting "large sporting events."[43]

Sports are a distraction from or even a substitute for quiet scholarship and academic achievement. Eliminating them would also reduce incidences of lewdness and vulgarity among young men. And that's what's really important.

Ultimately, even this is unsatisfying. If students can just cruise through primary, secondary, and continuing education and then still go on to play poisonous, strife-ridden sports professionally, what good are these reforms? Obviously, society's goal should be the total dissolution of institutional athletics.

"Professional sport" has "harmed public health," wrote Counter-Punch contributor Peter Bolton. Sports compel Americans to spend frivolously, consume vast quantities of "junk food," and make themselves captives to corporations hocking "unnecessary consumerist junk." But "of all the negative factors of professional sports," Bolton continues, "the most damaging of them all must be the ugly tribalism it breeds." Sound familiar?

To illustrate his points, Bolton cites Noam Chomsky, who once wrote of the confusion he felt over why he should care whether the team associated with the place he happened to be studying won or lost that weekend's contest. Both Bolton and Chomsky arrive at the same conclusion: Pro sports exist as "training in irrational jingoism" and a distraction from "things that are of real importance, like po-litical organizing for progressive social change."[44]

The very existence of sports is not compatible with developing a proletarian consciousness, organizing, and agitating for left-wing political goals. And that's what's really important.

By forcing sports fans to marinate in their own shame for the sin of indulging in the decadent spectacle of professional athlet-ics, today's progressive activists seek to restore the virtue of austere simplicity. But this isn't just an exercise in self-help. Amid unos-tentatious surroundings, we are free to devote our minds to higher pursuits. By committing to modesty, humility, and communitari-anism, we might dedicate ourselves to more important things than amusing distractions.

The Puritans would recognize all these arguments against team sports. Though Protestant reformers adhered strictly to the belief that men were the dominant sex, domestic violence was seen as a serious problem in Puritan society, and it was punished accordingly. Fines, whipping, or a time in the pillory were doled out to men accused of behaving cruelly toward their wives. Likewise, the Puri-tans looked down upon activities that encouraged factionalism and distracted impressionable young minds from their studies.

Few of today's socially progressive commentators would go so far as to endorse the Bolton/Chomsky view that all organized athletics—professional, semi, or scholastic—should be abolished. They don't believe that sociability, collegiality, and healthy physical exertion are bad for society. But then, neither did the Puritans.

In theory, our puritanical forebears were all for athletics. Simi-larly, the New Puritan looks just as fondly upon sports, but mostly in the abstract. In the real-world practice of athletic amusements, both the old and New Puritans see plenty they don't like.

The backlash against decadent sports is predicated on the princi-ple of simplicity—indeed, austerity—but the application of that principle isn't limited to games. Those aspiring to lead a moral life avoid garish and prideful displays in all things. It's a principle that applies as much to the aesthetics as it does to athletics.

To those who subscribe to this theory of social organization, fashion isn't just a stylistic choice. It must be a productive contribution to the progressive project. The clothing and accessories you wear have to communicate your station to the outside world. Your clothes must say who you are and to whom you are subordinate.

A similarly stern belief in the value of practical utility has found its way into the world of fashion. The practice of this spartan principle has transformed clothing into a statement that expresses more than just your sartorial choices.

A solid two thirds of consumers worldwide say that they would prefer to patronize brands that share their political beliefs and take firm stances on controversial issues, the consulting behemoth McKinsey and Company reported in 2019. That trend is particularly pronounced among younger consumers. For Gen Z and the millennial generation, "wearing your politics on your sleeve" isn't a euphemism for trite and shallow political values anymore. Wearing a uniform that reflects your politics is how you are expected to navigate society.

"Fashion companies are showing signs of getting 'woke' (a phrase defined as 'alert to injustice in society,' popularized on social media)," McKinsey stodgily advised those in the retail fashion space.[45] Nike, for example, took on former 49ers quarterback Colin Kaepernick as its chief brand ambassador in 2018, and that relationship produced a revenue bonanza. Consumers attracted to transgressive political ideals raced to purchase Kaepernick-branded shoes, and the press provided Nike with roughly $163 million in free advertising.

Later that year, an ad featuring the former quarterback leaned into his controversial comments and intimated that he had been cut from the roster because of his beliefs. "Believe in something, even if it means sacrificing everything," Nike's Kaepernick-inspired slogan declared. In 2019, that ad became the recipient of an Emmy Award.[46] By the end of the year, Nike's stock had increased by 18 percent, raising the value of the stock by $146 billion and adding $26 billion to the company's coffers.[47]

Elsewhere in the apparel sector that year, blue-jean producer Levi Strauss & Co. branded itself the official pants of the gun control movement. "It's inevitable that we're going to alienate some consumers, but we can no longer sit on the sidelines and remain silent on this issue," Levi's CEO Chip Bergh told *The Washington Post*.[48] But few seemed inclined to stop buying Levi's just because of the firm's politics, and the company's political stance attracted a variety of new consumers. In 2019, net revenues increased by 3 percent.[49]

"The president stole your land," the reflexively left-wing outdoor goods retailer Patagonia informed consumers in late 2017. That's a demagogic way to describe a Trump-era executive order that pared 2 million acres of federally managed land closer to the boundaries originally designated by Congress, which had been expanded by a series of presidential pen strokes over the decades.[50] But whatever Patagonia's table-pounding lacked in accuracy, it more than made up in sales revenue.

"CEOs are not just raising flags anymore," said Lesli Gaines-Ross, chief reputation strategist at the public relations firm Weber Shandwick. "They're actually taking action and asking their customers to do the same."[51]

These examples illustrate an industry-wide phenomenon. A study conducted by the consulting group Kantar found that brands with an explicit political purpose saw their valuations increase by 175 percent over the last twelve years—well beyond the median growth rate of just 86 percent over the same period. Marketing your fashion line as "moral merch" has evolved from a niche aspect of an effective promotional campaign to a foundational premise.

"Brand purpose also creates consumer loyalty based on shared values," *Vogue* reported in early 2020, "something a competitor's hot new product or lower price point simply can't overcome." Brands that capitalize on political causes célèbres are rewarded by consumers, *Vogue* added. Politicized fashion also underscores the fatalistic belief among young people that "the economic system doesn't work for them."[52]

That is an irrationally self-pitying thing to write. The economic system in which these young people are participating is working "for them" rather directly. It's selling their own fatalistic anxiety back to them at a premium price.

McKinsey observed that catering to "woke" consumerism was not without its perils. Fashion brands risk being labeled hypocrites if the values they preach conflict with best practices, particularly the use of cheap foreign labor common in the textile industry.

The European retailer Primark was singled out for criticism when it produced a piece of apparel advertising LGBT+ pride produced in Turkey, a nation with some of the most restrictive antigay statutes in the Atlantic Alliance.

Likewise, Nike was similarly castigated by some more-consistent consumers. Discerning fashion activists observed that the firm spoke out of both sides of its mouth when it backed minority rights in the United States even as it relied upon workers in China, a country implicated in the use of forced labor.[53] Indeed, this most "woke" of shoe brands has dedicated time and capital to lobbying American lawmakers against sanctioning Beijing for the alleged ethnic cleansing of its Muslim-dominated regions, forcing residents into reeducation camps where their religious convictions are deliberately violated.[54]

Those few thoughtful voices are usually drowned out by activists on social media, whose familiarity with the political causes they champion exhibit all the depth of a koi pond.

The New Puritans fancy themselves the vanguard of a new and exciting conception of the way we should outwardly express our commitment to social responsibility. In fact, they have merely rediscovered a very old code of communal conduct.

Sixteen-year-old Hannah Lyman was unrepentant when she was hauled in front of a Massachusetts court in 1676 along with thirty-eight other women. She and her fellow "overdressed" codefendants had violated the official Puritan dress code—specifically, the court charged, "wearing silk in a flaunting manner, in an offensive way." In a rare act of civil disobedience, Lyman appeared before the judge wearing the very same silken hood that landed her in court in the first place.[55]

Puritanical dress codes were not the result of an unspoken social compact that only those steeped in that culture could intuit. They were codified in law.

In 1639, the Massachusetts General Court, the body that served as an early colonial legislature, expressed its "utter detestation and dislike" for fashion statements that did not traditionally accompany—indeed, denote—the station into which an individual was born. "Immoderate great breeches, knots of ribbon, silk roses, double ruffles, and capes" were just some of the many stylistic choices that were denied the low born.

Arguably, Puritanism's distaste for anything other than ascetic garb originates with sixteenth-century Protestant reformers' mistrust of Catholic traditions. In particular, the ornate vestments worn by clergy. That distaste was only reinforced by Puritanism's opponents, who forced reformist ministers to wear the ornamental surplice as a display of obedience. The Puritans' austere principles would evolve into a doctrine that applied to, and tended to prohibit, the latest trend. Like so much else in Puritan life, apparel had to serve a grander social function.

Fashion was generally associated with social rank. That was particularly true when it came to lower-class women, for whom "new fashions, or long hair, or anything of the like nature" were strictly forbidden. Women were perceived to be more prone to vanity—a cardinal sin and a legacy of the fall of man to which Eve had consigned humanity in the Garden of Eden. As Cotton Mather preached, a woman's pride in her own appearance represented a peculiar "snare of her soul."[56]

Females of common status were prohibited from donning the silk hoods or scarves Lyman so ostentatiously flaunted. Nor were they allowed short-sleeved dresses, "whereby the nakedness of the arms may be discovered." These trends were reserved for the rarefied upper classes.[57] By the mid-1600s, embellishments of gold and silver, knee points, great boots, and other majestic accoutrements were only allowed to be worn by those hailing from estates with proven wealth in excess of two hundred pounds.

"In addition to concern for squandering money and engendering jealousy, sumptuary laws were intended to assist in the maintenance of virtue," wrote the author and historian Dorothy Mays. "A low-necked dress, dripping with expensive lace, was a sign of vanity, pride, and undue attention to material goods."

Sumptuary laws were hardly innovative when they were applied to New England. Historically, these laws were designed to preserve marks of wealth and status from adulteration by lower classes. By contrast, puritanical proscriptions against certain fashion choices took on a moral dimension.

The rigors of Puritan dress codes were both an effort to abide by the diktats of Scripture and an outgrowth of the belief that New England's splendid isolation from Europe's degenerate influences was under siege. "Increased trade with Europe was bringing prosperity" in the late seventeenth century, George McKenna observed, "and with it a new taste for consumer goods and fashions—early signs, it was feared, of worldliness and luxury."[58]

In 1679, in response to an outbreak of fancy hairstyles among the colony's more immodest women, the Massachusetts General Court felt compelled to update the rules governing acceptable fashion tastes. "Whereas there is manifest pride openly appearing among us by some women wearing borders of hair, and their cutting, curling, and immodest laying out of their hair," the legislature advised the colony's ladies to keep it simple.[59] Hannah Lyman did not. Though the records do not indicate that criminal punishments for violating colonial sumptuary laws were common, the stigma associated with being dragged before a court was not without social consequences.

"Puritans did not summarily reject the concept of beauty," Mays noted. "Indeed, they believed outward beauty often expressed inward virtue. Modest dressing for seventeenth-century Puritan America allowed for formfitting and flattering clothing, as evidenced by portraits of stunningly attired women. Clothing was considered immodest only when it displayed too much flash, too much wealth, or anything that blurred gender lines."[60]

"Clothing's most pervading function has been to declare status," Smithsonian Institution Division of Costume curator Claudia Kidwell observed.[61] This was as true in colonial America as it was in ancient Greece. And it was true in the United States, despite the egalitarianism that is baked into the American civic compact. But by the turn of the twentieth century, fashion was democratizing.

In postindustrial America, apparel was no longer strictly made to order. The mass production of clothing made style universally accessible, as did the popularization of mail-order catalogs like Aaron Montgomery Ward's and Sears, Roebuck and Co. On the eve of the Great Depression, the garment industry in the United States had moved out of the small sweatshops that peppered the urban landscape and into factories. Wealthy trendsetters and the stars of stage and screen set fashion tastes, and the sensibilities on display could be emulated by average consumers for an affordable price.

"Fashion, as we know it, is dead," said American designer Rudi Gernreich in 1971. "Status fashion is gone."[62] The clothing of the future, he predicted, would be "merely an instrument for the individual's own body-message." Liberation from the constraints ambitious fashionistas impose on themselves would "free us to think of more important things."[63]

"Clothes are just not that important," Gernreich said shortly before his death in 1985. "They're not status symbols any longer.

They're for fun."[64] Gernreich was wrong. Fashion is still a reflection of status. What's more, it is once again being subjected to the moral judgments of a hip, young vice squad whose members seem to believe that the clothes you wear should reflect your station in life.

Modern proponents of fashion as an extension of status have resorted to making arguments that would ring true to their puritanical forebearers. The primary distinction between Puritans old and new is that the accidents of birth today's fashion police believe your style choices *should* reflect are more ethnic than economic.

"I don't want white women asking me whether or not they can wear their hair in box braids or Bantu knots," *Teen Vogue* writer Antonia Opiah opened a 2017 essay. "Cultural appropriation would be the cultural *exchange* everybody wants and loves IF it were occurring on an even playing field, but it's not." Which is to say that cultural appreciation across ethnic divides is just not possible in a world where discrimination and inequality are facts of life. Thus, all cross-cultural trends are functionally oppressive, and you are obliged to avoid applying any discretion when evaluating them on their individual merits.

Opiah herself illustrates the oddness of this admonition when she later engages in the very same reasoned discretion she had just called insensitive. "White models wearing locs isn't wrong in and of itself," the author concedes. "But when it happens against the backdrop of the modeling industry lacking diversity, or makeup artists and hairstylists in the industry not being equipped to do a black model's hair or apply her makeup, and when the appropriation occurs with no credit, respect, or empathy, that's where things begin to feel like you're being kicked while you're down." Opiah later confessed that she isn't opposed to genuine cultural exchange, but that she wants to see more responsible voices in the fashion industry "asking me what we all can do to make things more fair."[65]

If we assume that Opiah doesn't mean that her in-box should be flooded with millions of requests from white women for dispensation to style their hair as they see fit, but rather that the definition of what constitutes appropriation should be the product of an open dialogue, her argument is unobjectionable. The problem, however, is that her compatriots are as hostile to the open exchange of ideas as they are to the exchange of culture and tradition.

In 2018, the website Fashionista attempted to define the distinction between appropriation and appreciation. The hairstylist and entrepreneur Vernon François, who has worked with a number of prominent black celebrities, suggested that one easy way to avoid criticism is to be open and frank about your intentions. "Don't [wear braids] for fun or because your African American boyfriend or girlfriend has them," he advised. "Learn about the story, find inspiration, and give credit where credit's due by explaining who or what has inspired you, like on social media."[66] You won't be surprised to learn that the audience for this sort of thing on social media isn't as discerning as François assumed.

Just shy of a year later, the model Nikita Dragun joined the likes of Kim Kardashian, Kylie Jenner, and the British pop group Little Mix's Jesy Nelson in the dock for appropriating black hairstyles. But Dragun had followed François's recommendations almost to the letter. After the runway model faced criticism for appearing at New York's Fashion Week with braided hair, she took to social media to describe who her inspirations were and explain that she adopted the style "to show my love and appreciation for all the gorgeous black women in my life." But the response from the internet grew only *more* vitriolic after she issued these sympathetic appeals.[67]

This is not to say that the racial and historical baggage associated with African hairstyles does not exist, or that whites may be unfamiliar with that history. From the often-exorbitant expense associated with black haircare today to the "pencil test" applied in places like apartheid South Africa, in which the writing implement was inserted into a head of hair to assess its tensile strength, ethnic hairstyling was politicized long before fashion bloggers got a hold of it.

Educating consumers around these issues isn't controversial. The controversy arises when the conversation shifts from being informative to being accusatory and separatist, and when the line between appropriation and appreciation is deliberately obscured to *preserve* rather than resolve social conflict.

Just as it is with appropriation in cuisine, the distinctions between appreciation and exploitation aren't all that hard to make. To wit, a January 2020 attempt by the Japanese fashion brand Comme des Garçons to enhance their brand by adorning its male models with the "Egyptian prince" look. The result was a thoughtless mishmash in which young white men paraded down the catwalk adorned in brightly colored blazers and cartoonish bleached-blond cornrow wigs.[68] Much like pornography, you know it when you see it.

Hairstyles are far from the only aspect of fashion that is aggressively policed by today's cultural Cheka. A variety of other, far more debatably controversial aspects of style are policed with similar enthusiasm but far less historical justification.

"Hoops exist across many minority groups as symbols of resistance, strength, and identity," *Vice* columnist Ruby Pivet wrote of a style of earrings that she believes are reserved for women of "Latinx" heritage alone. As supporting evidence of a trend, Pivet cites an episode of the television show *Broad City*, in which one of the white characters is scolded for adorning hoop earrings. "It's almost like you're stealing the identity from people who fought hard against colonial structures," the character says. "So, in a way, it's almost like you are the colonists."[69]

Pivet's column took off. The fashion-blogging world went to work bitterly condemning anyone who did not accept that "large gold hoop earrings" had been "culturally appropriated from Latinas who were told they were 'too ghetto' when they wore them."[70]

"White Girls, take OFF your hoops," read a mural spray-painted onto California's Pritzer College "free speech wall." The graffiti made national headlines, but its authors insist that it was misconstrued by the press. The "mural was not meant to police white women but serve as a form of education," read a statement produced by the authors of this admonition.[71] Apparently, the statement was made to be misconstrued. When questioned about its intent, the college's president of the "Latinx Student Union" informed her fellow students that she sees "our winged eyeliner, lined lips, and big hoop earrings serving as symbols [and] as an everyday act of resistance." So, "why should white girls be able to take part in this culture . . . and be seen as cute/aesthetic/ethnic? White people have actually exploited the culture and made it into fashion."[72]

So often, the offenses that allegedly constitute appropriation are a product of ignorance rather than malice. Ignorance is the only satisfying explanation for an insulting line of T-shirts produced by the online fashion giant Boohoo.com, which featured "Chinese text" in their designs. There was just one problem: The characters featured on these shirts were, in fact, Japanese.

"While this may seem like a 'simple mistake' on the surface, it actually has its roots in very serious racism and has an array of racist implications," Feiya Hu argued in Edinburgh's The Tab, "not least of all that all Asian cultures are the same or merely interchangeable." Her refusal to distinguish malevolence from incompetence is not an enlightened point of view. Precisely the opposite. It's a logical fallacy and a rejection of sounder methods for ruling out unlikely and, therefore, misleading explanations for human behavior.

Holding fast to the belief that you've been deliberately insulted when a more likely (and more innocuous) explanation suffices isn't a mark of sophistication. It's childish.

Distinct ethnic traditions in fashion aren't the only avenue that is ripe for conformist criticism. Women who adopt torn jeans as a fashion statement might be unwittingly appropriating the hard-won style choices of the working class, assuming for themselves the design trends that were the result of "thousands of hours of blue-collar work."[73] Even the "little black dress," a versatile staple of both the office and evening engagements, was stolen from nineteenth-century "domestic workers and shopgirls," for whom the uniform was compulsory.[74]

It has gotten to the point that chroniclers of appropriative fashion trends are so inundated with offenses that they've just thrown their hands up and declared all cultural traditions off-limits to those not born into a particular tribe. "So, basically just avoid wearing items of cultural significance if you don't belong to that group," *BuzzFeed* nervously informed its readers. That is the only way to avoid running afoul of the New Puritan tastemakers. "Because honestly," *BuzzFeed*'s shellshocked authors continued through gritted teeth, "who wants to be problematic?"[75]

"I think that fashion has and will always be a declaration of status. It relates where we are and how much social capital we have in the world, and it has always been that," said Ali Tate-Cutler, Victoria Secret's first plus-size model, when we spoke. "What I really believe is that these brands are trying to tap into the progressive left because, at this point in history, it's really seen as cool. It's this sense of, this is revolutionary, this is rebellious, this is subversive."

There's no arguing with that. But what are these consumers of "woke" fashion rebelling against? On a superficial level, they are likely to restate the premises of the high street fashion brands they're patronizing. Specifically, they are declaring their affinity for stylistic choices that stand in opposition to stuffy conservatism. But the ideals to which the New Puritans are most hostile aren't conventionally conservative so much as they are conventionally liberal. The adoption of a uniform that connotes a specific ethnic or socioeconomic status is a rebellion against the countercultural leftism of the late 1960s and early '70s.

For fashion industry professionals, there are consequences associated with violating this ideology's rigid tenets. In Tate-Cutler's experience, "You need to become an activist in something. You need to be vocal about it on your social media and, if you're not, you're not going to be booked as a model." But you can't advocate just anything. "You have to become an activist for things that are associated with the progressive left," she said. "And if you don't, you're done."

Tate-Cutler is sympathetic to activists who want to identify and stigmatize culturally appropriative trends. She sees the dearth of black models and black creators in an industry that thrives off the promotion of trends born of black culture as an "incongruity" that "needs to be addressed." But that well-intended mission has produced a minefield that fewer and fewer creators are willing to traverse.

"All of culture, especially with art or creative endeavors, we have consistently borrowed from other cultures to create new ideas. To create new art. To create new expression. And, at this point, what we're seeing is that a lot of people do not want to take those risks anymore," Tate-Cutler continued. "Which I would argue is not a good thing for art when we feel like we cannot take risks."

When I asked Tate-Cutler if she still found the profession to which she had dedicated her life fun, she answered curtly and without hesitation: "No."

Tate-Cutler described witnessing the transformation of her industry from one that focused on discrete presentations to a twenty-four-hour marathon in which "the performance of me" overtakes the work of modeling. And that is a game that cannot be won. "When we talk, it's almost as if, what I have to say now online has to become technically palatable for seven billion people," she added. "Because there is no cap on who might see this. And to make something palatable for seven billion people is a futile effort. You cannot do it."

If there is a backlash brewing, it is only because these trends toward a conformist fashion sensibility are nearing the point of diminishing returns. Literally.

Catering to "call-out culture" is valuable only so long as your firm isn't being called out. And when it is and the bottom line is jeopardized, fashion houses are less likely to play the game. Of this, controversy over the Instagram account "Diet Prada" is illustrative.

Armed with nearly three million Instagram followers and a gigantic chip on its shoulder, Diet Prada exists to scold fashion brands that offend anti-appropriation activists and reinforce the notion that taste should be the province of the progressive left.

Toward that end, the account's owners lampooned Gap after it announced a ten-year partnership with the iconoclastic hip-hop artist Kanye West, posting a line of satirical T-shirts and hoodies branded with obscene slogans like "Slavery was a choice," which mocked the rapper's dismissive attitude toward the legacy of human bondage.[76] The account's followers engaged in a merciless assault on Gucci after it posted images of a turtleneck-style balaclava with "red cut-out lips resembling blackface."[77] This social media juggernaut made international headlines when it charged Condé Nast with racism. Diet Prada justified this claim by citing one *Vogue* issue's cover art shot by Annie Leibovitz featuring NBA star Lebron James and model Gisele Bündchen, likening it to a World War I–era propaganda poster depicting a German solider as an ape brutishly ravaging a fair-haired American girl.[78] You see, if you didn't look at that stock glamour shot and immediately see century-old ethnic stereotypes, you're the racist.

This sort of deliberately obtuse and uncharitable maximalism is perfectly calibrated to generate social media engagement. But this Instagram account might have gone a step too far with its criticisms of Dolce & Gabbana.

Diet Prada was instrumental in the events that led to the cancellation of a 2018 Dolce & Gabbana fashion show slated to take place in Shanghai. The account homed in on a series of Chinese-language advertisements for the show featuring a Chinese model struggling to eat a variety of classic Italian dishes with chopsticks. Clearly, this was an attempt to humorously depict the follies associated with cross-cultural blending, like the sort that accompany an Italian fashion show in mainland China.

Not only did Diet Prada highlight the offense they took from these advertisements, they also posted an exchange with one of the

Italian fashion house's founders, Stefano Gabbana, who "appears to have engaged in a bout of insulting name-calling (including suggesting that the Chinese eat dogs) with a critic on Instagram," *The New York Times* reported. "Mr. Gabbana said his account was hacked."[79]

The ensuing controversy scuttled the show. But that wasn't the end of the story.

In 2019, Dolce & Gabbana filed a lawsuit in Italy against the owners of the Diet Prada account, Tony Liu and Lindsey Schuyler, seeking a staggering €450 million (roughly $600 million) in damages to "restore brand image since 2018." The fashion house argues that the constant indictments of their company by the Instagram account cost the company valuable partnerships with celebrities, and it seeks to recoup the lost revenue from both the Shanghai show and anticipated sales in the Asian market. For his part, Stefano Gabbana has filed a separate one-million-euro lawsuit alleging defamation.[80]

As of this writing, Dolce & Gabbana have not yet commented publicly on the lawsuit, which only became public knowledge after Diet Prada solicited donations to its legal defense fund in March 2021. The designers' quietness and their choice of venue—Italy, where standards to prove defamation are looser than they are in the United States—suggests that the suit may be more of a shot across their internet-based critics' bows. Nevertheless, the firm's willingness to mount an assault on one of the citadels of anti-appropriation discourse and court all the risks that entails suggests the game has changed.

For all the hazards associated with offending the very online consumers of the sort of content provided by outlets like Diet Prada, the threat to this firm's reputation and, thus, the bottom line had become even more intolerable.

What may look on its surface like a company observing its fiduciary responsibilities to shareholders could, in fact, herald a more serious backlash against the uncompromising call-out culture that has overtaken the fashion industry.

"The chances are that you will be taken down from backlash

by an angry mob. And so, people are privately feeling one thing and publicly saying another," Tate-Cutler concluded in our conversation. "And I would include myself in this. I do not say clearly how I feel about people wearing their value systems on their sleeves."

Dedicating yourself to an austere principle that maintains the clothes you wear should also weigh you down with the ever-present understanding of your place in the world and the crushing gravity of the history that put you there is a bleak way to live. That's a burden anyone would instinctually slough off were it not for the social pressure applied by this new class of moralizers.

For the New Puritan stylist, there is meaning and dignity in politically resonant fashion choices, and there is a self-righteous thrill to be found in imposing them on others. None of this is unique to this historical moment, nor is it hard to see where all this is going.

For most of its existence, the phrase "wearing your politics on your sleeve" was an insult, not a value proposition. It's not unreasonable to expect that the stigma around platitudinous and insecure expressions of fealty to political concepts you don't fully comprehend will one day make a comeback. How much damage this movement will leave in its wake, however, remains an open question.

FEAR OF GOD

THE EVIL OF BANALITY

The New Puritans' behaviors are predicated on the idea that this world can be perfected. Therefore, it *must* be perfected. That project demands clarity of vision and unity of purpose not just from themselves but from everyone else. The puritanical progressive is confident that they understand that vision and how to achieve it.

By now, we can safely conclude that this extreme interpretation of progressive politics, one that manifests in a mistrust of your trivial pleasures, is a result of ego run amok. These activists are living out a psychodrama in their heads. But why are they obsessing over the shadows on the wall? Why are they so convinced that they alone can discern the evil seductions within seemingly innocent occupations?

Beyond honestly believing they're doing the Lord's work, the New Puritans must also find it gratifying to think of themselves as uniquely perceptive. If you are so astute that you can see the hideous hidden workings of the world, you're a member of an exclusive club. And once you get a taste of that comprehensive vision—a theory of everything that reveals to you the secret, seedy underbelly of society—it can become intoxicating. Those who are attracted to this psychological orientation are likely to find that its applications are limitless. And when they apply this framework to just about everything, they find that just about everything is a problem.

This belief—a mystical decoder ring that unlocks doors that remain closed to the uninitiated—creates a handful of corollaries. Motivated by a passion for uncovering secret sins, New Puritans must engage in intense self-examination to make sure that secret sins do not also exist within themselves. This inquisition rejects the idea of private sin because there is no such thing as a private life. Practitioners of this rigid code must constantly analyze the most anodyne of customs and habits in the hunt for dangerous subversion. Every activity, no matter how banal, must be scrutinized under a microscope.

Among the most observant activists, few things are as dangerous as your trivial and diversionary hobbies, in part because you don't know just how wicked they are. You probably aren't even familiar with the sinful origins of your happy amusements. At the very least, you thought your hobby wasn't hurting anyone. Thankfully, the New Puritan is here to tell you how very wrong you are.

A July 2000 study aptly titled "Racism, Racism Everywhere" found that America's legacy of racial segregation tainted the act of baseball-card collecting.[1] More recent studies have invalidated these findings, noting that "player performance is the most important factor affecting the value of a player's card." Still, the more sensational study maintains its grip on the progressive imagination and is often cited.

"An increasing number of men are taking up sewing," *The New York Times* reported in 2020, "not only to break traditional gender stereotypes, but also [to] advocate body acceptance, racial justice, and more sustainable lifestyles."[2] Left unanswered: Do any of these men *enjoy* sewing? Who knows? We must assume that existing as a walking billboard advertisement for social justice is its own reward.

Maybe home decorating is your thing? Well then, your thing is racist. At least, it is if it involves organic cotton fiber.

In 2017, Tennessee-based Lipscomb University president Randy Lowry invited a group of African American students to his home for dinner. The purpose of the affair was to have a frank discussion about the concerns of the school's black student body in a comfortable and intimate setting. Lowry soon found himself at the center of a firestorm when one of his guests published an image on social media of the table setting, which included a jar filled with decorative cotton stalks.

One student who attended the dinner reported that Lowry's guests confronted him over his decorative choices. The university president allegedly defended the centerpiece as "fallish," adding that cotton cannot be "inherently bad if we're all wearing it." But that only set these already incensed students off even more.

The university president was accused, at the very least, of poor taste for overlooking the history of American slavery and its association with cotton crops. He soon issued an apology for the oversight. "The content of the centerpieces was offensive, and I could have handled the situation with more sensitivity," Lowry wrote.[3]

In their defense, these students weren't the first to react with indignation to the mere sight of cotton stalks. It somehow became a national news story when one Texas woman posted a comment on the arts and crafts retailer Hobby Lobby's Facebook page attacking their decision to sell cotton fronds. The retailer, she said, was "wrong on so many levels" because the commodity was once "gained at the expense of African American slaves."

The educational website Learning for Justice observed that anyone who dismisses these two incidents as innocent is ignorant of both the history of cotton and the undeniable fact that cotton balls *have* been used in genuinely racist efforts to intimidate black people.[4] That is true in the broadest sense, but it is not applicable to either of these two cases. We are once again being asked to subordinate elementary discretion to an ideological standard that rejects the consideration of context and intentionality.

Raw cotton isn't the only fabric that is proscribed in the new catechism. For some, yarn is similarly objectionable. At least, it is when it's used in the conflict-ridden practice of knitting.

It all started with a January 2019 blog post on the knitting enthusiast website Fringe Association. There, the blog's proprietor, Karen Templer, had the audacity to express her excitement over an upcoming trip to India—a locale so foreign to her that it was "like being offered a seat on a flight to Mars." In that stream-of-consciousness display of enthusiasm, Templer discussed her childhood fascination with the subcontinent's literature and history, the fantastically colorful dress that is common to India, and her childhood friend of Indian descent whose mother's cooking she regrets not trying in her youth.[5]

The internet proceeded to do what it does best: Come up with the least charitable interpretation of her remarks, attribute them to the most odious of motives imaginable, assign those motives to the blogger, and demand satisfaction.

According to her critics, Templer harbored racial hatreds toward the Indians she claimed to admire so much. "From what it sounded like she did not mean to be racist," one of her more gracious critics conceded. "However, there is no excuse for racism."[6] The outrage was loud enough that Templer felt compelled to apologize. "India is not a set or a backdrop for white people," the properly reeducated blogger wrote in a self-denunciation. "I'm coming to India from a place of respect for the relevance of textiles in the country's liberation from British rule." She inexplicably added that her remark about "Mars" was not intended to convey to her readers the impression that Indians were the equivalent of extraterrestrials. Presumably, some offense was caused along these lines.

But the damage was done. "The knitting community is racist," one outraged knitting enthusiast wrote in a statement on Instagram. "Keeping knitting, or anything else, away from 'political issues' is a privilege," she added. The world of recreational knitters was so riven by the controversy that it eventually found its way into a feature essay by *Vox*'s Jaya Saxena.

Saxena observed that Templer's post "was like bingo for every conversation a white person has ever had with me about their 'fascination' with my dad's home country," insofar as India seemed to exist as a "*colorful* and *complex* and *inspiring*" exotic location—and only "for them." Thus, Templer wasn't just guilty of "whitewashing" knitting; she was also thoughtlessly exoticizing India. What followed was a sprawling essay on the nexus between knitting, ethnic identity, and racism.

Eventually, Saxena arrived at one of the most pressing sociological conundrums of our time. "Social media also makes pointing out racism easier than ever," she observed without any discernable disapproval. Indeed, the author seemed to find this valuable. Social media venues have "allowed knitters of color to retain control over the conversation," she observed, while also relieving their users of the pressure to follow "the social norms of 'polite conversation.'"[7]

Saxena's observation is undeniably correct. Whether we are better off without the norms associated with "polite conversation" is, however, debatable.

If you are so well versed in the disguised forms evil takes that you can recognize it where others cannot, you're likely to feel a warm and fuzzy sense of exclusivity. Beyond the gratification individuals derive from the notion that they alone can decipher the world around them, subscribing to an idea that pulls back the curtain masking the world's scourges is useful from the perspective of a reform-minded organizer.

If the evils the progressive project seeks to extirpate are ubiquitous, there can be no boundary separating private and public life. This is an idea that allows its believers to embrace totalitarianism, by definition, because the problems that plague us are total. To circumscribe our renunciation of the Devil's works would be to tie one hand behind our back in this existential conflict. Moderation in the eternal fight against vice is no virtue.

The Puritans knew this as well as anyone.

• • •

When we think of a typical Puritan, our minds are likely drawn to stereotypes. A simple word-association game would lead most Americans to equate Puritanism with a caricatured bluenose: prudish, cloistered, cold, and dogmatic. Many of those clichés are derived from fictionalized accounts of the period. Perhaps the most famous, Arthur Miller's 1953 play *The Crucible*, is less a historical account of the conditions that prevailed in the seventeenth and early eighteenth centuries than a political parable about the early 1950s.

The story follows three young women who were accused of practicing the dark arts. They were hounded mercilessly by the magistrates tasked with adjudicating such claims. Miller did considerable research into the period before writing *The Crucible*, but he took some license. He toyed with the ages of his protagonists to justify a central plot device: an affair between John Proctor, one of the condemned, and his spurned accuser, the alleged witch Abigail Williams. This conceit was necessary not only to make the protagonist sympathetic (in reality, Abigail Williams was not yet twelve years old, and Proctor would have been in his sixties), but to establish the perversities of Puritanism.

Scorned by her ex-lover, Williams turns on Proctor in court. Alleging that he is the "Devil's man," she puts on a terrifying performance of demonic possession, and the court seals his fate. The author intended to make Puritanism the play's true antagonist. The moral of the story is that the ultimately murderous tenets of this paranoid system of social organization can be resisted by the wise and pure of heart.[8]

Miller's *The Crucible* was less an account of how the town of Salem, Massachusetts, prosecuted allegations of witchcraft than it was an allegory for Senator Joe McCarthy's efforts to expose Americans with alleged Communist sympathies.

Miller's conception of sin and free will appeal to the modern reader, but they don't much reflect the Puritan ethic. Proctor's ability to see through his coreligionists' superstitions is unrealistic. "In the seventeenth century, virtually everyone believed in witches," George McKenna wrote. "The trial record reveals no one, not even the defendants, expressing any doubt on that score."[9]

Moreover, as Michael Winship notes, trials for witchcraft were relatively rare and the general public was often keener to see harsh justice meted out than the presiding magistrates. While the jury's verdict tended to be informed by the fury of "religious populism" that prevailed at the time, more judicious minds empowered to overrule those verdicts were not shy about doing so.[10]

Ultimately, Miller's tale imparts to the reader a general sense that the all-consuming fear of God animating the average Puritan was an evitable phenomenon. All it would have taken was the courage to stand against a social tide you know to be wrong. This jury's verdict was a sin. And if Puritans rejected sin as readily as they claimed, this outcome should have been avoidable. In Miller's telling, it is easy for the virtuous to recognize superstition if you only apply a mental package of values and assumptions smuggled into the seventeenth century from the twentieth. But the Puritans did not simply abjure sin—sin was in the very air they breathed. It was pervasive and perceptible only to the most devout practitioners of the faith.

Even the victims of witch hunts believed in the omnipresence of sin and the existence of witches. It's unrealistic to believe that practicing Puritans could have recognized their own paranoias. It is equally unlikely that the New Puritans are aware of the social pressures exerting their influence all around them.

In McKenna's groundbreaking treatise, *The Puritan Origins of American Patriotism*, the author posits five propositions to which seventeenth- and eighteenth-century colonial Puritans generally subscribed.

They ranged from the belief in America as a land of providence, to proscriptions against idleness, to the notion that community activism contributed to one's personal salvation. But McKenna's fifth proposition deserves particular attention: what he called the puritanical orientation toward "anxious introspection."

"The Devil's works are not just external," he wrote. "Ultimately we are saved or damned by what is inside us.

"Our souls are constantly threatened by corruption, moral libertinism, hypocrisy, and, above all, pride," McKenna continued. "We need constantly to examine our hearts. There is no such thing as private sin; each sin adversely affects the commonwealth."[11]

This idea—the notion that there is no such thing as private life—animated the Puritan movement just as it has influenced the utopian progressivism into which it evolved. It does away with the special distinctions between the sin, the sinner, and the environment in which the sin is committed. All exist within the same continuum; all are interrelated and interdependent. As the mid-eighteenth-century Protestant preacher Jonathan Edwards taught his disciples, we are all "sinners in the hands of an angry God."[12]

He "abhors you," Edwards preached. "You are ten thousand times so abominable in His eyes, as the most hateful and venomous serpent is in ours." In our wretched state, we become worthy of redemption only when we observe absolute obedience, and unerring subservience cannot be but the product of fear.

God's judgment is not a capricious thing. It is well earned, whatever your fate may be.

In colonial Massachusetts, political reformers determined that virtue was not a subjective condition; it was empirically observable—both in the individual and society more broadly. For that matter, so, too, was vice. That which was not clearly one was almost certainly the other. As such, private practices that were not explicitly approved of were suspect.

Across the Puritan world, magistrates banned smoking tobacco products in public, forced households to destroy dice and decks of cards, and enforced observance of the Sabbath via edict, if only to preserve the outward appearance of propriety.[13] Puritan courts regularly fined those accused of suffering from the "itching disease" of gambling. Betting against the outcomes in games of chance was stigmatized and criminalized, and for theologically sensible reasons. Petitioning God to intervene in the pettiest of circumstances and only for pecuniary gain was, at minimum, a little gauche.[14]

During the English Civil War and under the Protectorate of Oliver Cromwell, Protestantism's most zealous reformers waged a ruthless campaign against proclivities that were thought to be a gateway to sin. Parliament passed laws closing all theaters, banning maypoles, and forbidding the celebration of religious holidays. Legislatures introduced fines for swearing that increased progressively based on the offender's social rank and imposed the death penalty on adulterers. On the Sabbath, it was forbidden to travel, dance, sing secular songs, play games, conduct commerce, or drink alcohol. "In 1657, Parliament was reduced to having a long and earnest debate over whether simply sitting at a gate or door should be added to the list of prohibited Sunday behavior—it was not, by two votes," the historian Michael Winship wrote.[15]

New England's Puritanism tended to burn hotter than even that of their zealous cousins in the Old World. The American Puritan's distaste for holidays was particularly instructive. On its face, the prohibition against the celebration of Christmas (and Easter, and Whitsunday, the festival of the Pentecost) was just another pincer in the faith's total war against Catholic practices and their pagan origins. And yet, Puritan clergymen and thought leaders of the time gave away the game when they admitted what they really hoped to achieve by banning the celebration of religious holidays.

"Men dishonor Christ more in the twelve days of Christmas than in all the twelve months besides," the preacher Hugh Latimer mourned. The famously stern Cotton Mather also dissented against "the feast of Christ's nativity," which is "spent in reveling, dicing, carding, masking, and in all licentious liberty . . . by mad mirth, by long eating, by hard drinking, by lewd gaming."[16]

It wasn't just that these diversions distracted revelers from God's mission, though that was a part of the problem. These unwholesome amusements could also twist and disfigure your soul, and they might corrupt those around you. The Devil's influence was a contagion that must be quarantined.

Recall from chapter 2 the preacher Benjamin Colman, whose treatise on what constitutes proper, wholesome mirth remains the most comprehensive document establishing the preferred forms of puritanical recreation. Colman preached that "mirth may and generally does degenerate into sin," and that humankind's highest calling was to emulate Jesus, who was more than anything else "a man of sorrow."[17] As such, decadent merriments were among the most sinful activities.

"Puritans wrote much about the need for recreation and leisure to have a positive side," Bruce Daniels observed, "but they wrote much more about the negative side always lurking just beneath the surface of even the most innocent appearing of activities." So, too, do the New Puritans.

For the old Puritan, it wasn't the holiday itself that was the threat so much as the revelry and impious thoughts that the holiday encouraged. For the New Puritan, the problem is pretty much the same.

The fear that haunts our modern moralists isn't just that holidays encouraged debauched merriment. Their concern is that these festivities allow you to stop thinking about the world's suffering and your contributions to that agony. It's your flippant disregard for "the importance of providing culturally sustaining, anti-racist holiday lessons, resources, and conversations" that has become intolerable. That is how the Center for Racial Justice in Education presents its itemized list of resources for instructors ahead of the annual "winter holiday season."[18]

This would be unobjectionable if this list of teaching resources was designed to help secular educators provide inclusive and nondenominational instruction around the holiday season. After all, the cultural and religious origins of the various midwinter celebrations are distinct. But this exercise is less about inclusion than exclusion.

As one of those resources—Everyday Feminism—observes, "Your Christian privilege grants you time off work for your religious holidays, a 'jury of your peers' who are likely to share your faith in court, and bias toward your religion in educational institutions." It's okay to celebrate Christmas, this essay grudgingly concedes. But you should probably feel bad about your tacit contributions to the "systemic oppression" associated with "the context of the dominant culture" when you do.[19]

The psychological torments Christianity and its signature solstice holiday have imposed on American minorities are legion, according to social-justice activist Paul Kivel. His admonishments range from the reasonable—like the fact that you've probably been instructed at some point by a Christian authority figure, like a minister or counselor or even vestigial Christian organization like the YMCA, which is not the experience of most non-Christians—to the absurd. If you "have ever heard heaven and good described as light or white and hell and evil described as dark or black," or if you measure time based on the Christian calendar, Kivel declares, you are contributing to the "dominant culture."[20]

Writing in *The Independent*, the left-wing writer and activist Jordan Uhl declared that the holidays are a waste if you don't spend those precious moments with close family bullying them over their indifference to society's injustices.

You should browbeat your grandma over "voter-suppression laws" and remind your uncle that "white homegrown terrorists, not Muslims" have killed more Americans than Islamic radicals. Don't let your family have a second slice of culturally appropriated apple pie before pointing out America's historical abuse of Native Americans. "Before everyone rushes to the couch for football and post-meal naps," Uhl adds, make sure you "disprove your relatives' false narratives of minorities committing most of the crimes" by reciting the FBI's hate-crime statistics.[21] Sounds like a joyous affair.

The transatlantic left has a long history of encouraging young activists to descend on their unlearned elders and inform them of their moral and political failings. This condescending tradition is as old as progressivism itself, likely beginning with the "settlement movement" of the late nineteenth century.

In 1884, the charitable institution Toynbee Hall was founded to address generational poverty in London's run-down East End. There, young and enthusiastic "university men" were encouraged to "settle" in working-class neighborhoods where they would proselytize their progressive values. The movement took off. In the United States, the Neighborhood Guild had a similar mission as Toynbee Hall. In Russia, this impulse manifested in young socialist revolutionaries decamping to the countryside to inculcate bitter class consciousness in the peasantry. In all its forms, the settlement movement had a strong whiff of condescension and naivete.

In the United States, the progressive activist class's arguments against thoughtlessly enjoying the December holidays sound like boilerplate secularism. Their true qualms are, however, less with uniquely religious affairs than they are with uniquely American festivities and the uniquely American ways in which they are celebrated.

Halloween—a North-American reimagining of what other cultures celebrate as All Saints' Day, All Hallows' Eve, All Souls' Day, or the Day of the Dead—has become grist for the content mill in left-wing media. Every year, the insatiable gaping maw of online click farms demand ever more costumes to be sacrificed upon the altar of cultural appropriation. We're well beyond the point of observing cultural sensitivities. We've transmuted inclusivity into something more closely resembling race essentialism, in which dressing up in clothing native to any nation but the one into which you were born constitutes a cultural crime.

This impulse verges on the farcical when it is applied to fiction and lore. According to the women's interest digital magazine Bustle, dressing your child up as an Egyptian god risks offending sensibilities—particularly if your costume is accompanied with an ankh. "This might just seems [*sic*] like a beautiful costume," they claimed, "but it's a symbol of a culture that was violently appropriated centuries ago." That would be news to the hippies of the 1960s and '70s, for whom the ankh was a life-affirming symbol of Eastern wisdom that communicated their distaste for consumerist materialism.

Moreover, Bustle continued, Halloween revelers should avoid dressing up as ninjas because it would be "essentially a parody of the real-life ninjas who existed in Japan." And please steer clear of anything resembling Middle Eastern garb, because such costumes "often incorporate items that imply violence, ultimately reducing a diverse group of people down to a single, stereotypic monolith."[22] It is apparently the height of sophistication now to assume that any homage to Middle Eastern culture is tantamount to likening all Middle Easterners to terrorists.

The Disney character from the eponymous film *Moana* is another source of apprehension. Writing for the nightmarishly named blog *Raising Race Conscious Children*, the author Sachi Feris describes the process of arguing her daughter out of her desire to wear a Moana costume because "Moana's culture is not our culture."[23] *Cosmopolitan* confirmed the wisdom of this neuroticism. "If your kid wears a racist costume," the magazine affirmed in 2017, "you're kind of wearing it, too."[24]

As University of Miami Law School professor Osamudia James reminded *Washington Post* readers that same year, "avoiding offense at Halloween requires thinking not just about stereotypes or discrimination but also about white supremacy."[25]

Of course, the promotion of cultural sensitivities—or just not being a jerk—is a deliberate exercise. But just as with fashion and stand-up comedy, we are now being asked to disregard intent when evaluating a potentially offensive act. What began as a well-meaning effort to make young adults more conscious of the feelings they might be wounding with their callous satire has become a campaign to rob young children of their innocence and impose on them their parent's racial anxieties.

If Halloween is such a fraught enterprise, you ask, why not just do away with it entirely? They're way ahead of you.

"Trick-or-treating in Milwaukee reflects and entrenches the city's deep racial and economic divides," former Harvard University Law School lecturer John Muller wrote for *Politico* in 2018. It is a holiday that "lends outsize importance to fears of violence and the unfamiliar," aggravates cultural and intercommunity tensions, and exacerbates "structural inequalities." Muller determined that neither "citywide Halloween events nor trick-or-treat schedules can solve that problem." Draw your own conclusion.[26]

The fourth Thursday in November, on which Americans celebrate Thanksgiving, is another source of consternation for those who allow holidays to irritate them.

Conceptually, there isn't much about Thanksgiving that puritanically inclined progressives would look upon fondly. It celebrates the establishment of the Mayflower Compact and the Plymouth Colony organized around it. That foothold in the New World would not have been possible without the aid of the local Native American tribes, who were subsequently displaced (albeit with a lot of intervening history of conflict, diplomacy, and intertribal politics). It is the forerunner to both Black Friday and Cyber Monday, two events that celebrate unadulterated consumerism. It was formally established by Abraham Lincoln in 1863 to commemorate what were at the time the Union's few and far between victories in the Civil War, forever coupling it with reverence for the Republic and its Constitution. If you find more to criticize than celebrate in the above, you're probably not going to see Thanksgiving as an absolute good.

"Thanksgiving Day should be known as National Land Theft and American Genocide Day," *Huffington Post* contributor Nicole Breedlove cheerfully submitted. She contended that the holiday's roots are embedded in soil soaked through with Pequot blood. Only after the 1637 massacre of one of this tribe's villages did American colonists begin to even think about providence or gratitude, Breed-love contended. "So when you sit down to dinner this year," she concluded, "think about the countless Native Americans who lost their lives so you can carve a turkey and get the best deals on Black Friday."[27]

The folk history of this holiday that children are (or rather, were) taught in elementary school is "socially irresponsible," the teachers' resource Learning for Justice advised.[28] They recommend educators teach Thanksgiving as a "National Day of Mourning," citing a recommendation in a 1970 speech by the Native American activist Wamsutta Frank James.[29] The lesson planners at ArtsAndJustice.org suggest renaming it "ThanksTaking."[30]

And if all that is just too much, you could do away with the holiday entirely. "One indication of moral progress in the United States would be the replacement of Thanksgiving Day and its self-indulgent family feasting with a National Day of Atonement accompanied by a self-reflective collective fasting," University of Texas at Austin professor Robert Jensen declared.[31]

That doesn't sound like a ton of fun. But then, if we're dedicating ourselves to the pursuit of "moral progress," fun is not the goal.

By the early nineteenth century, Puritanism's remnants in America had shed much of its religious character. The Puritans' progressive progeny were more invested in pursuing a morally righteous state within a liberal, secular order than in saving souls. Their objectives were no longer confined to a particular church or limited to one community or another. Their aspiration remained the extirpation of social sins, but religious conviction was less important than adherence to a moral code.

And yet, many of the old Puritan habits persisted. Though social reformers' goal was to improve and eventually perfect their external conditions, all the policy reforms in the world could not make for a more perfect social covenant if evil still lurked in men's hearts. Like their seventeenth-century counterparts, progressive reformers of the 1800s believed that unwholesome activities had the power to awaken a person's inherently evil nature and contribute to society's degeneracy.

In much the same way, the New Puritans are just as concerned that the banal preoccupations you amuse yourself with are corrupting you and defiling your surroundings. The great outdoors is just as fraught with the dramas and tensions that seem to plague every other aspect of society.

Following the sickening 2020 murder of Ahmaud Arbery by three white Georgia men while he was jogging, the historian and marathon runner Dr. Natalia Mehlman Petrzela took to the pages of *The New York Times* to allege that this extraordinary case was only the most vicious expression of a common phenomenon.

"Running," she averred, "has been a pastime marketed primarily to white people ever since 'the jogging craze' was born in the lily-white Oregon track and field world of the late 1960s." What's more, "Black people have not only been excluded from the sport," Mehlman Petrzela insisted, "they've also been relentlessly depicted as a threat to legitimate, white joggers." To support her thesis, the doctor claims that outdoor cardio was depicted in the twentieth-century popular culture—indeed, all her examples were from the twentieth century—as a white person's pastime. Nevertheless, in her view, Arbery's murder is just the latest example of the "glaring whiteness of recreational running."[32]

Gardening routinely ranks as one of America's most popular pastimes, and for good reason. It involves taxing physical labor, though you don't feel like you're burning calories and strengthening your heart while you do it. Soaking in the sun's rays is a critical source of vitamin D and exposing yourself to allergens strengthens your immune system. Most wonderfully, the healthy bacteria abundant in topsoil have physical properties that literally make you happy. One famous study published in the academic journal *Neuroscience* found that the microbial life in soil activates serotonin-releasing neurons in the brain, which happen to be the same nerves stimulated by the popular antidepressant Prozac.[33]

Of course, all this felicity must be alloyed with the understanding that your little garden is a modest contribution to society's most nagging inequalities.

In the summer of 2020, BBC presenter and botanist James Wong wrote about the racial antagonisms in the gardening industry he had endured in an op-ed for *The Guardian*. His experience with some unenlightened neighbors in England sounds harrowing, and his gentle admonition against making people feel unwelcome in any space was unobjectionable.[34] The op-ed would have attracted little notice save for a subsequent appearance on the BBC in which Wong elaborated on the systemic abuses that accompany gardening.

"Absolutely," Wong confirmed when pressed, "U.K. gardening culture has racism baked into its DNA." He added that racism was "so integral" to the British gardening experience that the two phenomena were not severable. That fact is "epitomized, for example, by the fetishization (and wild misuse) of words like 'heritage' and 'native.'" What's more, common misconceptions about what plant species are indigenous and what aren't exposes "often unconscious ideas of what and who does and does not 'belong' in the U.K." To be educated in local botanical conventions, Wong concluded, is to expose yourself to ideas that are predicated "on a bedrock [of] xenophobia and racism."[35]

Gardening's soiled past isn't exclusive to the U.K. The organization Green America notes that the urban gardening movement owes its origins to "victory gardening" promoted and widely adopted during World War II. But that movement is tainted by America's heinous historical crimes. "The colorful, upbeat, whitewashed victory gardening posters do nothing to hint at the over 6,100 farms that were taken from Japanese Americans," the advocates mourn. "They do nothing to show the forced labor of German prisoners of war and Japanese internees, and they ignore the fact that the government had to import thousands of Mexican workers to keep the United States food supply stable."[36]

As urban agriculture specialist Yolanda Gonzalez told Green-Biz, small-plot gardening can be part of our "anti-racist urban ag policies and advance land and food sovereignty for Black, Indigenous, people of color [BIPOC] urban farmers." But only if you are properly mournful when you do it.

Even the birds are racist. Well, at least bird-*watching* is pregnant with racist overtones. As *The Washington Post*'s Darryl Fears contends, "racism and colonialism are in ornithology's DNA." John James Audubon was a slave owner—the eponymous society he founded bears the name of an "oppressor." John Kirk Townsend, for whom the Townsend's Warbler and Townsend's Solitaire are named, was a practitioner of the racist theory of phrenology. The writings of the British naturalist Alfred Russel Wallace, who is responsible for classifying the *Semioptera wallacii* birds of paradise, are replete with racial epithets.

It's not just bird-watching that's suspect but most forms of amateur naturalism. "Conservation has been driven by white patriarchy," Clemson University professor and ornithologist Drew Lanham told Fears. Birds, generally, "are a reminder that this field that I work in was primarily developed and shaped by people not like me, who probably would have viewed me as lesser," University of Hawaii ornithology student Olivia Wang agreed. As one ornithology activist observed, "White people were the ones to name the birds after other White people." Ornithological societies are listening to these critics. They have promised that offensively named species will one day soon have new monikers. In the meantime, bird-watchers can and should find more innocuous ways to spend their time off.[37]

You won't find any respite in the meditative solitude that was once available in simple pastimes like fly-fishing either. Not if *Angling Trade* magazine can help it.

Writing for the magazine in the fateful summer of 2020, contributor Joel R. Johnson noted that one of the biggest recent developments for the sport was that the fishing, hunting, and sporting-goods company Orvis had signed on with the "Brown Folks Fishing initiative." That campaign has the commendable goal of building relationships with communities of color and expanding interest in and access to fishing equipment, licenses, and sites. But after he wrote about this valuable initiative, Johnson made the mistake of reading the anonymous online comments under the article. The notoriously provocative comments section informed him that most fishing enthusiasts weren't happy about this development. They were only provoked by the encroachment of politics into their hobby.

"Reactions ranged from 'I go fishing to get away from this' to 'I hope this is a joke, I've never seen racism in fly-fishing,'" Johnson wrote. He was repulsed. Johnson, a black man, informed his readers that he had experienced not only racism on the water but violence, too. Those are the most overt manifestations of racism. Still, racial discrimination also takes the form of white readers who become annoyed by the demand that they must confront racism during their leisure time, too. "It continues to work when no one thinks it does (kinda like the Devil)," Johnson wrote. "You may not believe in the Devil, but racism believes in you."[38]

This sort of thing could be written off as a little overwrought, but a product of bitter experience and good intentions. These avid hobbyists only want to promote the observance of basic human decency in their respective pastimes, which would be not only unobjectionable but praiseworthy. That certainly describes DriveTribe contributor Jesus Garcia's thoughtful piece asking himself and his fellow gearheads if sexism had become a lamentable feature of car culture.[39] But that thoughtfulness becomes something else when questions about sexism devolve into diatribes about "toxic masculinity."

"Car culture didn't create the toxic masculinity," Streetsblog USA contributor Kea Wilson conceded. "But it's certainly used its worst tropes to its advantage from its start." By backing up her argument with a variety of mid-twentieth-century car advertisements that leveraged male sexual fantasies to sell automobiles, Wilson's argument seems sufficiently supported. But she didn't stop there.

"The rhetoric that lead [*sic*] to the approval of the Federal Highway Act was deeply infused with toxic masculine tropes of no-expenses-spared nationalism and the importance of achieving economic dominance over our foreign rivals," Wilson continued. The claim that a national highway system to facilitate the movement of road-mobile military assets during America's great power competition with the Soviet Union represents a Freudian expression of misogyny is, to put it mildly, a huge stretch.

Wilson goes on to note that the automotive industry's lobbying for harsher penalties against jaywalking pedestrians is indicative of men "bodily dominating" women. "Motorized vehicles, by definition, are dominant, violent, environment-destroying machines," Wilson averred. If we want a more "healthy masculinity," she concludes, "we may need to find another way to get around."[40]

Car culture isn't just sexist. Automobiles, it turns out, are equal-opportunity bigots.

In 2016, Harvard University economics professor Roland Freyer published a surprising study that dispelled a narrative preferred by antipolice activists. The notion that black Americans are more likely to be fatally shot by police than whites, he found, had no empirical basis. What Freyer did find was that African Americans were more likely than whites to be touched, pushed, handcuffed, or intimidated during encounters with law enforcement.[41] Many of those interactions are the result of routine traffic stops for a litany of offenses that defy reason (prior to the summer of 2021, for example, the Minneapolis Police Department could pull you over if you had an object like an air freshener dangling from your rearview mirror).[42]

What's the solution? Well, *Sierra* magazine senior editor Paul Rauber conceded, society could invest gobs of money improving police training, recruiting diverse officers into the force, and paring back the legal immunities afforded law enforcement. "But there is another, perhaps simpler way," he posited. You'll never guess. "The solution," Bay Area racial justice activist Darrell Owens told Rauber, "is more bike lanes, more public transit, less driving. That's the solution that ultimately curves traffic violations down to zero."

For some, the conundrum associated with police interactions gone wrong is a function of too many laws. For others, it's a matter of insufficient police training. For the New Puritan, the problem is the existence of cars.

The tendency among the puritanically inclined to see evil lurking in the mundane and everyday complements their desire to unite all these hidden transgressions as part of one vast conspiracy. But in rejecting the nuances that typify so much of the human condition, these activists have overlooked the good and emphasized the bad. Theirs is not a fuller but a narrower understanding of these traditions and the value of our pastimes.

All of us are to some degree susceptible to this. It's a deeply human trait to seek out the simple and comprehensive and abjure the complex. The trick is to have enough self-awareness to recognize this psychological predilection and catch yourself in the act of succumbing to it. That's much easier said than done, especially when it entails bucking social pressures to adopt a preferred narrative that simultaneously explains the world around you and absolves you of any fault for contributing to its woes.

In the New Puritan imagination, our appealing amusements that disguise evil have evolved beyond dancing around the maypole and ambling heedlessly on the Sabbath to include even the most benign hobbies. And yet, the rationale behind what we would otherwise chalk up to neurosis is the same today as it was four hundred years ago: a fear of idleness. Or, more specifically, a fear of what the indolent are capable of. There are few activities that both encourage sloth and hold the idle captive to wicked stimuli as much as video gaming. As such, modern moral reformers across the political spectrum have come to regard this practice with a mixture of hostility and outright dread.

In 1958, the physicist and Manhattan Project scientist William Higinbotham manipulated a cathode-ray tube display used in radar systems so that a little digital dot bounced from one end of a screen to the other. On that day, he created what is believed to have been the first video game. Higinbotham called his game *Tennis for Two*, and the technology paved the way to the first commercially successful video game, *Pong*, in 1972.[43]

The technological advancements in the fourteen years that separated *Tennis for Two* and *Pong* weren't that profound. But what did change in the intervening years were society's attitudes toward this new technology.

In 1976, the coin-operated-amusements manufacturer and game developer Exidy released an arcade game based on the 1975 Paul Bartel action film, *Death Race 2000*, starring David Carradine and Sylvester Stallone. That movie took place in a dystopian future in which the United States played host to a murderous cross-country auto race, wherein contestants were required to run down pedestrians for points.

But while this bloody action classic featured plenty of gore, the video-game version of the film was little more than a series of barely recognizable black-and-white blobs that could only represent cars and their humanoid targets (deemed "gremlins" by the game designer) if you squinted hard enough. Nevertheless, behavioral scientists, safety consultants, and, of course, politicians determined that the game was an instrument dedicated to the incitement of real-world violence.[44] It was the start of a trend that has yet to abate nearly fifty years later.

In the decades that followed, video games would become a convenient scapegoat to explain otherwise senseless acts of violence.

The early 1990s arena fighting game *Mortal Combat* was attacked by then Democratic senators Joe Lieberman and Herbert Kohl due to its realistic (for the time) depictions of gore. The game's popularity inspired the creation of a ratings system to regulate the marketing of games with mature themes.

When two high school students killed twelve of their classmates and a teacher at Colorado's Columbine High School in 1999, some public figures blamed the event on the popular first-person shooter game *Doom*. "For a generation, Hollywood and computerized games have undermined the core values of civility and it is time they were stopped by a society that values free speech enough to protect it," said former house speaker Newt Gingrich, to the applause of the federal lawmakers he was addressing.[45]

In her 2000 campaign for U.S. Senate, Hillary Clinton argued in favor of legislation that would impose penalties on retailers that sell adult-rated games to minors. California followed her lead, only for the Supreme Court to later rule that the state could not restrict the sale of a legal media product without violating the First Amendment.

Following the 2012 massacre of elementary school students in Connecticut's Sandy Hook Elementary School, Democrat-turned-independent Senator Lieberman said the shooter had an "almost hypnotic involvement" in "particularly violent video games." Then-president Barack Obama appeared to agree. He later called on Congress to fund research into the psychological effects of video gaming as part of his plan to seek systemic remedies for gun crime in the United States.[46]

As recently as 2019, lawmakers like the Republican lieutenant governor of Texas, Dan Patrick, and GOP House minority leader Kevin McCarthy were blaming video games that "dehumanized individuals" like the *Grand Theft Auto* series for mass shootings, even though the series hadn't had a new entry in six years at the time of these allegations.[47] "We must stop the glorification of violence in our society," then-president Donald Trump said in the wake of two mass shootings that year. "This includes the gruesome and grisly video games that are now commonplace."

We've now had several decades to study the links between gaming and violence, and researchers have failed to establish a connection. "Scant evidence has emerged that makes any causal or correlational connection between playing violent video games and actually committing violent activities," read a 2017 statement from the media psychology division of the American Psychological Association. "Efforts to 'link' violent crimes to violent video games and other media may persist due to a well-known phenomenon called 'confirmation bias,' or the tendency to pay attention only to information that confirms prior beliefs and ignore that which does not."[48]

In sum, the belief that violent games produce violent people persists because the figures who look upon these games with suspicion reinforce their preexisting prejudices by disregarding evidence that conflicts with their priors. But the data just doesn't add up. "The data on bananas causing suicide is about as conclusive," Stetson University psychology professor Chris Ferguson told one reporter. "Literally. The numbers work out about the same."[49]

That's an important corrective. Unfortunately, those who are most inclined to accept these researchers' conclusions have just replaced one bias with another. Gone is any support for the idea that games give way to real-world violence. But still with us is the equally subjective notion that video games promote depravity—racism, homophobia, and misogyny.

"Video games do have a big problem, but it is not stylized virtual violence," wrote *New York Times* contributor Seth Schiesel in a 2018 op-ed. "Rather, it is the bigotry, social abuse, sexism, and other toxic behavior to which players too often subject one another when gaming together online."[50]

"Just as white people must grapple with their own privileges and complicity in systemic racism that hurts Black people, video games must also come to terms with the harm they've caused," *PC Magazine*'s Jordan Minor contended in 2020, citing the unregulated online forums in which anonymous users transgress against social norms by expressing bigoted sentiments.[51]

The portrayal of people of color in games, a 2020 PBS investigation revealed, often appeals to stereotypes. Black characters are "confined to the fighting genre," the report contended, and "Latinx

characters have often been portrayed as gangbangers and drug deal-
ers, as seen in the *Grand Theft Auto* franchise."[52]

The problem of stereotyping in games isn't limited to race.
Women in the world of games are depicted as "hypersexualized,"
cultural reformers contend, with unrealistic body shapes and excessive displays of skin. Moreover, female developers have complained
of a "toxic work" environment in their industries of choice. "It has
become undeniable that women working in video games are routinely abused and undermined in the workplace as well as by online
trolls," *The Guardian*'s Keza MacDonald wrote.[53]

These complaints have prompted game designers to act. Developers have formed alliances in the effort to combat "toxicity" in
the online environment, hire diverse programmers, and generally
improve the gaming experience. Users now have the option of reporting abusive players when utilizing the online networks offered
by console producers like Microsoft and Sony. But for some, these
voluntary measures don't go far enough. For them, the frustrating
constitutional protections afforded Americans are the real obstacle
to addressing gaming's seedy underbelly.

"Ambiguities within the U.S. legal system have played a role in
constraining the efforts of law enforcement during the era of online
gaming," read a 2019 *Washington Post* dispatch.[54] Worse, "many of
the titles cited most for toxic players remain the industry's most
popular," a correlation that some see as an indictment of American
society.

Our Puritan forebearers had nothing like video games, but they
did have playthings like cards and dice—and they despised them.

Plymouth Colony governor William Bradford denounced these
seemingly harmless amusements as "fooleries," and not just because
they could be used to gamble.[55] In the 1650s, the overbearing Massachusetts General Court passed a variety of laws banning the use
of these gaming instruments in what Michael Winship described as
an effort to "rein in young people's fondness" for these insidious diversions.[56]

The Puritan moralists of the seventeenth and early eighteenth century drew a bright line between children's games and what Increase Mather, father to Cotton Mather, called the "sinful sports and pastimes" of a young adult.[57] Thus, public houses were prohibited from offering patrons access to activities like bowling and shuffleboard because they contributed to idleness and all the wicked inclinations that arise from that condition.

In all things, the God-fearing Puritan must be mindful of the great project to which he should be dedicated. "We must constantly and continually, in everything, and at every time, perform service unto God in all our actions and throughout our whole course and conversation," the Congregationalist minister John Downame preached in London prior to his emigration to New England. "In the meanest duties of the basest calling, yea even in our eating and drinking, lawful sports and recreations, when as we do them in faith."[58]

Replace the great project of Puritanism with that of progressivism, and the glaring similarities are hard to ignore.

Moral crusades do not end in victory. They rarely end at all. Devilry can never be vanquished. Its influence merely transmutes into unfamiliar forms, whereupon the battle against evil begins anew. And so it was that the organs dedicated to stigmatizing the combustion of tobacco products turned their attention to a device that contains no tobacco and involves no combustion: specifically, the practice of "vaping." And their moralizing forebearers, the campaign's objectives relating to public health are, at best, a secondary consideration.

At the dawn of the seventeenth century, London was a tobacco town. The herb was smoked ubiquitously, sold in commensurate quantities, and talked about as though it were a miracle cure for everything from toothaches to venereal disease.

This conventional wisdom had its dissenters. Perhaps the most successful among them was the anonymous author of a 1602 pamphlet, *Work for Chimney-Sweepers; or, A Warning for Tabacconists.*

The tract alleged that smoking led to a variety of maladies, and it scoffed at the notion that tobacco had any medicinal value whatsoever. But the arguments within the document that appealed to the sensibilities of Protestant reformers maintained that the English should not smoke because they were a special breed. Native Americans and sailors can consume tobacco because of their distinct constitutions and "corrupt humors." The delicate and refined inhabitants of the British Isles, not so much.

"Tobacco derives from the devil and his priests in the Americas," David Harley wrote of the pamphlet's conclusions for the *Bulletin of the History of Medicine*. For Puritans, the assault on the practice of smoking represented an alternative avenue to attack the aspects of English society with which they took issue. "Both moderate and radical Puritans could unite under the banner of the reformation of manners," Harley added, "and tobacco made a new topic to vary the traditional diet of attacks on brothels and alehouses."[59]

The proscriptions in Puritan society against smoking were numerous. It was disfavored for the careless handling of fire that it encouraged—an ever-present threat that led to restrictions against the practice of smoking outdoors well beyond the borders of Puritan New England.[60] Its poorly but intuitively understood negative health consequences were also a concern. Cotton Mather, both a scholar of Puritan thought and a practitioner of the medical arts, inveighed against the "caustic *Salt* in the *Smoke*" which "may lay Foundations for Disease in Millions of unadvised People."[61]

But one of the most compelling reasons to proscribe the practice of inhaling tobacco smoke from the Puritan perspective was the curtailment of "hedonistic enjoyment." Smoking wasn't formally banned in the Massachusetts colony until 1683, but there is evidence that smokers were prosecuted for the offense prior to the ban. "Goodwife Lambert," read one account from an Ipswich court report dated April 17, 1662, "being presented for taking tobacco in the street, confessed it."[62]

American society's healthy distaste for puritanical moralizing presented an obstacle to the adoption of antismoking laws well into the twentieth century, as a 2000 Surgeon General's report, "Reducing Tobacco Use," attested. By the late 1930s, "the Puritan temperament that had fueled anticigarette activity early in the century was on the defensive," the report read. "Antipathy to Puritan moralism was strong enough to weaken faith in any research tainted by it."[63]

Because the antismoking campaign "necessarily seeks to alter personal behavior, it is cast by some as a moral reform movement." Following the discovery that smoking had "secondhand" health effects on the people in a smoker's general vicinity, the movement absolutely did assume aspects of a moral crusade.

As Richard Klein wrote in his subversively titled 1993 exploration of the history of smoking, *Cigarettes Are Sublime*, the time in which he lived was "one of those periodic moments of repression when the culture, descended from Puritans, imposes its hysterical visions and enforces its guilty constraints on society, legislating moral judgments under the guise of public health, all the while enlarging the power of surveillance and the reach of censorship to achieve a general restriction of freedom."[64]

Today, the battle to banish tobacco smoking from polite society has largely concluded in victory. The weed has been rendered taboo— at least, among the upper classes and in popular culture. But public-health advocates, antitobacco activists, and the institutions they control have become victims of their own successes.

By the end of the first decade of this century, efforts to make smoking into a vulgar and expensive habit had done all they could to reduce tobacco use. In the mid-2000s, rates of smoking that had declined steadily since the 1970s leveled off. Then, in 2007, the first commercially successful nicotine aerosolizer, "NJOY," entered the marketplace.

The personal vaporizer wasn't a new invention. The first patent for such a device was filed in the 1920s. But it wasn't until Chinese pharmacist and bedeviled smoker Hon Lik invented a rechargeable device that reliably dispersed nicotine in a cloud of propylene glycol or vegetable glycerin mist that the product took off. The device satisfied smokers insofar as it delivered both the addictive chemical they wanted and simulated the sensation of smoking. Soon enough, smoking rates began to decline once again. In 2010, adult cigarette-smokers represented 21 percent of the population in the United States. By 2015, just 15 percent continued the practice.

There is no established correlation between the rise of vaping and the decline of tobacco use, but a U.K.-based study published in *The New England Journal of Medicine* found that "e-cigarettes provided greater satisfaction and were rated as more helpful to refrain from smoking than nicotine-replacement products." Promisingly, "those in the e-cigarette group had less severe urges to smoke than did those in the nicotine-replacement group." The vaping group coughed less and produced less phlegm at the end of a year, and its members had fewer severe urges to smoke than those using traditional nicotine replacement therapies (NRTs).[65]

All good news, right? Not if you're in the antismoking business— an enterprise that is composed of nonprofits, advocacy groups, and the pharmaceutical industry, which owns the patents on almost every recognized NRT.

From vaping's inception, it came under withering assault from the antismoking industry and its allies in government, as many assumed that it was simply smoking in another form. Harvard Medical School's Jonathan Winickoff likened vaping to "bioterrorism." Matthew Myers, president of the Campaign for Tobacco-Free Kids, claimed a CDC study found that "e-cigarettes could be a gateway to nicotine addiction and use of other tobacco products," when the researchers' reached the precise opposite conclusion.[66]

When vaping opponents couldn't prove that vaping was a gateway to tobacco use, they simply deemed it so. "Hundreds of thousands of those young people will develop a nicotine addiction and ultimately switch to smoking regular cigarettes," the *Los Angeles Times* reported in 2020. The article cited a study that used a Monte Carlo simulation—a simple probability algorithm—to justify the claim.[67]

Ultimately, efforts to restrict access to vaping products enjoyed the most success after a panic erupted following an outbreak of undiagnosed lung dysfunction among vapers—so-called "popcorn lung." It was later determined that the cause of this sudden epidemic wasn't nicotine vapes, but marijuana products produced and sold primarily on the street. Those devices substituted traditional emulsifying agents like glycol and glycerin with vitamin E acetate—a synthetic form of vitamin E used in topical skin creams. That's what was making people sick.

Nevertheless, the epidemic lit a fire under preexisting efforts to take the product off American shelves. Within a year, anti-vaping groups had successfully banned "flavored" products in many American states and prohibited the sale of certain vaping products by the manufacturers directly to consumers.

The inadvertent result of the efforts to impose regulations on the vaping industry akin to those associated with "tobacco products" was to force much of the industry into the arms of Big Tobacco. NJOY was the last major market vape that wasn't owned, wholly or in part, by a tobacco company. In the years that followed, vape producers would be systematically bought out by tobacco manufacturers as it became increasingly difficult to compete in the highly regulated marketplace. Among the first firms to call for the banning of flavored "e-liquids," for example, were tobacco companies like Reynolds American (manufacturer of the e-cigarette Vuse). They could survive without that revenue while their upstart competitors in the vaping marketplace could not.

But maybe these consequences were not so inadvertent after all. Even though anti-vaping advocates' claims regarding the negative effects on users' health couldn't be duplicated in more clinical environments, their concerns about the corrupting influence these products were having on society weren't so easily refuted.

"Anna started vaping for fun during her sophomore year at a local high school," the *Texarkana Gazette* reported in 2019. "She never expected to get addicted."[68] Well, Anna should have. It's a nicotine product, and nicotine is an addictive chemical (a fact the FDA requires every producer of these products to advertise on the packaging).

The chroniclers of Anna's story observed that it's wickedly easy for children to get their hands on this product, despite the prohibition of its sale to minors. But the same could be said for lottery tickets or alcohol—both of which are proscribed to minors, and both of which have found themselves in the crosshairs of aspiring social engineers.

To be clear, no study has determined that vaping is "safe," which is a relative condition anyway. There is virtually no such thing as a risk-free activity. Studies have indicated that vaping is *safer* than habitual tobacco use, though that isn't a high bar to clear. No one, however, is affixing a stamp of approval onto this practice. You swim at your own risk.

So, if you're inclined to dissuade your children from using nicotine products, as most health-conscious parents would be, the group Very Well Family advises parents to acknowledge the obvious: People vape because they enjoy it. "To gain credibility," the wellness group notes, "acknowledge the reasons teens may want to vape—all their friends are doing it; vaping seems like the cool thing to do; the flavors sound interesting and fun." Once you make note of these realities, you can argue against them.[69]

In what may be the loudest echo from a bygone age, a 2019 study conducted by University of Texas at San Antonio criminal justice professor Dylan Jackson established a link between childhood vape use and degeneracy in adults.

"Using a nationally representative sample of 8th and 10th graders in 2017, Jackson found that adolescents who vape are at an elevated risk of engaging in criminal activities such as violence and property theft," ScienceDaily's summary of the study's abstract read.[70] Armed with the assumption that minors who vape are at increased risk of criminality in adulthood, America seems to have determined that the proper course is to saddle children with a felony charge now before they can commit a worse offense later in life. "As vaping continues to outpace traditional smoking among the nation's youth, students who a few years ago may have been charged with at most a misdemeanor for smoking a joint are now facing felony charges for having a vape pen in their backpacks," *The Texas Tribune* reported.[71]

We're not just talking about red-state reactionaries. A ban on the use of aerosolized nicotine products in public in Ocean City, Maryland, is so strictly enforced that it routinely results in the arrest of violators, including minors. In one viral video, seventeen-year-old Brian Everett Anderson was tased by police for "disorderly" conduct—an allegation the video of this event does not back up. What it does support is the "violation" of the city's anti-vaping ordinance, which the teen had disregarded in full view of the law enforcement officers who had warned him against such depraved behavior in public.[72]

This is nothing less than a collective mania.

American society's response to the popularization of vaping has all the markings of a moral panic. It's a reflection of our inherited capacity for what George McKenna called the puritanical tendency toward "anxious introspection." The concerns that inspired this absurd overreaction would be familiar to the Puritans who witnessed the witch trials with some trepidation, even if they believed that devilry was an omnipresent force. Evil's insidiousness is a particularly powerful influence over the young and indolent, and keeping an eye out for its temptations is a task without end.

We flatter ourselves today when we assume that our society has advanced beyond such superstitious pursuits. We most certainly have not.

6

TEMPERANCE

SOBER, CHASTE, AND PENITENT

The puritanical progressive is deeply suspicious of enjoyment for enjoyment's sake. That much is clear by now. But so far, the why of it all has been rooted in abstract principles. The prescriptions for a wholesome society preferred by the New Puritans do not always arise from theory alone. There is a practical dimension to their strict preferences, one that is informed by the wisdom accumulated over the centuries mankind has spent experimenting with different models of social organization.

Harmonious social relations are difficult to maintain if your highest aim in life is pleasure-seeking. That is especially true if that pursuit of self-gratification is contemptuous of the boundaries others have established for themselves and their loved ones. The preservation of a functional community demands that we impose some limits on ourselves.

That which leads us to lose control—to forget ourselves amid intemperate desire—can tear a community apart. For a brief moment in this nation's history, a movement that embraced self-indulgence as a virtue tested our unspoken but deeply engrained commitment to preserving social comity. That moment is all but over.

What we have instead is a moralistic revolution. Its vanguard isn't just seeking to root out reckless excess but anything that could possibly lead to it. This movement has whipped up a panic that is as imprecise in its aims as many of the old Puritan inquisitions were. And as is often the case, it's the poor and disempowered who consume the minds of well-heeled moral reformers. It's also the poor and disempowered who feel the sting of their panics most acutely. Thus, we're being subjected to something akin to a new temperance movement. And much like the old temperance movement, its sharpest edges are reserved mostly for those farther down the socioeconomic ladder.

Lockhart Steele was fired in October 2017. "Terminated effective immediately," read the internal memo updating all *Vox* staffers about the status of their one-time CEO and editorial director. "Lock admitted engaging in conduct that is inconsistent with our core values and is not tolerated at Vox Media."[1]

Steele found himself at the center of a familiar firestorm, one that dominated headlines in the autumn of 2017 and became the #MeToo movement. Across the spectrum of American society, powerful men who used the license afforded by their status to proposition and harass their female subordinates were being systematically exposed. For his part, Steele was accused of making a physical pass at a web developer while the two rode in the back of an Uber.

"I reported what had happened with the VP," Steele's accuser, who had since left the company, wrote in a public blog post. "A year later, I found out that an investigation had been done. That he had multiple victims within the company. That his punishment was being told he could not drink at corporate events any longer."

Curtailing Steele's access to intoxicating beverages was deemed a shockingly insufficient response given the allegations against him. Oddly, *Vox* employees sought to remedy this injustice by demanding that they, too, be denied booze.

"At the request of many of you, we will ramp up the food and cut down on the drinks," read a subsequent Vox Media memo ahead of that year's annual Christmas party. While the company knew "that alcohol isn't always the reason for unprofessional behavior," it was nevertheless their responsibility to avoid fostering "an environment that encourages overconsumption," which "certainly contributes to it." As such, the open bar was going the way of the dodo. Employees would be allowed only two "tickets" that could be redeemed for alcoholic beverages. After that, they were free to pay for more drinks if they wanted, so long as they were willing to endure the shame of their irrepressible dipsomania.

Vox might have just been ahead of the curve. That same year, the global consultancy firm Challenger, Gray & Christmas conducted a poll of 150 human resources department representatives across the United States and found that fewer than half of surveyed employers would serve alcohol at their holiday parties. That represented a dramatic decline from the 62 percent of employers who planned on providing alcoholic beverages just one year earlier. But what could they do? As the vice president of one surveyed firm confessed, "Employers are currently very wary of creating an environment where inappropriate contact between employees could occur."

That year, the essayist Matt Labash studied the emerging best practices regarding the provision of alcohol to anyone who could later sue you. What he found was a risk aversion that bordered on the pathological. Employers were advised by their lawyers to "issue tickets, if they must serve alcohol, with employee names, while making staffers show an ID card so that non-drinkers don't give tickets to heavy drinkers." They were told to ask bartenders to "water down the drinks" and "avoid serving salty food, which makes people drink more." But to really be safe, it was best to "nix the alcohol altogether," because the sauce is a "veritable Pandora's box of potential issues."[2]

Seeing as alcohol's primary social function is to facilitate uninhibited interactions that are sometimes as risky as they are entertaining, it's reasonable to assume that 2017's relatively dry office holiday parties weren't much fun. That's what we must conclude given Challenger, Gray & Christmas's 2018 survey, which found that more companies were planning to cancel their holiday parties altogether than at any point since 2009, when economic collapse had rendered lighthearted engagements a tad callous.[3]

As the wake left by the #MeToo movement settled, the office holiday party made a comeback. By 2019, businesses were once again ready to celebrate, and they were beginning to do so with booze again.[4] But that is cold comfort.

The movement that exposed the abuses of powerful men and the lengths the institutions to which they belonged would go to shield them from the consequences of their actions should have given way to soulful introspection. Instead, the professional class projected their guilt, placing the blame for very specific personal indiscretions not on the individuals responsible for them but on externalities like the demon liquor.

Why did these institutions take such uncompromising measures to avoid the risks inherent in social situations where sexual tension is both present and bathed in alcohol? To reduce the prospects for conflict.

Limiting alcohol intake and prescribing rigid codes of conduct that govern interactions between men and women is a tried-and-true formula for reducing intercommunity tensions. It has been both tried and proven true throughout the centuries. The Puritans didn't invent this formula, but they sure perfected it.

Around the turn of the seventeenth century, the austere preacher John "Decalogue" Dod elaborated on some of the beliefs that contributed to Puritanism's prudish reputation. As his nickname suggests, Dod's sermons tended to focus on the Ten Commandments. He specialized in teasing out the penumbra of meaning within them that only the keenest of trained eyes could discern. One seemingly straightforward commandment, "Thou shalt not commit adultery," was to Dod a deep well from which a shrewd biblical scholar could draw whatever he wanted.

In Dod's estimation, the Seventh Commandment implicitly forbade almost anything that could conceivably lead to temptation. It disallowed "wantonness" that might encourage carousing. It precluded most dancing, "because the action is nothing but a profession of an unchaste heart." Indeed, the "unchaste touches and gesticulations" encouraged by the act of mixed-gender dancing struck one heir to Dod's maximalism, Increase Mather, as having a "palpable tendency toward evil" due entirely to the impure thoughts stimulated by the act.[5]

But that's not all. Dod believed that the Seventh Commandment also tacitly objected to theatrical performances, "which serve for nothing but to nourish filthiness." It proscribed indolence, including everything from "lazing in bed" to "vain sports," and it vetoed all but the most productive carnal pursuits. "The Seventh Commandment," Michael Winship observed, "forbade not only adultery, but any kind of non-marital sex, including masturbation, sodomy, and bestiality. Even thinking about illicit sex, Dod warned, was 'hateful to God.'"

Even if all these elaborate criteria for respectable intercourse were met, the potential to offend God still loomed large. "Even within a loving marriage, sex had to be moderate," Winship added. "The medical science of the day had it that women did not conceive without orgasm, but excessive sexual indulgence, Dod warned, often resulted in monstrous, stillborn births and mentally crippled or 'ungodly and stubborn' children."[6]

In our mind's eye, we can now conjure up the image of the typically devout Puritan plagued by crippling performance anxiety. He must not even think about the prospect of sex until the moment of intimacy. He must engage in the act with workmanlike expediency. He must bring her to climax, but with as little tactical creativity as possible. If you pity the plight of our perplexed Puritan, just imagine what his poor wife had to endure.

In the uncompromising communities that comprised colonial New England, Dod's maximalist prescriptions for proper inter-sex relations were backed by the force of law. "Disorderly sex—all sex outside marriage, was vigorously, if not completely, repressed," Winship continued. For instance, "a couple simply seen with the man's arm around the woman's neck late at night or just acting in an 'unseemly and suspicious manner' could draw a court's attention." Courtship, as you can imagine, was an involved affair.[7]

Nevertheless, the idealized Puritan conception of what sex *should be* bore little resemblance to its practice in the real world. Sex for fun within marriage was not uncommon, and there was no social stigma around such pleasures. As John Cotton, a congregationalist minister and émigré to the colonies, observed, "Life is not life if it be overwhelmed with discouragements." Thus, "thy wife beloved and she to be joyfully lived withal, all the days of thy vanity."[8]

Likewise, Cotton continued, "wine it [is] to be drunken with a cheerful heart." The Puritan relationship with alcohol was similarly complicated because, like sex, this was not a temptation that could be entirely avoided—not when the mass consumption of untreated water was a more pressing threat than the occasional reprobate.

In New England, the cultivation of palatable wine-grape varieties was hindered by the failure of imported vines to take to the rocky native soil. The vines that did root themselves in the local terroir bore fruit that wasn't nearly as tasty as their European cousins. But where wine failed, beers and ciders succeeded. The cultivation of corn, oats, barleys, and fruit-bearing trees encountered few of the obstacles that hindered the production of grapes in America, and colonial kitchens were ubiquitously equipped with brewers' tools.[9]

The Puritans were a communal people. And just as it is today, alcohol served as a social lubricant. That rendered drink a pivotal feature of community functions and made the tavern central to

Puritan life. "Nearly every occasion, from harvests and barn raisings to college commencement ceremonies, became occasions for prolonged drinking bouts," George McKenna detailed.[10] "Beer, ale, and cider played the same role as bread and cakes did at the dinner table," Bruce Daniels observed. "Both alcohol and food promoted conviviality—a virtue as well as a necessity to people living in cramped houses and austere ideological quarters."[11]

It wasn't the often necessary and enjoyable consumption of mildly fermented beverages that invited the ire of seventeenth- and eighteenth-century moralists but gluttonous drinking and the debauchery that so often followed. "The wine is from God," Increase Mather conceded, "but the Drunkard is from the Devil."[12]

The low alcohol content in this period's preferred boozes made abject drunkenness a strenuous activity to which the aspiring inebriate must devote several hours of dedicated labor. It's a wonder, then, that reports of public intoxication were not all that rare.

In the early 1630s, Massachusetts Bay Colony's governor, John Winthrop, marveled woefully over the way in which the colony's young people "gave themselves to drink hot waters very immoderately." As one strait-laced member of New England's Congregationalist establishment observed, no fewer than forty ministers "were drunkards, or so far addicted to drinking" that they were an embarrassment to themselves and their church.

Just as "gluttony was a sin," Daniels observed, "drunkenness was a crime." As such, New England municipalities forced barkeeps to avoid overserving their patrons—a convention that is still with us today. What's more, purveyors of drink were obliged to ensure that their customers were not diverted from midweek church meetings, and the sale of stronger spirits was capped at "two pence a person."[13] While it was rare for overdrinkers to find themselves before a court, those who did were subject to penalties ranging from stiff fines to whippings or pillorying.[14]

But as the decades progressed, so, too, did the proof of intoxicants. By the turn of the nineteenth century, the ciders and beers that American colonists consumed with abandon were eclipsed in popularity by distilled spirits. By 1820, "the annual per capita consumption of spirits by those fifteen years or older," the historian Joyce Appleby observed, "was four times that of today." It's no coincidence that it was only six years later when Lyman Beecher founded the American Temperance Society, which, by 1834, advocated not just moderation but total abstinence from the consumption of alcohol.[15]

Scholars of American Puritanism are regularly frustrated by those who confuse Puritan values with Victorian mores, though the distinctions between two often complementary philosophies have grown hazy over the years. While they were *rhetorically* hostile toward drunkenness and casual sex, the historical record suggests early Puritans didn't practice what they preached. As American Puritanism evolved, however, it became more restrictive. By the mid-nineteenth century, puritanical codes of conduct governing the arts and recreation, sex and alcohol, and a dozen other taboos that were mostly notional in the colonial period had become absolutist maxims.

Just as the temperance movement cannot be divorced from the religiosity that prevailed in Puritan America, the prohibitionist movement took its cues from the period's progressivism.

Before it was a political juggernaut, American progressivism was first a fashion. It arose from the moneyed classes and famous surnames that populated the Midwest and the Northeast, many of whom had family ties to Puritanism. Progressives championed causes like the eight-hour workday, restrictions on child labor, racial egalitarianism, creating safe housing standards, and giving women the vote. In contrast to this period's populism, with its origins in Democratic Party politics and its geographic affinities for the South and West, progressives of the late nineteenth century largely rejected socialistic policy prescriptions and toxic class-consciousness.

As Harvard sociologist Talcott Parsons observed, the puritanical tendency to which progressives were most attracted was the spirit of "instrumental activism"—the idea that politics can be a source of identity and enlightenment. There was no political crusade more illustrative of this tendency than temperance and its signature achievement, Prohibition.

The temperance movement's members were mostly middle class. They sought to rein in the commercial and political "interests" that preserved alcohol's place of prominence in American society. They were progressive crusaders, yes, but by no means secular. Yale University professor and historian Sydney Ahlstrom called Prohibition *"the* greatest Protestant crusade of the twentieth century."[16] And while their cider- and beer-swilling forebearers might have stopped shy of advocating total abstinence from alcohol, temperance's absolutism derives from a puritanical belief that drunkenness gave way to bad outcomes both for individuals and society as a whole.

"The morals and values that the religious revivals of the Temperance and Prohibition Eras promoted were steeped in Puritan ideology," Brown University's Leah Rae Berk observed. Her study of the arguments made by those who supported the abolition of the liquor trade found recurring themes familiar to students of puritanical thought.

"Dry" advocates attributed alcohol consumption to virtually every other social evil that plagued late nineteenth-century America—from disease and poverty to crime and domestic violence. Alcoholism was considered a by-product of excess idleness and neglectful parenting. Those who consume intoxicating beverages were accused of being "enslaved" by drink, reigniting the fires that so animated Puritan antislavery activists. Prohibition advocates likened their work to a "crusade," harkening back to the utopianism inherent in Puritanism's providential ideals.

And when their great work was finished, prohibitionists seemed to genuinely believe they would have helped restore the paradise lost in Eden. "Once complete abstinence is achieved," Berk wrote of the prohibitionist outlook, "prisons will empty, crime will cease, humanity will be saved, and the kingdom of heaven will reign on earth."[17]

The temperance movement and the prohibition of alcohol represented the zenith of puritanical progressivism. It was all downhill from there. Their well-intentioned labors produced one of the greatest legal debacles in U.S. history. The Eighteenth Amendment and the laws that followed its ratification did not eliminate temptations to venality, hypocrisy, and degeneracy. Those aspects of the human condition were only exacerbated by Prohibition.

In the end, temperance's crusaders had mistaken one symptom of the disease they were fighting for the malignant affliction they so desperately wanted to cure. Bound up in the temperance movement were questions about what constituted proper activities outside the workplace, a healthy work-life balance, and wholesome education, to say nothing of marriage, family life, and relations between the sexes. These matters preoccupy social reformers even today. They probably always will.

Modern progressive activists do their utmost to foist the moralism that culminated in the nation's failed prohibitionist experiment onto the shoulders of the American right. But what should we expect? So great was the backlash against sanctimonious moralism in the 1960s and '70s that even the New Puritans are eager to avoid the stink of it. And yet, they persist in their crusaderism, which is increasingly "dry" in disposition if not policy.

The backlash against hooch among the formerly permissive left complements many of the values and first principles central to a progressive political orientation. Not only is drinking a habit that contributes to the mistreatment of women, it also facilitates the mistreatment of minorities. That is, in essence, what *New York Times* opinion writer Nicholas Kristof alleged in a 2012 essay that accused the brewing powerhouse Anheuser-Busch of the "devastating exploitation of American Indians."

"The human toll is evident here in Whiteclay," read Kristof's dispatch from that Nebraska town. "Men and women staggering on the street, or passed out, whispers of girls traded for alcohol." Kristof's charges echo the allegations in a popular 2008 documentary, *The Battle for Whiteclay*, a town in which four liquor stores served approximately a dozen residents.[18] The disparity here arises from the neighboring Pine Ridge Indian Reservation. Liquor sales are outlawed in Pine Ridge. The retail alcohol industry in Whiteclay, where four million cans of beer and malt liquor were sold annually, circumvents that prohibition.

"So, Anheuser-Busch and other brewers pour hundreds of thousands of gallons of alcohol into the liquor stores of Whiteclay, knowing that it ends up consumed illicitly by Pine Ridge residents and fuels alcoholism, crime, and misery there," Kristof alleged. "It's as if Mexico legally sold methamphetamine and crack cocaine to Americans in Tijuana and Ciudad Juárez." Kristof observed that the tribe had filed a lawsuit against the beermaker, but that petition was subsequently dismissed by a federal judge.[19] Lawfare was unequal to the scale of the challenge posed by this unscrupulous purveyor of drink.

So, what was Kristof's proposed remedy for the exploitation he alleged? The author was coy about that. But he did leadingly observe that, where there is less available liquor, studies have shown that there is "less drinking and fewer alcohol-related crimes." That seems logical enough. But how would you secure such a reform? "I'm pretty sure a nationwide boycott of Budweiser would wake the company up," he wrote in the pages of the *Times*.[20]

The op-ed failed to mobilize the nation to boycott America's largest brewing company, but it did get the attention of Anheuser-Busch's lawyers. "Beer producers are prohibited from selling beer directly to retailers or consumers in Nebraska, and we obey all laws wherever we operate or sell beer," the brewer averred. The statement added that the matter that preoccupied Kristof "involves deeply complex, societal, cultural and sometimes physiological issues," which is a lawyerly way of accusing Kristof of vastly oversimplifying the problem he sought to address.[21]

That is not to say that the *Times* columnist didn't have a point about the disparate social costs of alcohol consumption. A 2014 study published in the *Psychological Bulletin* posited that African Americans report a generally healthier relationship with alcohol than Americans of European descent, in part as a by-product of the "complex interaction of residential discrimination, racism, age of drinking, and lack of available standard life reinforcers (e.g., stable employment and financial stability)." As a result of these adverse social pressures, black Americans, apart from "low-income African American men," begin drinking later in life and have lower rates of alcoholism than American whites.[22]

There is a palpable sense of existential conflict here. Sure, discrimination is nothing to celebrate, but what if it contributes to healthier lifestyle choices? No progressive in good standing could ever endorse private discrimination, of course. But what about the public sort? That's a far less complicated inducement for our New Puritans.

"Alcohol is something that people enjoy drinking. It's pleasant," said Emily Owens, University of California, Irvine professor of criminology, law, and society. "But at a certain point, alcohol consumption really is problematic for society." It is, therefore, worth considering the positive social consequences associated with artificially increasing the price of alcohol through taxation. In that way, we might "discourage people on the margin from consuming as much as they might currently choose to."[23]

Owens, who holds a secondary appointment at UC Irvine's Department of Economics, dismisses the regressive effects of "sin taxes" like the one she proposes here. As with all consumption taxes, lower-income Americans are less likely to purchase a commodity in bulk and will end up paying more than higher-income Americans. But would that really be such a bad thing? "In this case," a 2012 academic paper published in the *American Journal of Preventative*

Medicine opined, "that larger financial impact might lead to greater reductions in drinking and a larger public health benefit for those same individuals."

To state the proposition as clearly as possible: Forcing poorer Americans to pay more for alcohol isn't such a bad idea because poorer Americans are more likely to have drinking problems.[24] Therefore, targeting them with higher taxes would have the most pronounced social benefits.[25] In this regard, the prohibitionist mind-set is little changed from the 1920s.

While prohibitionists were progressives in good standing, they were also products of their time. And their time was one in which Anglo-American Protestantism was under siege amid an influx of Irish, German, and southern European Catholics. It was also a time when the terrifying intellectual temptations of class envy and revolutionary Marxism gripped the imaginations of the underclasses.

It's no accident that groups like the Anti-Saloon League and the Women Christian's Temperance Union were financed by some of the nation's most well-heeled interests. Meanwhile, their opponents, the staunchest of whom were of immigrant or minority stock, languished in the fundraising department. The Volstead Act that proscribed alcohol sales contained loopholes designed to mollify wealthy interests. Among them were provisions that allowed Americans to maintain personal stockpiles of alcohol purchased before the act went into effect and the legalization of costly "medicinal" alcohol prescriptions. And, of course, the laws proscribing alcohol sales were routinely undermined by corruption in the nation's police forces, so long as you could afford the privilege.[26]

"An unprecedented campaign of selective enforcement lurked beneath the surface glamour of the roaring '20s that left the urbane elite sipping cocktails in swank, protected nightclubs," observed author and historian Lisa McGirr, "while Mexicans, poor European immigrants, African Americans, poor whites in the south, and the unlucky experienced the full brunt of Prohibition enforcement's deadly reality."[27]

• • •

Despite all the costly threats to social and civic health presented by Prohibition, "the noble experiment" is still being attempted today, albeit on a smaller scale. As recently as 2015, New Hampshire-based Dartmouth University banned from campus the possession, distribution, or even consumption of alcohol with a proof harder than 30. In other words, no distilled spirits allowed. The school's stated rationale was to curb "binge drinking" among students, particularly the upperclassmen who belonged to fraternities or sororities.[28] The ban was also designed to suppress "extreme behaviors," including "sexual misconduct and blatant disregard of social norms."[29]

But the law of unintended consequences is not subject to repeal. The ban did little to curb reported incidents of sexual misconduct, which increased year over year after its implementation.[30] And the fear that the ban would lead students who drank illicitly to avoid seeking medical attention if they over imbibed—a fear addressed in the school's 2017 "Good Samaritan" policy—proved well founded. Dartmouth's student paper reported that from 2016 to 2019 there had been 352 "Good Sam" calls to the college's public safety office. Nor did the ban do much to curb "extreme behavior." A 2019 internal audit found that "the vast majority of student crime was related to alcohol: Over 250 students from 2016 to 2018 received a disciplinary referral for liquor law violations, and nearly 40 were arrested each year."[31]

Some believe that America's conflicted relationship with alcohol and the taboos around its consumption contribute to its abuse on college campuses. The common refrain goes something like this: In places like Western Europe, where children as young as fifteen years old are allowed access to light beers and wines, there is a much healthier drinking culture. The data doesn't entirely support that claim.

In this century, reports of "drunkenness" among teenage minors in Europe are routinely higher than in the United States, and Europe's rates of death due to cirrhosis of the liver are far greater than America's.[32] And yet, binge drinking among Europeans in the key college-age demographic (age twenty to twenty-four) declined by a precipitous 10 percent from 2005 to 2016.[33] Studies have routinely shown that, in Europe, the likelihood of hospitalization as a result of alcohol poisoning falls off a cliff by the age of eighteen and settles into a negligible range by the time you turn twenty.[34]

So, what are we to make of this? Perhaps nothing more than alcohol, like any other age-restricted vocation, becomes a rite of passage. And when it is not deliberately administered by responsible adults, it will be abused. To seek the extirpation of this evil is to go to war with human nature, which is always a losing game.

Ultimately, the emerging argument for abstention from alcohol that is the most compelling centers on personal responsibility and personal enjoyment.

One of the more popular and commercially successful proponents of this philosophy is the memoirist Sarah Hepola. Her bestselling book, *Blackout: Remembering the Things I Drank to Forget*, details a messy and revealing journey to sobriety and the perils of chronic alcohol abuse.

In a deeply personal reflection on her unrequited love affair with the bottle, Hepola describes frequent blackouts, embarrassing displays of indecorous behavior, and sexual encounters with complete strangers. All this was a lot of fun, right up until it wasn't.

"I was so scared when I quit drinking that my life would be over and that everything would be worse and that I'd never have fun again," Hepola told NPR. "And I really just feel like it has been this extraordinary new path that I've gotten to take which is to deal with life on life's terms and to find self-reliance in myself."[35]

Framing abstention from drink as a way to recapture life's most enjoyable aspects rather than sacrificing them for the sake of personal health or a noble social principle is compelling. It's an argument that won't attract many followers among those who derive satisfaction from the performance of their self-discipline, but gratification and self-interest are powerful motivating factors for most everyone else.

And yet, the personal consequences of excessive drinking are fueling only part of the backlash against booze. It isn't just the terrible things alcohol does to women that have proven so convincing. It's the troubling things alcohol does to men that have scared some progressive activists straight.

Alcohol makes men into menaces. The intoxicant that predatory men use most frequently to get what they want from unsuspecting young women isn't Rohypnol, ketamine, or Methylenedioxy-methamphetamine (aka, MDMA, which is commonly found in the street drug Ecstasy). It's alcohol. "Quite honestly, alcohol is the No. 1 date rape drug," one law enforcement officer told *USA Today*. "Roofies are very rarely—if ever—seen in real life."[36]

Alcohol makes men into brutes. In 2019, a sixteen-year study conducted in Sweden determined that men with alcohol dependency were six times more likely to be arrested for threatening, attacking, or sexually assaulting their wives or girlfriends than the general male population.[37] "Men are the victims of alcohol-fueled violence, too," read a resource via the activist charity CAIS, "but the disproportionate manner in which women are harmed by this powerful, intoxicating, addictive drug sure makes the availability, pricing, and aggressive promotion of it one of the key issues in women's rights today."[38]

Alcohol makes men into bad providers. In 2014, Vox Media observed a profound increase in the number of poll respondents who blamed "drinking" as a "cause of trouble in your family." This was presented as yet another compelling reason to support "stringent alcohol taxes," as researchers concluded that "alcohol tax would significantly reduce violence, crime, and other negative repercussions of alcohol use."[39]

There is a rationale to all this, but these arguments are not new. They would sound familiar to any temperance advocate active around the turn of the twentieth century.

"There are so many references to the degradation of Saturday night," the historian Catherine Gilbert Murdock told PBS documentarians in 2011. "This is a time when there is no divorce, when the concept of police protection for domestic violence doesn't exist, when the concept of marital rape can't be discussed. But you *can* discuss it through alcoholism, and what alcohol does to men."[40]

Indeed, one of the chief innovations of the national president of the Women's Christian Temperance Union, Frances Willard, was to couple abstention from alcohol with the concept of "home protection."[41] Both temperance and extending the vote to women, in her view, were vital to the preservation of domestic tranquility. It's no coincidence that the Women's Christian Temperance Union also maintained a "Department for the Suppression of Impure Literature," as crusades against moral impropriety tend to sprawl.

It's not as if the New Puritan doesn't know that they are giving voice to age-old arguments. Some of them are fully aware of the parallels they're inviting, and they're not at all self-conscious about it.

"Rather than a regressive movement consumed with moralist disdain for alcohol use, many of [Temperance's] most ardent supporters wanted alcohol banned for a much more practical reason: women's safety," wrote Moira Donegan, the creator of a list of "Shitty Media Men," which arguably served as the catalyst for what became the #MeToo movement.

"What is the price that women pay in enduring sexual violence, sexual harassment, and domestic violence, for men's good time?" she asked. "Is all this female suffering worth it to us for the male privilege to drink? Should men, really, be allowed to drink alcohol?"

Donegan didn't dwell on who, precisely, "allows" men to drink alcohol. Nor did she speculate as to the methods that could conceivably take that freedom away. Rather, she embarked on what she claimed was only a thought experiment: "What if we took women's safety as seriously as we took men's pleasure? What would such a commitment obligate us to do?"

Donegan is left to mourn the Western world's casual disregard for the protection of women to the point that we live in a society in which intoxicating beverages flow freely. Perhaps the time has come for more extreme measures? Donegan concludes with a kind word for the diminutive temperance activist Carrie Nation, who rose to prominence (and notoriety) through her propensity for destroying saloon property with her trademark hatchet.

"When she took her axe to the bottles, she saw herself as taking an axe to the forces that enabled domestic violence, sexual harassment, and rape," Donegan concludes. "That goal, at least, is worth raising a glass to."[42]

For moral reformers, few threats are as urgent as the temptations that have the power to undermine our collective dedication to building the ideal society. That is as prominent a feature of moral reform movements today as it was in the 1600s. And if attacking disruptive and corrupting distractions is your passion, prescribing proper relations between the sexes is just as important as avoiding the beguiling lure of alcohol.

Throughout history, sex and alcohol have been coupled in the minds of the moralizers. These enticing and intemperate seductions encourage sensualism and hedonism, and they threaten to break communities apart.

While a healthy mistrust of alcohol and its effect on intersex relations has always been part of our collective heritage, it isn't always the most pronounced feature of our culture. And yet, no matter how hard libertinism's advocates try, they cannot erase the old moral codes. For evidence, we need look no further than the rise and fall of the sexual revolution.

In 1948 and 1953, respectively, the zoologist and sex researcher Dr. Alfred Kinsey published two profoundly influential studies exploring behavioral norms around sex. At the time, these were the most exhaustive studies of both "normal" sexual behavior and the aberrant sort—both heterosexual and homosexual; subjects so taboo they still couldn't be discussed in polite company. What made

Kinsey's research so influential wasn't just that he dared to delve into sex's unmentionable aspects—most influentially, his finding that premarital intercourse was quite common—but that he crafted an easily digested visual way to convey to the lay public that human sexuality is not a binary thing.

The complicated human species, his studies contended, inhabits a sexual spectrum. Moreover, an individual's place on that continuum is not fixed; people can migrate along it over the course of their lifetimes and in whatever direction they please.

Dr. Kinsey's research determined that homosexual experiences were far more common than the public generally believed (or, perhaps, was willing to acknowledge). His work contributed to the normalization of homosexuality, and it broke down the strictures around casual sex. But not everyone celebrated Kinsey's work.

The Lancet editor David Sharp wrote that a credulous consumer of Kinsey's research would likely conclude that "everything was normal" when it came to sex, including quite a lot that should not be.[43] For example, Kinsey's critics contend his research produced conclusions that were, at best, ambivalent toward pedophilia and incest.

Another critic of Kinsey's work found the doctor's favorable outlook toward the "considerable affection" found in one incestuous relationship he studied made for "sickening reading."[44] The sex scholar's research was described as methodologically flawed, given that the subjects of his study were not randomly selected but volunteers. That self-selected sample included a disproportionate number of gays, prostitutes, and deviants including convicted sex offenders, which likely produced skewed conclusions.

But even the most caustic critic of Kinsey's work was forced to concede that his research set the stage for a paradigm shift. It laid the foundation upon which the sexual revolution was built.

"Naturally, our parents obeyed the law fastidiously—and the law made crimes out of obscenity, pornography, 'indecent' exposure, nudity, all kinds of sex outside marriage, some kinds of sex *within* marriage, crossing a state line for immoral purposes, abortion, divorce, desertion, and numerous types of behavior which they defined as perversions or sins against nature," Allan Sherman wrote in his 1973 exploration of the emerging countercultural ethos bawdily titled *The Rape of the APE*—an acronym for the American Puritan Ethic.[45]

Sherman's coarse, insolent, acid trip of a book, published auspiciously enough by Playboy Press, did manage to capture the high esteem in which Kinsey's work was held among activists and political theorists. Whatever the academic merits of the doctor's research, which were probably quite limited, their liberative social value could not be dismissed so easily. "In spite of the antiseptic conditions of our heredity and environment," Sherman observed, "we discovered we had dirty minds."

Kinsey's had many prominent admirers. Among them, the "Playboy Philosophy's" premier champion, Hugh Hefner. "When you do get scientific evidence, as Kinsey has supplied," Hefner told *National Review* publisher William F. Buckley in a 1966 interview, a rational observer must commit to "questioning the old morality." According to Hefner, those old morals had been exposed as hypocritical, unnatural, and even unhealthy.[46]

Hefner articulated a world view that explicitly sought to bury America's puritanical heritage in the past. He ascribed his own libertine ideals to his belief in "anti-Puritanism." Hefner maintained that Puritanism itself was a reactionary response to the less constrained sexuality that used to be a part of the "Judeo-Christian ethic," but which "kind of got lost."

Playboy's publisher proposed a "new morality." It would be centered around "situation ethics," replacing the restrictive and, frankly, unrealistic codes of conduct that governed relations between the sexes prior to the mid-twentieth century. The puritanical ideal is just "not a proper approach in a society that is supposed to be pluralistic and is supposed to be secular." Hefner's moral code rejected the idea that "chastity is more important than human welfare," and he coupled "female emancipation" with "sexual emancipation."[47]

"What I attack is the notion that right and wrong should be related simply to the notion of sin," Hefner concluded. "We are going through a period of moral transition in relation to sex, and we will not be going back to the old concepts."

The sexual revolution and its vanguard in which Hefner served did succeed in burying the old mores—for a time. But Hefner was not the first to challenge those codes of conduct, and his blindness to the activism that preceded him also blinded him to the prospect of a backlash against his own beliefs.

By the early 1920s, the United States had become an archipelago of sometimes competing but often complementary "Comstock laws." Named for the Gilded Age anti-vice campaigner and native Bostonian, Anthony Comstock, those laws established vice squads that policed the dissemination of lewd, pornographic, or even just provocative literature. In 1868, Comstock launched a crusade to anathematize "obscene literature," which had become a lucrative industry in America.

Comstock's campaign became a sensation, attracting many followers and producing a consensus around the need to police immoral speech. In 1873, he and his allies convinced the YMCA in New York to rechristen its preexisting anti-vice committee as the New York Society for the Suppression of Vice, on which Comstock served as a secretary and which later became the model for a variety of other regional societies.[48]

These assaults on free expression offended many, but few dared to challenge them in as public a manner as the legendary cofounder of *The American Mercury*, H. L. Mencken.

Though he was often more a source of pithy quotes than wisdom, Mencken was among the foremost intellectual critics of "Comstockery" and the Puritanism from which it presumably derived. "The original Puritans had at least been men of a certain education, and even of a certain austere culture," he wrote. "They were inordinately hostile to beauty in all its forms, but one somehow suspects that much of their hostility was due to a sense of their weakness before it, a realization of its disarming physical pull."[49]

In 1926, Mencken and the *Mercury* resolved to test the limits of these laws. Toward that end, they published two stories designed to shock. The first effectively satirized organized religion's rigidity and its unintended consequences: popularizing the unmentionable carnal pleasures it proscribed. The second, entitled "New Views of Sex," described casual, premarital sex as a simple "diversion of man, a pastime for his leisure hours."[50]

Mencken got his wish. The essays resulted in his arrest for provocation, but he was eventually acquitted of the criminal charges against him. Mencken later sued the society that had agitated for his arrest and won.

Another suit brought by Mencken targeted the U.S. Post Office, which was empowered by Comstock and his supporters in Congress to ban the transmission of "publications of an indecent character" and literature that was "obscene, lewd, lascivious, or filthy."[51] Not only had Congress weaponized the U.S. Post Office against immorality, the federal legislature tapped Comstock himself to serve as Special Agent of the Post Office Department, providing him with police powers. Mencken's protest eventually compelled the federal judiciary to begin critically reexamining the constitutional propriety of the nation's obscenity laws.

But what Sherman denounced as our inherited "antiseptic conditions," Hefner dismissed as the "old morality," and Mencken condemned as "hostility" to all things beautiful are not entirely Puritan. The buttoned-up sexual inhibition commonly attributed to seventeenth-century Protestant zealotry owes itself more to later generations of Americans.

Abstinence and celibacy weren't something Puritan society encouraged among men and women of marrying age, and marrying age arrived early. If you hadn't entered into matrimonial bonds by your midtwenties, you were decidedly overripe. Insofar as marriage was an absolute good and sex within marriage was godly, being chaste past a certain point was a personal failing. Marriage was so important to Puritan society, in fact, that it was facilitated in ways that would have offended the staid Victorians that succeeded Puritanism.

"Puritan settlements encouraged marriages satisfactory to the participants by permitting divorces for those whose spouses were impotent, too long absent, or cruel," the author and historian Carl N. Degler wrote. "Indeed, the divorce laws of New England were the easiest in Christendom" at the time.

While premarital sex was a sin prohibited by statute, "the literally hundreds of confessions to premarital sexual relations in the extant church records" Degler cites suggests it was a common one. So much so, in fact, that the confessors were often the congregation's most upstanding "visible saints." And those confessions did not prevent the offenders from ascending to full membership within the church and Puritan society writ large.[52]

The thread that connects seventeenth-century Puritanism, the straightlaced moralists of the nineteenth century, and the new Puritans of the twenty-first century isn't a strict ethical code governing proper sexual relations. It is the belief that carnal pleasures can't just be enjoyable; they must serve a greater political purpose.

For progressive political activists who came of age when the tenets of the sexual revolution were unchallenged and its revolutionaries held the reins of political power, eroticism has no stigma around it. These activists are still pushing the boundaries of what society considers "normal." For them, though, quaint crusades like normalizing homosexuality and erasing the taboos around casual intercourse are largely over. The battle has shifted to popularizing polyamory and legalizing prostitution. And yet, these forms of coupling all serve a purpose beyond self-gratification. They also advertise one's membership within a political tribe.

Natasha Lennard, a veteran of a variety of left-wing publications, is indicative of this sort of outlook toward sex. Her essay "The Uses and Abuses of Politics for Sex" describes the mission before the modern sexual revolutionary as dismantling the "heteronormative social order." The social conventions that actively or passively promote heterosexuality as "normal" must be done away with, in part, because anything that "punishes desires, identities, and sexual practices outside of its narrow remit" deserves to be anathematized. This doesn't sound like a puritanical outlook at all.

And yet, the essay devotes particular focus to the many ways in which sex is and should be *transgressive*. Lennard describes a partner who talked "a big game about queering," but he used the phrase to describe "a political subjectivity" designed to attack conventional sexual frameworks. What her partner meant, Lennard continued, was "queer-as-disruption, as opposed to gay-as-assimilation: 'Not gay as in happy, queer as in 'fuck you.'"[53]

She goes on to confess an internal struggle over her desire to avoid engaging in an amorous escapade with someone to whom she was not attracted. "The arguments that followed didn't focus on the problematics of him assuming my desires for me," she pondered. "They turned on the fulcrum of why my desires weren't somehow better." Lennard describes the arduous process of "questioning and challenging" her own desires and the struggle to rationalize avoiding intercourse with people she didn't find attractive but who "share my political diagnoses."

Ultimately, the essay ends with some thoughts on the ubiquity of online dating services and pornographic venues, which have robbed sexual activism of its political shock value. "To be blunt," she concludes, "when there's a popular app for organizing your next queer orgy, how rupturous [sic] of our political status quo can the mere fact of such an orgy be?"

You can say a lot about this sort of outlook, but you cannot say that it doesn't regard sex as an instrument of political utility.

Lennard draws much of her analysis from the work of the late

Franco-American philosopher Michel Foucault, whose political theories sought to expose the "fundamental link" between power and sexuality. Foucault coupled sexual repression with political repression in his effort to "define the regime of power-knowledge-pleasure that sustains the discourse on human sexuality."[54] The Foucauldian "theory of desire" maintains that, where there is sexual attraction, the "power relation is already present." Thus, he sought to lift the stigmas around sexual enterprises because they exist only as tools the powerful wield to censor and control.

Given the 2021 allegation that Foucault routinely sexually abused "scores" of prepubescent boys while he lived in Tunisia in the 1960s, this philosophical outlook might have been more self-serving than he let on.[55] But at least he talked about sexual liberation as a means of personal fulfillment—"the proclamation of a new day to come and the promise of a certain felicity."[56] The students of his ideas seem incapable of describing the act of lovemaking as something as trivial as fun.

"So many of us believe that the work of our genitals is far less noble than the work of our minds," *The Guardian*'s Dave Madden ponderously declared. The "shame" of our own desires "diminishes us as individuals" and augments the political power of the ("primarily") men "who use sex as a weapon." After all, "sexual desire can be one of our most revolutionary political tools."[57]

The "quietly revolutionary" act of polyamory—having multiple consensual sexual relationships at once—is also less about individual happiness than pissing off the right people. Quartz science reporter Olivia Goldhill described the political theory associated with bedding multiple partners "as a mixture of socialism—a respect for a non-hierarchical society that values collective, community decision-making—and a libertarian belief that everyone should be free to make their own decisions without government interference."[58]

If you wanted to sacrifice the time, you could mine the boundless internet for similar essays on the political program associated with the many rapidly proliferating sexual orientations. There is power in bisexuality (attraction to both genders), pansexuality (attraction to everyone), asexuality (attraction to no one), autosexuality (attraction to yourself), demisexuality (attraction only once a romantic bond has formed), sapiosexuality (attraction to intelligence), skoliosexuality (attraction to the nonbinary or trans), and so on.

The only sexual preference that tends not to receive this apple-polishing treatment is heterosexuality. Those who are unfortunately and ineluctably straight have noticed their exclusion. There's even a term that describes the guilt they feel for failing to contribute to the revolution between the sheets: "heteropessimism."

"Heterosexuality is nobody's personal problem," *The New Inquiry*'s Indiana Seresin counseled after recalling how a friend confessed to the humiliation she felt as a result of her own attraction to the opposite sex. "Sure, some heteropessimists act on their beliefs," she continued, "yet most stick with heterosexuality even as they judge it to be irredeemable." While most who admit to being ashamed of their heterosexuality manage to reconcile the contradictions, Seresin notes that there is a thriving subculture dedicated to reinforcing that self-hatred.

The author does, however, appear to have more sympathy for the women who suffer with this condition than ailing men. "Heteropessimism has become a framework through which men process both demands for gender equality and the quotidian experience of romantic harm as evidence of a global female conspiracy," Seresin observed.[59]

These ruminations on sex as a form of political expression do not comport with our stereotypical assumptions about Puritanism's stuffy attitudes toward coitus. They align with the Puritan ethic only insofar as sex is perceived to be an activity that helps cement a broader social covenant. And yet, the outlook that views sex as a positive force is under assault from within the left-wing coalition.

• • •

In 1975, the journalist and activist Susan Brownmiller published the wildly successful book *Against Our Will: Men, Women, and Rape*. It was a groundbreaking work, though it was more a source of curiosity than an ideological manifesto at the time of its publication. It argued earnestly and without pretension that rape is "a conscious process of intimidation by which *all men* keep *all women* in a state of fear."[60]

This cognitive leap—widening the scope of sexual violence from a discrete criminal act committed by one person against another into a form of deterrence in the Cold War between the sexes— thrust open a breach through which a more radical feminism would rush. Among their ranks was the radical feminist Andrea Dworkin.

"Any violation of a woman's body can become sex for men," Dworkin wrote in her 1987 book *Intercourse*. "This is the essential truth of pornography." Along with her colleague Catharine Mac-Kinnon, Dworkin's activism manifested in political campaigns against pornography. This feminist crusade was once so antithetical to the liberal mission to defend freedom of expression in whatever constitutionally protected form it took that it attracted few followers on the left. Not anymore.

To many modern progressive activists, Dworkin's view of sex as an indelibly exploitive act makes perfect sense. There cannot be, for example, "feminist pornographers," notes *The Guardian*'s Julie Bindel, because such a thing cannot "be made in an ethical way" and should therefore not constitute protected free expression.[61] But curbing legal freedoms for producers of erotica was not the limit of Dworkin's ambitions.

"Intercourse is not necessary to existence anymore," Dworkin's *Intercourse* continued. "The hatred of women is a source of sexual pleasure for men in its own right. Intercourse appears to be the expression of that contempt in pure form, in the form of a sexed hierarchy; it requires no passion or heart because it is power without invention articulating the arrogance of those who do the fucking. Intercourse is the pure, sterile, formal expression of men's contempt for women."

Therefore, she continued, the likelihood that we can foster the development of a healthier sexual culture that puts a premium on mutual respect and satisfaction is nil. That's "because there is a hatred of women, unexplained, undiagnosed, mostly unacknowledged, that pervades sexual practice and sexual passion."[62]

Although it is festooned with fashionable misandry, the essence of Dworkin's argument is that sexual liberation's truest form is abstinence. Heterosexual intercourse can never be an expression of "sexual equity." It is an act of occupation because penetration requires female "submission."

"If objectification is necessary for intercourse to be possible, what does that mean for the person who needs to be fucked so that she can experience herself as female and who needs to be an object so that she can be fucked?" she asks. A woman who seeks out and enjoys sex with men "needs to be wanted more than she needs integrity or freedom or equality."

With the revitalization of prudish temperance as a progressive value, the idea that women who enjoy sex like to be "degraded" and cannot be devoted feminists has found a new audience today.

When she isn't arguing for curbs on the libations enjoyed by men, "Shitty Media Men" list creator Moira Donegan is making the case for neo-Dworkinism. In her review of Dworkin's anthologized works, Donegan adopts what readers could forgivably mistake for a conservative view of prostitution. She recalls how Dworkin experienced sex work as "not fully a choice" but an abusive form of economic slavery. Donegan notes that *Intercourse*'s famous seventh chapter, cited above, is widely misinterpreted by its critics as a condemnation of all sex as rape. And yet, if rape is not the only form heterosexual activity takes, it sure is "common."

"Rape is not exceptional but common, committed by common

men acting on common assumptions about who men are and what women are," Donegan writes of Dworkin's thought. If Donegan disagrees with this belief, she's coy about it. When women *do* make their own choices regarding sex, "we make those choices under unfairly constrained circumstances." Though women *do* initiate and enjoy sex, they are also "more vulnerable to sexual coercion, exploitation, and violence" than men. Thus, it "should not be hard to say that heterosexuality as it is practiced is a raw deal for women and that much pornography eroticizes the contempt of women."[63]

Following Donegan, *New York Times* opinion writer Michelle Goldberg published a similar reflection on Dworkin's theories. "Indeed," she wrote, "some of Dworkin's ideas have been reincarnated in #MeToo." Among them, the idea that consent could be subject to postcoital revocation. That idea was applied to the actor and comedian Aziz Ansari, who was accused of sexual assault by a partner long after the fact and much to his surprise, as the affair seemed to him both consensual and mutually enjoyable at the time. But Ansari's partner did not enjoy herself, and later accused the actor in texts of ignoring "clear non-verbal cues" betraying her discomfort.

The actor apologized for having "misread things," and that was that. At least, it was until this mutual misunderstanding became the subject of a national scandal when the couple's personal communications were published months later on the website Babe.net.[64] Goldberg accurately observed that Dworkin would have deemed this episode "presumptive rape"—or, at the very least, "a violation."

"I think Trump's victory marked a shift in feminism's relationship to sexual liberation," Goldberg wrote. "As long as he's in power, it's hard to associate libertinism with progress."[65] That is a lot of power to grant a president you oppose—too much, in fact, to be convincing. Donald Trump is long gone from the Oval Office, but what Goldberg alleged was only a reaction to him persists. As naked as Trump's disregard for female autonomy was (reflected best, perhaps, in the infamous *Access Hollywood* tape, in which the future president described the ease with which a person of his stature could commit sexual assault), the intellectual beachheads were long ago prepared for Dworkinism's resurgence.

"Consent, Dworkin understood, is an essential but insufficient tool for understanding the political realities of sex," Donegan contended. Well before Donald Trump quit his day job as a game-show host to become a politician, the idea of "consent" was being reimagined by progressive activists and the institutions they control. No longer was this a mere social contract. Suddenly, it became more of a real, binding, physical contract.

The advocacy group Affirmative Consent Project got into the business of distributing "consent contracts" to college students across America as early as 2015. "YES," the agreement reads in letters large enough to be legible in mood lighting. "We agree to have SEX!" Aspiring participants are encouraged to sign the document and take photos of it as proof, should any Dworkinesque retroactive "violations" become actionable.

But can't that signature also be the result of coercion? Who is to say whether that contract was entered into under duress or because of one or both participants' impaired judgment? After all, as the project's founder, Alison Berke Morano, wrote for its website: "Consent is to be determined from the perspective of the complainant."[66]

Morano didn't invent the consent contract; she just capitalized on it. By 2014, hundreds of colleges and universities around the country had adopted legalistic language defining consent in some form in their charters.[67] According to the standard the University of Minnesota adopted in 2015, for example, both parties must agree to sex via "clear and unambiguous words or actions." Anything less comports with the university's definition of sexual assault.[68] By the middle of the last decade, campuses around the country had signed on to the "Consent Is Sexy Campaign," which sought to dismiss the apparently widespread perception that contractional negotiations are a mood killer.[69]

Erasing any ambiguity from sexual engagements isn't the preoccupation of activists alone. States have gotten into the act, too.

In 2014, California passed and implemented its version of a "yes means yes" law, which sought to codify the terms that constitute mutual agreement to engage in intercourse. The law relies on the "affirmative consent" standard, a concept that renders any sex act performed under the influence of drugs or alcohol or if someone is asleep nonconsensual.[70]

On its face, that doesn't sound objectionable. Nonconsensual sex is a crime that should be prosecuted to the fullest extent. But as is often the case with interpersonal relations, it all became complicated quickly.

To establish consciousness in both participants, the law states that consent must be "ongoing throughout a sexual activity." Reporting from a California high school, which was required to teach the law and the best practices it prescribes, The New York Times summed up the confusion neatly: "What does that mean—you have to say yes every ten minutes?" one confused student asked his instructor. "Pretty much," the teacher replied.[71]

Writing on Vox, the site's former cofounder and current New York Times opinion writer Ezra Klein observed that this statute will cause college-age men "to feel a cold spike of fear when they begin a sexual encounter." Moreover, the law "will settle like a cold winter on college campuses, throwing everyday sexual practice into doubt and creating a haze of fear and confusion over what counts as consent." Most shockingly of all, he wrote all this approvingly.[72]

Klein conceded that the law was "terrible," but only because it was terribly written. It would encourage legal challenges, but its ambiguity was necessary because the behaviors it sought to criminalize were just as ambiguous. California's courts didn't seem to agree. The ad hoc conditions the law created and the extrajudicial prosecutions it (and the Obama administration's revisions to Title IX after 2011) encouraged routinely denied those accused of sexual assault on campus their civil and constitutional rights.[73] Millions of dollars in judgments were awarded to the people who were deprived of their Fourth and Sixth Amendment rights as a result of this overcorrection.[74]

By early 2020, no less a venue than *Teen Vogue*, an outlet that has rebranded itself the bleeding edge of radically progressive thought, rediscovered an essential feature of human sexuality: It's complicated. "Some students do practice affirmative consent, but many others use a range of social cues to make sense of whether or not a sexual encounter was consensual or nonconsensual," they observed. Of course, no one wants to be thought of as "the pleasure police," but that was a consequence of what amounted to an intimidation campaign.

Teen Vogue found that affirmative consent standards hadn't changed the "implicit framework" in which "men are the ones who move the sexual ball down to the field, and women are the blockers." But fear and confusion have made men more reluctant to perform their traditional gender role. "For most heterosexual men, the fear of doing consent wrong and unintentionally assaulting someone is deeply held and part of their everyday experience of sex," the outlet conceded.[75]

You can see why innocent and well-intentioned young people might be dissuaded from a casual sexual experience with someone who isn't a long-term partner, given these inducements. Plagued by self-doubt, inhibition, and a fear of real legal consequences arising not from deliberate malfeasance but miscommunication and regret, young people are increasingly concluding that the only way to win this curious game is not to play.

Much as we could conjure up in our minds the image of a dutiful Puritan whose efforts to abide by his society's complicated and often conflicting messages around sex rendered him impotent—figuratively, if not literally—we can easily imagine something similar testing today's committed young progressives.

She inhabits a strange world that is rhetorically accepting of almost any sexual appetite, but she also knows that the behaviors that constitute sexual aggression and even sexual violence are far more nebulous than criminal statues allow. He understands that the rituals he must observe when engaged in courtship are labyrinthine but not unnavigable if you treat people with respect. Yet the outward manifestations of that desire, from flirtation to physical displays of affection, involves the risk of accidentally contravening those standards. Wooing a prospective partner boldly and assertively is fraught with implication. And there are real consequences—social and legal—if a signal is misread or a cue is overlooked.

This anxiety-producing set of circumstances has led many young people toward one obvious conclusion: It's just not worth it.

Between 1991 and 2015, the Centers for Disease Control and Prevention's Youth Risk Behavior Survey found that the percentage of high school students who had engaged in intercourse declined from 54 to just 40 percent.[76] Many don't see this as an undesirable trend. After all, less sex at such a confusing age means fewer social complications, less teen pregnancy, and the reduced spread of sexually transmitted diseases. But this trend doesn't begin and end with young people.

By the end of the last decade, San Diego State University psychology professor Jean Twenge found that people in their early twenties are also increasingly abstinent. Compared to the members of Generation X, the younger generations are two and a half times more likely to say they refrained from sex in their early twenties.

The number of Americans aged eighteen to twenty-nine telling survey respondents they had not had any sex within the last year doubled between 2008 and 2018 to nearly a full quarter of the young adult population.[77] By 2018, the number of young women who report having no sex at all had jumped by 8 percent, while the share of sexless young men under the age of thirty tripled to reach 28 percent. And while this phenomenon is more pronounced among the young, the trend is visible across the board. "The share of people who are having relations once a week or more now sits at 39 percent, compared with 51 percent in 1996," *The Washington Post* reported.[78]

According to Twenge, the primary culprit for the decline is the drop-off in the number of young adults who "have a live-in partner," which translates to fewer opportunities. Others blame the post-2008 economic recession and declining workforce participation among young people for a reduction in the number of attractive mates and, thus, fewer sexual encounters. Still more insist that the digital revolution is to blame. It's hard to find a partner when your face is buried in a screen. While these are all likely contributing factors, none are as satisfying as what my *Commentary* magazine colleague Christine Rosen identified as the primary culprit: fear.

"A 2017 poll by the *Economist* found that among Americans ages 18–29, 17 percent believed that a man asking a woman out for a drink 'always' or 'usually' was sexual harassment," she wrote. "Twice as many young respondents as older ones thought commenting on a woman's appearance was harassment." Sociologist W. Bradford Wilcox and behavioral scientist Samuel Sturgeon note that the trend toward abstinence corresponds closely with a paradigmatic shift among young adults who now "view behavior related to sex and dating as troubling."[79]

If young men are becoming quietly terrified of women, young women are loudly concluding that heterosexual coupling—or coupling at all—isn't worth the effort. "I think a lot of hetero women are waking up to the fact that sex, not all but a lot, with a man is often less fulfilling, orgasm-wise, than going solo," twenty-six-year-old "Rachel" told a *Vice* reporter in 2018. "Romantic love is great, but it isn't everything," twenty-six-year-old "Niki" agreed. "If your friendships fulfill you emotionally, and your hand or a toy fulfills you sexually, what's wrong with that?"[80]

To some on the left, these are entirely positive social developments. "The sexual revolution liberated a generation," the late English writer Jenny Diski said. "But men most of all." Thus, a sexual drought could only be a boon to young women, who some observers seem to believe derive no satisfaction from most sexual encounters. "No sex, for many young women, may be better than bad sex," *The*

Guardian's Yvonne Roberts wrote in an article headlined: "The Sex Revolution of My Youth Wasn't So Great. Maybe Today's Celibacy Is a Sign of Progress." She adds, "A more positive analysis of increasing sexual abstinence may also be part of the mix." After all, "some individuals may also be happily asexual—hardly a tragedy."[81] Not at all, but only so long as the emphasis in that sentence is on "happily" rather than on self-deprivation. More often in modern discourse, that order is reversed.

The enforced isolation associated with the onset of the pandemic in 2020 surely exacerbated a trend toward chastity, but this proclivity is still informed by political incentives. In an op-ed for *The New York Times*, Haili Blassingame described her mid-pandemic decision to break up with the boyfriend she still loved amid her pursuit of a "political" identity—"something nontraditional." She found it in the oxymoronic status she stumbled across online and subsequently adopted: "solo polyamory."

"I liked how solo polyamory cherished and prioritized autonomy and the preservation of self, and I found its rejection of traditional models of romantic love freeing," Blassingame wrote. She describes her new identity as one that allows her to "experience the expansiveness of love" in isolation. But while "solo polyamory" still allowed Blassingame at least the possibility of a nonmonogamous sexual relationship, her peers are taking the leap into outright celibacy.

The ever-expanding initialism is, as of this writing, "LGBTQIA+." The "A" refers to a sexual identity that is abstemious—the asexual or "ace." Asexual people embrace "the ability *not* to have sex," according to Angela Chen, the author of *ACE: What Asexuality Reveals About Desire, Society, and the Meaning of Sex*. But this is not an outgrowth of suppressed urges. In Chen's telling, asexual people are capable of both romantic and platonic love, and they desire affection. What they do not experience is sexual attraction.

"Compulsory sexuality is the idea that all normal people want and desire sex, that everyone has this baseline level of sexual desire," the author explained. "But the truth is not everyone has that base-line of sexual desire."[82] Though Chen describes both an orientation and a lifestyle choice, her book draws heavily from "critical queer theory," a discipline not far removed from feminist theory, in which the works of Andrea Dworkin and her colleagues feature prominently. Ladening this lifestyle with academic theory renders Chen's convictions political, and her philosophy is being accurately described by her allies as a "movement."

In 2021, *The Guardian* described a growing sensation among "younger activists" whose vocation revolves around popularizing the idea that "it's possible to live a fulfilling life without sex." Those activists describe "being celibate" as a state of being that provides "a position of clarity." They lead a life that is not complicated by "sex clouding their vision."[83]

Sexlessness isn't just rewarding but enlightening. As one user of the online forum Asexuality.org confessed, he had encountered "a sort of spiritual levity upon realizing" his celibacy. "I know that being asexual doesn't make me more spiritual than anyone else," another forum participant concurred, "but I think there's a reason that religions the world over have practices and traditions that encourage celibacy."[84]

Maybe there's something to that old-time religion after all.

7

ORDER

THE COMPANY WE KEEP

The progressive activist class has rediscovered the value of older ideas about how societies should organize themselves, even though they are repudiating an earlier generation of radical leftists for whom social structure itself was regarded as a form of bondage. But what catalyzed the old morality's renaissance?

As we've seen in the previous chapter, the old mores don't just encourage healthy interpersonal relationships. They also preserve order. The chaos that results from individual autonomy is no longer seen as such a desirable condition for those within the left-wing ecosystem. That which is unsystematized cannot be optimal, almost by definition, because it has not been molded by the capable hands of enlightened men and women. Carving order out of the spontaneous social structures people make for themselves is just another offensive in the left's campaign against the forces of entropy.

The haughty impulse that leads society's aspiring engineers to perfect personal relationships cannot observe any constraints. Private spaces and personal conduct, too, must be reconfigured so that they comport with the progressive Puritan's overarching program.

In 2013, *The New Republic*'s "Fatherland" columnist Mark Oppenheimer identified a disquieting trend among his left-leaning peers. In a column auspiciously titled "The New Puritans," Oppenheimer found that the countercultural ethos he grew up with was fast disappearing. No longer were his ideological compatriots contented with taking it easy. The consensus that had formed around breaking down structure and avoiding stress was evaporating before his eyes.

Gone was the "hippy ethos" of just letting go, Oppenheimer wrote. "The Puritan parents I encounter are nearly all liberals."

Those puritanical parents all exhibit two "unfortunate" traits: "The first is the fun-smothering tendency of Progressive-era moral uplift, the tendency that brought us Prohibition and the first laws proscribing opiates and narcotics," Oppenheimer wrote. The paternalism he identified took many forms, but the most visible and controversial at the time of Oppenheimer's essay was the crusade mounted by former New York City mayor Mike Bloomberg to limit the sale of sugared beverages to no more than 16 fluid ounces and to restrict the purchase of gigantic soda fountain drinks to those paying for them through supplemental nutritional assistance programs (aka, food stamps).[1]

"The second is an interest in hygiene that could be quite salutary," he continued, "but could also fetishize symbolic, pernicious forms of sanitation and purity, as in Margaret Sanger's support for eugenics."[2] Oppenheimer's observations had merit, and they sparked a brief bout of introspection on the left.

"Known as helicopter parents," *The Atlantic*'s Arit John wrote, picking up where Oppenheimer left off, "these moms and dads monitor everything their children eat, watch, and read. Their parenting habits are as illiberal as their politics are liberal."[3]

Only a few years earlier, policy makers began catering to the demands of a hyper-engaged parenting philosophy, which transposed parental responsibilities onto more public entities. No longer was the progressive parent content with dropping out and letting go. Quite the opposite. They now sought to file down life's sharp edges for the sake of the children, and they assumed that it was the state's responsibility to do just that.

This tendency sparked its share of backlashes. Perhaps the most memorable was led by columnist, author, and activist Lenore Skenazy with her "Free Range Kids" movement. Skenazy drew national attention in 2008 when she had the audacity to allow her nine-year-old to ride the New York City subway system unaccompanied. The successful experiment led national media outlets to brand her "America's Worst Mom."[4]

But the backlash did not last, and more permissive parenting techniques continued to fall out of favor. In their place arose an overbearing philosophy centered on the notion that it was the community's responsibility to raise children.

Today, the authorities are called into action wherever neglectful parenting is even presumed.

Danielle and Alexander Meitiv, ten and six years old respectively, were taken into custody and their parents disciplined when the two kids were allowed to walk to their homes alone from a park situated only a mile and a half away.[5]

Forty-six-year-old Debra Harrell was arrested for "unlawful conduct toward a child" and processed for allowing her nine-year-old daughter to play by herself at a local park before she arrived home from work.[6] Her daughter was briefly placed in protective social services.

Eight-year-old Dorothy Widen was just walking her dog around the block when a neighbor called the cops. "She was gone for five minutes," Widen's mother told a local paper. "I was in the backyard, and I could see her through the yard." Cleared of wrongdoing by the police, Widen was nevertheless subjected to a humiliating interrogation by the Department of Children and Family Services several days after the incident.

Julie Koehler was investigated by police for child abuse because she left her three girls alone in a car on a 70-degree-day with the windows open just long enough to run into a local Starbucks. Her "negligence" led to her children being taken into custody and examined for signs of sexual abuse.[7]

Maisha Joefield put her five-year-old daughter to bed one night and, exhausted, settled into a bath with her headphones on. When she emerged, her daughter, Deja, was gone—she had meandered over to her grandmother's residence nearby. "Police officers removed Deja from her apartment and the Administration for Children's Services placed her in foster care," *The New York Times* reported.[8]

"Each year, child protection agencies, sanctioned by juvenile courts, remove around twenty-five thousand children from their homes who spend less than thirty days in foster care," read a 2016 University of Pennsylvania Law School study on a conspiracy of anxious neighbors, trigger-happy courts, and indiscriminate bureaucracies diligently traumatizing children and parents alike. "The distribution of these data tells us that most of these children spend fewer than two weeks in foster care before being returned to their original caretakers."[9]

These abuses by the state in the name of child safety aren't occurring in a vacuum. They're the outgrowth of an emerging civic consensus that the state should take on an outsize role in the administration of family affairs. You might think that everyone would be outraged by such misuses of authority. But if you delve deep enough into the intellectual currents on the left that helped to produce this phenomenon, you'll encounter general agreement around the idea that overzealous Child Protective Services departments are not doing *enough*.

The backlash against disorder in public and private life isn't irrational or nefarious. Not entirely, at least. Predictability gives way to stability, easing the disorienting sense that we are all rudderless agents unmoored to anything sound and durable. Establishing inviolable social hierarchies involves control, and control creates a sense of mission.

Like their ancestors, the modern Puritan ethos is a reaction to a perceived crisis. The only remedy for our presently chaotic state is to impose order on it—a newer, better order.

The old Puritans were so focused on order that they saw the most basic unit of society—the family—as just another political institution; indeed, an institution that was valuable only so far as it advanced the broader Puritanical social program. The New Puritan would emphatically agree.

Popular mythology maintains that the average Puritan was a one-dimensional tyrant devoid of human warmth. Of course, they were more complicated than that.

Sixteenth- and seventeenth-century Protestant reformers were anything but monolithic in their beliefs. Indeed, transatlantic Puritanism was rocked by periods of profoundly divisive theological and social conflict. They were superstitious, yes, but also inclined toward rationalism and empiricism. They were totalitarian, insofar as theirs was a totalistic belief structure that could not abide distinctions separating public from private life. But they were also radically egalitarian. The Puritans were complex, enigmatic, and often inconsistent. In short, they were human beings.

The Puritan existence was defined by struggle: struggle against wickedness, injustice, and our very natures. The state, in their view, was not an enemy in that struggle but an instrument of moral agency that not only could but *should* enforce society's ethical covenants.

Although they were prone to superstition and valued the old ways, the Puritans were not hidebound Luddites. Puritan thinkers, particularly those that emigrated to America, would be profoundly influenced by Enlightenment-era liberalism.

The Puritans were democratizers. They were compelled by their antipathy toward Catholic practices to break down the barriers between the priestly class and the laity. In Puritan society, the individual's interpretation of Scripture was as valid as the next man's, to say nothing of the clergy. Congregational voting, a system by which church members had individual input on both religious affairs and matters that we would today regard as the province of government, was arguably the progenitor of American democracy.[10]

The puritanical ideal of autonomous self-determination for private interests set the foundations upon which America's republican institutions were built. Yes, Puritan theology was invested in communitarianism as the natural state in which mankind was born, and its members adhered to a somewhat bleak view of humanity. But they did not reject modernity or the concept of social progress. What the Puritans rejected was disorder.

A range of scholars have tried to explain why New England's colonial experiment was successful in ways that competing settlements were not. Some have attributed the success of these colonies to puritanism's uniform political culture. Others have suggested that the homogenous religious makeup of these societies created conditions for sustained stability. In either case, conformity was the goal, and equilibrium was the result.

In the seventeenth century, the Massachusetts, Plymouth, New Haven, and Connecticut colonies were model settlements. They were largely free from serious epidemics. They experienced significant population growth despite a dearth of immigration from England following the first wave of migrants. New England had lower rates of mortality (both in infancy and adulthood) than its colonial competitors or even England itself. By the middle of that century, life expectancy surged into the early seventies for both men and women.[11]

The average Puritan community by the mid-1620s was relatively small and homogenized. And that's just the way they liked it. The first wave of migrants to New England embarked on that parlous voyage in part because they despised the social evolution that was being imposed on English society, to say nothing of the Crown's imperious interventions into daily civic and religious life. The New World they sought to create was designed to be an idealized reflection of the Old, conforming as closely as possible to what the historian Jack P. Greene described as romanticized conceptions of a "well-ordered commonwealth."[12]

Puritans organized themselves into "tightly constructed and relatively independent communities in which inhabitants formally covenanted with each other to comprise unified social organisms," Greene continued. "Although they were by no means disinterested in achieving sustenance and prosperity, they put enormous emphasis upon establishing well-ordered communities knit together by Christian love and composed only of like-minded people with a common religious ideology and a strong sense of communal responsibility."[13]

Social stability was maintained not just by the conditions that were present in the early colonies but by those that weren't—in particular, the lack of income disparities that can produce pronounced class divisions. The early colonies were not riven by the disruptive and disaggregating force of commerce. Most early settlers cultivated cereal grains or livestock and subsisted on modest profits. Puritanical laws that enshrined the privileges of the elite, like dress codes, were rarely visible to the average Puritan. Thus, any inclination toward class envy was kept in check. This all contributed to the promotion of egalitarianism, but with limited potential for social discord.

Puritan communities sought and secured a striking degree of social stability, in part through the preservation of uniformity— uniformity of faith, uniformity of dress, uniformity of behavior, and uniformity of thought. Puritanism scholar Stephen Foster noted that the mechanisms used to police trespassers against this social contract weren't the methods to which Europeans appealed. There were no monarchs, landed lords, hereditary nobility, or even a church hierarchy around which society could be organized. What enforced social uniformity was a "radical volunteerism" expected of Puritan society's stakeholders, and almost everyone was to some degree a stakeholder.

It wasn't all roses for Puritan society. With democratization came dissension. The autonomy of individual congregants made resolving disputes—be they religious, legal, social, or otherwise—an ordeal. As the generations progressed, declining adherence to Puritan religious dogma among the children of the elect presented a real problem for a society in which the church served as the primary venue for conflict resolution. So it was that Massachusetts' incipient legislature, the General Court, began to involve itself more actively in private affairs. "In the 1650s," Michael Winship wrote, "the Massachusetts General Court repeatedly passed laws to rein in young people's fondness for drinking, gaming, strolling around on the Sabbath, and acting disrespectfully during the church services."[14]

The native born, dispossessed of their parents' zeal and raised in stable conditions, continued to drift away from their orbits around the church as the century progressed.[15] Thus, out of an "impulse for consensus" and following prolonged debate over the matter, the standards for ascending to full voting membership within a congregation were relaxed. This reform did little to rein in New England's unruly sons and daughters. "By the early decades of the 18th century, it was a general lament among ministers that they 'did not enjoy the prestige, influence, and social status' of their 17th century predecessors," Greene observed.[16]

With the development of a thriving trade economy in more populated settlements on the colony's coast, the stability that had once typified Puritan society began to dissolve into discord. That was visible in rising rates of degeneracy, evinced in the record by increasing criminal prosecutions for deviance and, most glaringly, by the moral panics catalyzed by this social breakdown. Most notably among them, the Salem witch trials of 1692.[17]

Ultimately, economic competition, rising rates of individual wealth, the acceptance of debt as a necessary evil, diversifying social structures, and the deterioration of communal units began to break tight-knit Puritan society apart. This trend only accelerated after England passed the so-called Navigation Acts in 1651, which forced Britain's colonies into a monopsonistic relationship with the mother country by barring colonial producers from selling many key resources to any buyer other than England. The acts also made early America dependent upon British producers for most manufactured products.

Eventually, the Puritans were compelled to look less to the church to resolve social disputes and more to the law. Rising rates of litigation, particularly involving property and debt, scared traditionalists. They even coined a term to describe this menace: "creeping '*Rhode Islandism*.'"[18] Even today, the very concept is enough to strike fear into the hearts of anyone who doesn't live in Rhode Island. But as the historian David Thomas Konig chronicled, the transition from "communalism to litigation" was a compromise that nevertheless preserved the Puritans' conception of themselves as a "well-ordered people."

And yet, the seeds that would one day bring about the extinction of fire-breathing Puritanism as the essential characteristic of New England society had been sown. The rise of mercantilism in the early eighteenth century and its associated financial rewards set the stage for what the author and academic Bernard Bailyn called "a new spirit of the age."

"It's guiding principles were not social stability, order, and the discipline of the senses," he wrote, "but mobility, growth, and the enjoyment of life."

Imagine that.

None of this is to accuse all of today's more puritanical progressives of being control freaks, though the bill surely fits for some. It is to accuse them of being human.

Belonging to a stable covenant is one of mankind's most innate desires. Those who thrive in disorder and isolation are so few and far between that it is reasonable to assume that is not our ideal state.

One of the hallmarks of an ordered society are at least a handful of norms and conventions around which an unquestionable consensus has formed. A fondness for consensus—or, at least, a distaste for dissension within their ranks—certainly informs modern progressivism's moralistic streak.

Today's progressive activists pride themselves in their support for diversity in all spheres of public life—all spheres, that is, save intellectual life. The New Puritan mistrusts the legal and technological advents that give way to disunity. One of the chief inventions responsible for the breakdown of the conventions that kept dissenters quiet (or, at least, not so visible) is social media.

The distribution of a microphone to anybody who wants one is probably not an unalloyed good. The number of venues that publish entirely unedited thought that is not curated by an institutional gatekeeper has its rewards, especially if you're suspicious of those institutional gatekeepers. But if mankind is a tribal animal, being exposed to all the variated forms in which tribes organize themselves offends on an instinctual level.

Foreign ideas, unfamiliar manners, and distinct customs that may be perfectly normal in one community could be entirely anathema to another a thousand miles away. And in an earlier age, those two communities would almost never interact. Today, divergent, insulting, and even threatening thought patterns are readily available. Indeed, they're hard to avoid.

"A funny thing happens when you take young human beings, whose minds evolved for tribal warfare and us/them thinking, and you fill those minds full of binary dimensions," university professor and author Jonathan Haidt said in a 2017 lecture. "You tell them that one side in each binary is good and the other is bad. You turn on their ancient tribal circuits, preparing them for battle. Many students find it thrilling; it floods them with a sense of meaning and purpose."[19]

This observation is illuminating not just of young people's instincts but their desire to impose order on an unruly world. The New Puritan's foremost supposition about itself is that it is righteous and moral. Thus, anyone who is not a coreligionist falls somewhere outside the purely ethical spectrum. And they must be stopped.

"The conspiracy theories, the lies, the distortions, the overwhelming amount of information, the anger encoded in it," Yale Law School lecturer Emily Bazelon wrote of social media with palpable exasperation, "these all serve to create chaos and confusion and make people, even nonpartisans, exhausted, skeptical and cynical about politics." She doesn't dwell on the distinction between that which is outright false and premises that are merely debatable, but blurring that line establishes an urgency that justifies her extreme remedy for the "chaos" that prevails today: curtailing rights to free expression codified in the First Amendment.

Those rights "are simplistic," she writes, and "inadequate for our era." In Europe, for example, such liberties are not afforded the general public. There, you can be prosecuted for saying the wrong thing to the wrong person. Therefore, Bazelon claims, those countries "have created better conditions" for an informed citizenry to determine "what they want their societies to be."

Bazelon makes this author's life that much easier by establishing a connection between her censorious impulse and the censorship sought by the likes of Catharine MacKinnon and Andrea Dworkin, who advocated legal restrictions on pornography, and critical race theory advocates who support reading "racist hate speech" limits into jurisprudence around the First Amendment.

In the end, though, Bazelon doesn't rest her argument on the constitutional propriety of restricting certain forms of speech but the more arguable claim that the private firms administering internet-based proprieties should become more active censors. "In the last several years," she concludes, "some liberals have lost patience with rehashing debates about ideas they find toxic." If that's the case, they are no longer "liberals," according to any commonly understood definition of the word. They have become something else entirely.

Those who are incensed by the conduct of social media users argue that the legal protections afforded the owners and operators of those services need to be pared back. Here, and unlike the initiatives proposed by progressives in this book's preceding chapters, the left has allies within the post-Trump right.[20]

Some Republicans, too, want to strip social media companies of the protections they enjoy in Section 230 of the Communications Decency Act, which shields firms like Facebook, Google, and Twitter from the legal liabilities imposed on more conventional publishers. Thus, a curious alliance between the likes of progressives like Senator Elizabeth Warren and conservatives like Senator Ted Cruz—indeed, between Donald Trump and Joe Biden—has formed.[21] And though their gripes with these media companies diverge, their remedy does not.

The arguments against Section 230 are not devoid of all merit, but those arguments cannot (and should not) be evaluated in the absence of a full consideration of what has fueled this new activist cause: the unfiltered access to a credulous audience social media provides their political adversaries. What these platforms allow and what they do not isn't the whole problem; it's the assumed influence they wield that so rankles.

Tensions between the free expression enjoyed by the lay public and the expert classes has been a subject of debate since the concept of free expression emerged. True Puritans sided definitively with the laity. After all, in their time, speech policing was a tool used by the state and the clergy alike to enforce religious dogma that was antithetical to Puritan thought. But the New Puritan is more inclined toward the sort of propriety that evolved from puritanism in the nineteenth century. It is a propriety that regards thought that is not curated by the enlightened with suspicion.

"Free Speech Is Killing Us," read the hysterical *New York Times* headline gracing a 2019 op-ed by *New Yorker* staff writer Andrew

Marantz. "I no longer have any doubt that the brutality that germi-nates on the internet can leap into the world of flesh and blood," he wrote.[22] And while his prognosis might have been overwrought, subsequent events confirmed Marantz's prescience among those already inclined to agree with him. The January 6 riots in 2021 that led to a siege of the Capitol Building are proof, according to Mic, that certain public figures cannot have access to an "unfettered megaphone" on social media.[23]

The fetter, a shackle usually affixed around the ankles, is an apt metaphor. "Unfettered" speech is a threat that haunts would-be gatekeepers everywhere. "Does our traditional commitment to un-fettered free speech still serve democracy?" asked NPR host Dave Davies.[24] In 2021, *New York Times* readers were alerted to the exis-tence of "unfettered conversations" taking place on the "invitation-only app" Clubhouse.[25] There, users have the option to "block" unwanted participants, which is precisely what happened to *Times* reporter Taylor Lorenz. This exclusivity has "created disputes about access, including with a *New York Times* journalist," read the *Times*'s strangely detached reporting on itself.

These laments betray the extent to which online social media applications do, in fact, fetter their users. They block, they de-platform, and they censor. They brand that which they subjectively deem misinformation as such, often based on the judgment of the manifestly unqualified and at the expense of these platforms' cred-ibility. This is all quite fettering.

Ultimately, social media's worst contribution to the discourse, its puritanical critics maintain, is that it facilitates an unmoderated dialogue in which racism, sexism, classism, homophobia, and half a dozen other bigotries can be expressed without fear of consequence.

The U.K.'s Birmingham City University professor of criminol-ogy Imran Awan outlines this indictment in detail—and I don't use the word "indictment" figuratively. The professor identified a hand-ful of cases in which hateful content and even indications of violent intentions expressed online justified the arrest and prosecution of some careless social media users in Great Britain, where protections on "unfettered" speech do not exist. And you don't have to be a dedicated bigot to be a passive participant in the expression of those hateful views.

"My research showed some people simply join in with conversations targeting vulnerable figures," Awan explained. "Others post messages that don't say anything specifically racist but that they know will inflame racial tensions." He goes on to illustrate the phenomenon by showing how a perfectly banal post asking users to describe the "typical British breakfast" devolved into a bidding war among social media users to publish the most vile, savage expressions of racial antagonism they could come up with.

"In this way, social media acts as an amplifying echo chamber for such hateful rhetoric and racist views," Awan continued. "It makes the way some people imagine the world seem more real." True enough, but that goes for social media's critics, too. That is, unless you believe that casual face-to-face conversations between perfect strangers routinely degenerate into shockingly racist performance art. Such a theory demands a certain amount of condescension from its proponents—an understanding that they're just a little bit better than the average Joe.[26]

In the real world, racially insensitive slights are often far subtler than the deliberately provocative spectacles pseudonymous internet users make of themselves. There's even a word for that sort of thing among progressive social reformers: "microaggressions." Those are exactly what they sound like: minor, perhaps even unintentional offenses, which could conceivably be construed as racial even when likelier explanations for individual acts of thoughtlessness exist.

A primer on the subject and its "implications for clinical practice" published by the education school at Columbia University describes how fiendishly difficult it is for "therapists to identify" racial microaggressions in the wild. Nevertheless, this document prescribes best practices for those who hope to interdict unwittingly antisocial behavior. Their foremost recommendation is to avoid passively condoning that behavior by letting it slide.

"A simple comment—'I'm sorry; what's so funny?'—can jar someone from their rudeness," the document advises those who have been exposed to humor that comes at someone else's expense. "When a friend poses a question that feels hurtful, let protracted silence do the work for you," it continues. If the offending incident occurs at a place of business, "leave," but "before you walk out, let the managers know why you're leaving." If you have family members who offend with insensitive jokes, let them know the extent to which their bigoted behavior is "creating distance" between you. What if you've become the unwilling recipient of a prejudiced email? "Reply to all," the primer suggests, "sharing your thoughts with everyone on the email list. Others then may follow your example."[27]

This is all sound advice for those who don't appreciate rudeness or want to avoid being thought of as a jerk (except for that "reply all" one. No one appreciates a "reply all"). Curbing antisocial behaviors in our neighbors without resorting to street justice or the pursuit of professional consequences is a project of perennial importance. It certainly preoccupied Puritan reformers.

Recall the words of the stern minister John "Decalogue" Dod, whose oeuvre involved delving into the Ten Commandments to fish out an untold number of social proscriptions. We've discussed his work when it comes to the Seventh Commandment and the ways in which "Thou shall not commit adultery" was interpreted to include virtually any sexual appetite. His thoughts on the Third Commandment, "Thou shalt not take the name of the Lord thy God in vain," were just as creative.

Dod applied this commandment to the many irritating "microaggressions" of his time. It didn't just warn Protestant reformers against blasphemy; it forbade anything even remotely approaching profanity.

"If you claimed to be a Christian while failing to show it in the way you led your life," Michael Winship observed, "you took God's name in vain just as fatally as you did by swearing." But if the demands on the elect were to model Puritanism's preferred behaviors so they would be more widely adopted, you couldn't simply hector your rude friends, relatives, and neighbors into submission. That would only push them away from you and lead them to ignore your advice. So, Dod crafted his own primer for congregants confronted with unwanted lewdness or blasphemy.

"If you found yourself in a situation where rebuking swearing would be too socially awkward, Dod advised, the next best thing was to walk out," Winship summarized. "And if that was not possible, you should make a conspicuously grimacing face, or at least cover your ears."[28] The methods for providing the tasteless among us with a gentle rebuke have not improved much over the centuries.

While Dod was not above delivering a stern lecture to any and all who offended God, regardless of the social graces he risked contravening, he nonetheless recognized that a lasting and meaningful reproach had to be delivered with sincere compassion. A "sour look and an austere contemptuous gesture," Dod preached, "alienates men's hearts from us."[29]

Though it comes from the same place, Dod's advice is markedly more tolerant than modern-day efforts to shame inadvertent microaggressors. We are left to wonder whether alienating those they regard with contempt is something the New Puritan is all that worried about.

Throughout this book, the theme of family has been a constant. After all, family is a constant source of frustration for the progressive Puritan.

Their preferred code of social conduct would force you to berate your relatives during holiday functions. It compels the state to take on a more active role ensuring that you and your neighbors are providing proper parentage. It forces matrimonial bonds to serve a social function, and it prescribes certain forms that a wholesome relationship should take. Whether that's good for your relationship is immaterial; it's not about you, but society as a whole.

If the family is a source of unalloyed joy for puritanical progressivism's most committed advocates, that happiness is buried under a mountain of exhortations and commandments. Here, too, the links to the past are too obvious to ignore.

Early American Puritans retained a certain fondness for what the scholars Steven Mintz and Susan Kellogg deemed a "deep sense of cooperative commitment" and a "communal responsibility" not just toward one another but also toward the great work of building a new Zion.

Toward this end, the family served an irreplaceable purpose.

"The Puritans never thought of the family as purely a private unit," Mintz and Kellogg explain. "To them, it was an integral part of the larger political and social world." The family's nuclear structure was not self-governing. "Family ties and community ties tended to blur," these scholars note. The family was society's primary economic and educational unit.[30]

Political order was an outgrowth of those family ties. They, therefore, could not be left to organize themselves. Familial relationships were policed by "tithingmen" whose job it was to oversee households. This constabulary ensured that "marital relations were harmonious and that parents properly disciplined unruly children." And there were penalties for the men, women, and even children who failed to live up to their responsibilities or succumbed to the temptations of sin.[31]

"The puritan religion taught that even newborn infants were regarded as embodiments of guilt and sin," Mintz and Kellogg continue. "In their view, the primary task of child rearing was to break down a child's sinful will and internalize respect for divinely instituted authority through," among other tools, "repeated admonitions, physical beatings, and intense psychological pressure."

After the age of two, childlike impetuousness stopped being cute and started to be a sign of intolerable insubordination. According to one Pilgrim pastor, a child's "stubbornness and stoutness of mind arising from natural pride" must be "broken and beaten down so the foundation of their education" can be built up around "humility and tractableness and other virtues."[32]

Puritanical society in the colonial period saw the family as the state in a microcosm. It therefore followed that the state should oversee that contract and guarantee the social compact. To the extent that the New Puritan disagrees with this conception of family life, it is only on the margins.

If the New Left has an inception date, it is June 15, 1962. On that day, the political manifesto that came to be known as the Port Huron Statement was completed.

"Many of us began maturing in complacency," the student-written document affirmed. That complacency, the statement's authors averred, must end. "We regard *men* as infinitely precious and possessed of unfulfilled capacities for reason, freedom, and love," the statement continued. "In affirming these principles, we are aware of countering perhaps the dominant conceptions of man in the twentieth century: that he is a thing to be manipulated, and that he is inherently incapable of directing his affairs. We oppose the depersonalization that reduces human beings to the status of things."[33]

This testament's discernably religious tone struck a powerful chord, and it received favorable coverage in both countercultural and legacy media venues. The document's nondenominational spiritualism was reflective of an emerging left-wing ethos that gravitated toward the mysticism and incorporeality of Eastern religious traditions while retaining classical liberalism's fondness for individual liberty. But the drafters of this document within the Students for a Democratic Society were soon replaced by a more radical cohort that became progressively more illiberal.

As George McKenna noted, the SDS's early egalitarianism was replaced with an all-consuming pursuit of "honesty, authenticity, sincerity," and, above all, purity. "Eventually, purity overrode everything else, including effectiveness and engagement with the rest of American society."[34]

As the Port Huron Statement foreshadowed, this was also the period in which the earliest forms of New Age thought came into vogue—a movement with quasi-religious foundations in secular humanism and Eastern spirituality. Its prescriptions focused to a prohibitive degree on self-gratification, because to be in touch with one's own desires was to take one step closer to a higher consciousness. This was the ether in which "progressive parenting" techniques were incubated. Those techniques de-emphasized discipline in favor of self-actualization, ontologism, and uninhibited indulgence in the pursuit of a spiritual awakening.

This theory gave rise to a more laid-back parenting style. It placed a premium on drawing out children's innate potential, nurturing their instinctual aptitudes, learning through discovery (and the mistakes that accompany inquisitiveness), and reducing the potential for conflict between kids and their overweening parents. This devil-may-care parenting movement appealed primarily to middle-class white households in the postwar years.

Countercultural parents came from "cultured, sophisticated, and economically advantaged homes," according to University of California, Los Angeles professor of psychology Thomas Weisner.[35] Some of the subjects of his early 1970s study of families raising children in unconventional ways chose to withdraw from conventional society altogether. Others put down roots in more prototypical urban and suburban environments. But the countercultural family shared some universal traits. Their family structures were fluid, and their ideological affinities were integrated into many otherwise apolitical aspects of daily life. But most of all, they shared a particular outlook on parenting, which, like those who were moved by the Port Huron Statement, emphasized self-actualization and authenticity.

"Weisner's counterculture subjects emphasized shared feelings, honesty, expressiveness, intimacy, and physical contact with their children," the University of Montana's Eva Dunn-Froebig observed. A companion analysis by sociologists Robert Rath and Douglas Mc-Dowell found that parents emphasized directness and honesty, and they encouraged their kids to be open to experimentation and change.

"They wanted to instill counterculture ideals in their children, like being open toward sex and sexuality, questioning authority, and being committed to peace and nonviolence," Rath and McDowell concluded. "They also said they wanted their children to have the freedom to develop and define their own values and ways of life."[36]

This is all a rather overt rejection of the Puritan tradition—both substantively and stylistically. But like the sexual revolution, it was not to last.

As it was in the seventeenth century, so it is today: the nuclear family remains Anglo-American civilization's primary social unit. That is a source of frustration for those who dislike both primary social units and Anglo-American civilization. For that irascible cohort, the atomistic family and all the trappings around it exist to maintain intolerable systems of oppression that must be dismantled.

You might not be aware, for example, that the nuclear family is classist.

It and the architecture that has been built around it—most notably, the single-family home—represents a "tool of repression and social control," according to author and architectural theorist Phineas Harper.

"Designed to enforce a particular social structure, nuclear housing hardwires divisions in labor, gender, and class into the built fabric of our cities," Harper wrote. That home's placid facade masks a horror show of abuses. Among them, domestic violence, the "subordination of women," and the maltreatment of domestic labor.[37]

The alternative to this family home is, of course, a more collectivized conception of both the "nuclear household and family itself" and the world outside those structures. Harper tasks architects not just with the work of reimagining houses but with the epochal charge of ushering in "an alternative type of society." No sweat.

The nuclear family isn't just classist. It's also racist.

In 2020, the Black Lives Matter organization hosted on its official website (blacklivesmatter.com) a manifesto entitled "What We Believe." And what they believed was that the nuclear family was an oppressive construct.

"We disrupt the Western-prescribed nuclear family structure requirement by supporting each other as extended families and 'villages' that collectively care for one another, especially our children, to the degree that mothers, parents, and children are comfortable," the passage read.

That section was soon deleted from the website, along with much of the manifesto. It had been inadvertently publicized by the fact-checking outfit PolitiFact, which set out to contextualize this statement beyond the point of recognition in the effort to suggest that the document did not say what it quite plainly said.[38]

But even if the wrong sorts of people were privy to this manifesto—that is, anyone who wasn't predisposed to nod credulously along with it—BLM's intended audience heard their message loud and clear.

"We are committed to disrupting the Western-prescribed nuclear family structure requirement by supporting each other as extended families and 'villages' that collectively care for one another, and especially 'our' children to the degree that mothers, parents, and children are comfortable."[39] That passage, a near verbatim recitation of BLM's reconceptualization of the family, was included in a resolution adopted by the United Federation of Teachers union in November 2020. It passed with the resounding support of 90 percent of the union's Delegate Assembly.[40]

As well as being racist and classist, the nuclear family is also sexist.

The American feminist philosopher and author of *The Feminine Mystique*, Betty Friedan, famously likened the life led by the average housewife to a "comfortable concentration camp." Those women who placidly consign themselves to their own subjugation "are suffering a slow death of mind and spirit."[41]

In her famous book *Sexual Politics*, Kate Millett maintained that "patriarchy's chief institution is the family." Beyond facilitating reproduction, its primary function is to socialize children into an oppressive male-dominated social milieu. As one "student of the family" insisted, "the family is the keystone of the stratification system, the social mechanism by which it is maintained."[42]

"The nuclear family must be destroyed, and people must find better ways of living together," New York University humanities professor Linda Gordon wrote. "Whatever its ultimate meaning, the break-up of families now is an objectively revolutionary process."[43]

"If we want to talk about equality for children, then the fact that children are raised in families means there's no equality," wrote Mary Jo Bane, the Thornton Bradshaw Professor of Public Policy and Management at Harvard's Kennedy School and former Department of Health and Human Services assistant secretary under Bill Clinton. "In order to raise children with equality, we must take them away from families and communally raise them."[44]

The notion that the American family is a shackle around the ankles of women and an obstacle on the pathway to a more evolved conception of child-rearing is neither new nor especially fringe, depending on the intellectual circles you frequent.

The question before radical progressives isn't whether the family as we know it is headed for extinction. Their theorists have moved on to the matter of what should replace the family. The founder and executive director of the nonprofit Family Story, Nicole Sussner Rodgers, has many, many suggestions.

"'Mother' and 'father,'" she writes, "have increasingly less meaning and utility today when so many children have two moms or two dads, single parents, blended families, or even three legal parents."[45] Sussner Rodgers's fragile assumption here seems to be that if a person is not raised in a traditional two-parent heterosexual household, he or she will be regarded by society as illegitimate in some ill-defined way.

If you fully internalize this logic, you end up with the conclusions drawn by administrators at New York City's elite Grace Church School. "While we recognize hateful language that promotes racism, misogyny, homophobia, and other forms of discrimination are already addressed in our school handbooks, we also recognize that we can do more than ban hateful language," read the private school's "Inclusive Language Guide." Toward that end, the school banned the use of allegedly divisive words like "mom" and "dad."[46]

If the logic justifying these neurotic linguistic prescriptions was just to be as polite as possible, they would only be a curiosity. But that rationale is strained to its breaking point when you get down into the details.

"Sexuality can be fluid along the course of a person's life," Grace Church School's guidance read. Along with gender, sexual self-identification can change over a lifetime, so avoiding these words is only practical. But that also assumes that someone who changes their gender identity will retroactively take offense at the way Grace's administrators correctly referred to them all those years ago. Such a person, if he or she exists, is also quite probably a self-obsessed hysteric who is easily offended. It would be impossible to satisfy such a person, and the energy expended in that effort would be more productively dedicated to almost any other pursuit.

And yet, Family Story's executive director has a point insofar as the definition of what constitutes a family is no longer so tightly constrained. As evidence, she cites the example of Sarah and Kae, two good friends who are both straight and sought to adopt a child together. In a landmark ruling by a Canadian court in 2018, they won the right to co-parent. "And that's how we became a family," said Sarah.[47] The phenomenon of platonic co-parenting is taking off in the United States, too, where adults are skipping the laborious process of dating and mating and moving right along to having children. Of course, some of those children are the product of a rather conventional conception, which leaves the "platonic" nature of these relationships subject to interpretation.[48]

At least these couples (or whatever they consider themselves) decided to bring a child into a loving and, hopefully, stable environment. That's more than you can say for an increasing number of addled narcissists who hide behind a fashionable sort of anxiety as an excuse to avoid having children. Self-imposed childlessness wouldn't be worth caring about if advocates of this lifestyle were not also trying to convince their peers, some of whom desperately long for the joy that children bring into the world, to abstain from procreating.

Not only are kids the manacle that keeps women paddocked in social structures designed to oppress them, making new people is bad for the environment. The "small family ethic" was proposed by James Madison University's Travis Rieder as early as 2016. "Dangerous climate change is going to be happening by then," Rieder told NPR when asked what the world would look like twenty years in the future. "Here's a provocative thought: Maybe we should protect our kids by not having them."[49]

This recommendation aligns with an observation offered by progressive Congresswoman Alexandria Ocasio-Cortez. "Basically, there's a scientific consensus that the lives of children are going to be very difficult," she asserted. "And it does lead, I think, young people to have a legitimate question: Is it okay to still have children?" Although the paralyzing fear that having children will contribute to undesirable environmental conditions has led some to voluntarily submit to childlessness, the infecund have not found a perpetual state of crippling anxiety to be a suitable replacement for the fulfillment found in child-rearing.

"I feel like I can't in good conscience bring a child into this world and force them to try and survive what may be apocalyptic conditions," one woman told *The Guardian* reporters. That mentality contributes to the findings of a study published in the academic journal *Climatic Change*, which found that 14 percent of those surveyed cited climate change as a "major reason" for their decision to remain childless. And for many of them, this is an agonizing experience. "Climate change is the sole factor for me in deciding not to have biological children," another young woman confessed. "I don't want to birth children into a dying world [though] I dearly want to be a mother."

Those women who do take the plunge and still retain some fondness for the progressive project are increasingly regarded by their fellow progressives as heretics. Take, for example, *New York Times* opinion writer Elizabeth Bruenig.

On Mother's Day 2021, the self-described socialist published a moving essay about the experience of having children in her midtwenties—a young age relative to those who share her ideological affinities. In the op-ed, she confronted many of the misconceptions about motherhood that she hears from young, single women. "It isn't a chore but a pleasure," Bruenig wrote, "not the end of freedom as you know it but the beginning of a kind of liberty you can't imagine."[50]

This apostasy was met with a barrage of vitriolic attacks on her character and motives. Bruenig was accused of "discouraging abortion," which is an unforgivable sin on the left. Her decision to have two children was deemed a manifestation of her "white extinction anxiety." *Salon*'s Amanda Marcotte likened Bruenig to the antifeminist activist Phyllis Schlafly and attacked the *Times* for publishing something that only appeals to "dudes so shitty they worry they won't get a wife until they trap someone who's too young to know better." The writer Jude Ellison S. Doyle insisted that this work was a "grift," though it's not at all clear who is being conned here. "The greatest trick the Devil ever pulled was convincing this woman it was a tremendous personal achievement to be repeatedly knocked up by an internet troll she met in high school," she added with puzzling vitriol.[51]

The full-throttle rage spiral Bruenig's casual expression of contentment sent these and many other critics of her essay into is instructive. She did not attack anyone. She didn't display any racial animus, trans- or homophobia, or hostility toward abortion rights. What so aggravated her inquisitors was that she found in motherhood a measure of happiness. And to her critics, happiness cannot be anything other than derivative of observing cultural progressivism's conceits.

If you do decide to have children, you certainly cannot be trusted to raise them. Not according to the left's haughtiest social engineers.

"It's a central idea to feminism anyway, that mothers aren't natural entities," the author Sophie Lewis said in a 2019 interview with *The Nation*. "Mothers nurture, but they also kill and abuse their wards. That's why it's so valuable to denaturalize the mother-child bond."

This idea, Lewis added, is critical to opening a new frontier in "revolutionary politics." And the first step in that Long March involves popularizing the idea that the family structure is unhealthy for all involved.

"We know that the nuclear private household is where the overwhelming majority of abuse can happen," Lewis continued. "And then there's the whole question of what it is for: training us up to be workers, training us to be inhabitants of a binary-gendered and racially stratified system, training us not to be queer."

That process begins by challenging the notion that "babies belong to anyone." Children belong to the collective. Thus, Lewis hopes to popularize the concept of "gestational surrogates," whose attachment to their children is functionally reptilian. Kids are conceived, they're born into conditions as comfortable as surrogacy allows, and the hive takes it from there. "If everything is surrogacy," Lewis continued, "the whole question of original or 'natural' relationships falls by the wayside."[52]

Lewis's crusade to break up the family unit and turn us all into figurative "surrogates" isn't entirely ideological. Her peculiar policy preference, she admits, arises from a trauma she experienced within her own family.

In her book, *Full Surrogacy Now*, Lewis describes a childhood car trip with her family after seeing an amateur theatrical production, the plot of which revolved around one of its characters discovering that his children were not biologically his own. "Musing incredulously on its themes, I recall cheerfully asking from the back seat: 'But, Dad, it's ridiculous. If you found out that we (my brother and I) were actually the biological children of the milkman, you wouldn't love us any less all of a sudden, would you?'" Lewis wrote. "I had meant it as a rhetorical question only. But there was a stony, awkward silence that made clear to me I was not going to get the answer I needed. I felt so devastated that, for the rest of the drive, I could not speak."[53]

This emotional injury led Lewis to gravitate toward an abject hatred for the very idea of family. It is "stratified, commodified, cis-normative, and neo-colonial," she wrote. It fetishizes reproduction, which is really the pathologically bigoted fixation with making more able-bodied, upper-middle-class white people who identify with the gender of their birth. And, as we have learned, the single-family house is also home to a cacophony of horrors: "Discomfort, coercion, molestation, abuse, humiliation, depression, battery, murder, mutilation, loneliness, blackmail, exhaustion, psychosis, gender-straitjacketing, racial programming, and embourgeoisement," Lewis wrote. "The private family is the headquarters of all these."

Lewis isn't a rare or obscure crank. Well, at least she isn't rare or obscure. The marketplace of ideas on the left is increasingly rife with family abolitionism.

"The idea of family abolition may invoke visions of violent interventions," writes Open Democracy's Sophie Silverstein. It's really about love. The nuclear family "as an institution . . . is built on intersecting racism, sexism, and homophobia." It, therefore, doesn't generate but actually withholds affection.[54]

"If we were used to the idea that we belong to each other, we might act as if the crises that threaten the most vulnerable also posed a danger to the most comfortable," *The New Republic*'s Nora Caplan-Bricker mused. "That may sound like a utopian pronouncement, but it's closer to the inescapable truth."

"One way philosophers might think about solving the social justice problem would be by simply abolishing the family," the British philosopher Adam Swift opined. "If the family is this source of unfairness in society, then it looks plausible to think that if we abolished the family there would be a more level playing field."[55]

But how might we achieve this radical redefinition of the family unit—a construct so universal (even in tribal societies) that it must be an evolutionary adaptation? The magazine *Commune* provides a step-by-step instruction manual.

"The best starting point to abolish the family is a massive insurrection," the guide dauntingly begins. Amid the death and destruction wrought by civil warfare, aspiring family abolitionists are advised to establish "protest camps," organized (as you might have guessed) communally. Those encampments should include common sleeping areas where the group protects its members from the potential rapists in their midst, and "syringe exchanges" to provide care to "active drug users." This is surely temporary. The process of natural selection in an anarchic war zone is likely to weed out the rapists and heroin addicts rather quickly.

Of course, breaking up the family is a process. Those who want to form "intimate, family-like units" should be allowed to do just that—at least for a while. But individual child-rearing is out of the question. "Childcare areas become crèches," *Commune* advised. There, access to your little bundle of joy will be monitored and constrained. Those who resist this new order will be regarded as "counterrevolutionaries" to be treated with all the severity this term implies.

Congratulations! "If you've reached this step, you have succeeded in abolishing the family," this radical flow chart concludes. "You have freed queer love and feminist care to create a basis for human flourishing."[56]

If this all sounds to you like warmed-over Marxism, you're not wrong. Marx and Engels picked up where Plato left off, reiterating his belief that the optimal social structure would lead to the dissolution of the nuclear family. But when the Soviets attempted to implement the *Communist Manifesto*'s prescriptions for free love and communal child-rearing, they found that it—like just about everything else in the book—didn't function as advertised.

The Bolsheviks were quickly inundated with thousands of fatherless infants and neglected children, who were suddenly the state's problem. The existence of tens of thousands of homeless youths soon resulted in widespread juvenile delinquency. Children in the young Soviet state were introduced to crime and drugs at an early age. Children's sex lives often began well before the point of sexual maturity and delinquency was rampant. Rape was common and sexually transmitted diseases proliferated.[57]

Soon enough, the old bourgeois morality began to make a comeback in the worker's state, but only out of absolute necessity.

A dystopian future in which you deposit your newborns into the children's crèche to be cultivated like crops may be a long way off. In the meantime, there's still plenty to be miserable about.

Take, for example, what well-adjusted people took to be a heartwarming episode in 2017 when Robert Kelly, a professional political analyst with an expertise in inter-Korean affairs, was making an appearance on the BBC via his home office. During a live interview, Kelly's three-year-old daughter burst into the room and confidently marched her way toward her father in full view of the camera.

The clip went viral. "BBC Dad" and his family became a sensation, and all the world cooed over the adorable display. All, that is, except for *The New Statesman*'s "Media Mole."[58]

"There's nothing worse than watching everyone else crease with mirth while you're left thinking: but . . . no?" the British tabloid magazine's culture critic "Moley" Tant admitted. The author confessed that it's impossible to enjoy such a display of cuteness because it failed to remind viewers of the awfulness of existence.

"Basically, the message this video delivers to me is: Being a man is playing life on the easy setting," Tant added. That is an odd thing to say of a man with a doctorate in international relations who speaks multiple languages and makes a living as a professional geopolitical affairs analyst.

It was the fact that Kelly gently nudged his daughter away from the camera during a live, globally broadcast television news appearance that proved so irritating. Not because that wouldn't be anyone's instinct in that situation but because, in Tant's imagination, a woman could never get away with such behavior.

At least Tant seemed to be consciously miserable. "Once again, the yawning awareness of the patriarchy shits on my ability to enjoy something," the missive concluded.[59]

"Of course, this is all cruel projection," Tant added with some long overdue self-awareness. "It's not his fault that the patriarchy exists, and also annoys me so much." All right, fleeting self-awareness.

In the end, Tant asks us for our "pity." And we should provide it. This immiserating world view has stolen away a simple joy—one of life's many small and forgettable daily pleasures that, cumulatively, make it worth living.

Here is as good a place as any to start breaking all this down. It's not a natural choice to hoist the crushing weight of the world on your own shoulders. That burden must be imposed on you, and your instinctual desire to cast it off must be conditioned out of you. You must be coerced and cajoled into participating in this joyless project.

As you have likely concluded by now, it's just not worth it.

8

REFORMATION

SLOWLY AT FIRST, THEN ALL AT ONCE

The puritanical predisposition is one that leads its adherents to carve out order from chaos, enforce and observe consistency, and reject the distractions that diminish your usefulness to the cause.

The puritanically minded today are waging a campaign against disorganization. It's reasonable to conclude, therefore, that entropy of the sort that provides for maximum liberty within legal bounds is the proper remedy to this patronizing arrogance. The good news here is that entropy doesn't need to be cultivated to flourish.

It is a sound bet that the New Puritan belief system is destined to one day be as ridiculed and reviled as the old Puritan ethos, in part because it attracts adherents through coercion. The movement's primary manifestation is small groups of people taking things away from larger groups of people. Your first encounter with this movement is likely to be when that activity or artist or product you enjoyed has been adulterated or even proscribed for your own good. Blindly and with the utmost pomposity, a puritanically inclined minority is courting the resentment of a much larger host. We know how that usually ends.

Even as you read this book, the New Puritan revolution is busily creating its own counterrevolutionaries. That's not to say we should just sit back and count on the revolution to plant the seeds of its own destruction. Skeptics of the original Puritans' excesses—including some of their society's most prominent members—later regretted their complacency. But the best defense against severe earnestness, it turns out, has the added advantage of being enjoyable.

Self-seriousness is not the same thing as seriousness. One needn't become a prophet of doom to also be perceived as sober and rational. A hopeless pessimism that arises from obsessing over how wrongly your neighbors are living their lives isn't a shrewd outlook at all. Desperately trying to control that which you cannot and, by rights, should not is enough to drive anyone a little mad.

The alternative to policing moral conformity is as simple as *not doing that*. This not only renders you marginally less annoying but has the advantage of making fewer demands on your time. It doesn't require you to filter your experience of the world through a rigid political framework. It doesn't force you into a defensive crouch. And it doesn't lead you into a hopeless state of gloominess over the inexorable decline to which we've consigned our children. It allows you to become a little less political and, as an inevitable consequence, more joyful. What's not to love?

The assumption that the new puritanism will ultimately consume itself is an expectation we can draw from the devolution of similar movements in transatlantic history. The paradigm that led earlier generations of moralizers to strip you of your worldly pleasures was eventually discredited and displaced by a more successful paradigm that made fun of that effort. That is the story of one American city's failed moral crusades. It was an enterprise that can be summed up in the loaded phrase: "Banned in Boston."

In 1878, inspired by a speech delivered by the anti-vice campaigner Anthony Comstock, a variety of prominent Bostonians founded the

New England Society for the Suppression of Vice, which was modeled on the New York society of the same name. Their mission was the promotion of a unifying civic morality native to mainline Protestantism and the suppression of alternative forms of moral virtue. Their cause was an urgent one because the threat they were organizing to combat was imminent: a book of poems.

By the end of the 1870s, proponents of "free love"—the propolyamory movement of the late 1800s—had organized a campaign designed to challenge Massachusetts' Comstock laws and its proscriptions against the publication and dissemination of lewd material. Those challenges had all failed. The moral reform movement in Boston had reached the zenith of its power.

Emboldened as they were, the forthcoming publication of the final edition of Walt Whitman's celebrated book of poetry, *Leaves of Grass*, lit a fire under moral reformers. Whitman's most famous work was, in his own words, "avowedly the song of Sex and Amativeness, and even Animality."[1] He sang the praises of the prostitutes he'd bedded and described in excruciating detail (by the standards of the nineteenth century) the carnal act's most agreeable aspects. The book was not intended as a political statement, but it became one in short order.

In 1879, the New England Society helped to strengthen Massachusetts' obscenity proscriptions, expanding prohibition to all forms of media "containing obscene, indecent, or impure language" that leads to the "corruption of the morals or youth."[2] Local officials mounted a campaign targeting Whitman's Boston publisher, eventually forcing it to withdraw publication of the book in 1882.

The objectives shared by moral reformers in late 1800s Boston are by now quite familiar. One of the New England Society's most prominent members, Yale College president Noah Porter, expounded on the principles animating anti-vice crusaders in terms any Puritan would recognize. Valuable works of fiction, Porter wrote in 1882, "rightly used cannot but elevate the soul." By contrast, dangerous literature had the capacity to "beguile to sin" and promote "foul and vicious passion."[3]

Literature that compelled us to think about sex as an act of "indulgence" leads us to forgo our earthly responsibilities in the pursuit of personal pleasure. Free love and the literary contributions to that movement, Porter wrote, "dethrones the will from its appropriate dominion over the feelings and releases the emotions from their responsibility to the conscience." It therefore undermines "a wholesome and most necessary discipline to the duties of good citizenship and of personal responsibility."[4]

We have an ethical obligation to "reclaim and recover" our friends and neighbors who are tempted by vice, Porter maintained. Every aspect of society must be directed toward this pursuit, as the "public order" cannot last "so long as a lower stratum is becoming ignorant and brutalized from one generation to another." Every social unit, from the state to the family, must be conscripted into this fight. In fact, these two societal poles are not really all that distinct. "It is superfluous to say that the state naturally grows out of the family," Porter concluded, "inasmuch as every family is already a state in miniature."[5]

The Puritans were long gone by the time Porter wrote these words, but they could have been written by any proponent of the seventeenth century's prevailing morality. Moral reformers of the 1800s had, however, updated the doctrine by adopting a more modern set of tactics to enforce puritanical sensibilities.

As the scholar and theologian P. C. Kemeny observed, the moral reformers of the nineteenth century employed "quasi-scientific discourse" to give the "social hygiene movement" a more scientific feel. Noah Porter, for example, authored a book on human nature and the corruptions to it represented by "licentious literature" entitled *The Elements of Moral Science.*

In the book, Porter expanded on the conventional Victorian ethical wisdom while burdening his arguments with pseudo-scientific language. In doing so, he made them sound superficially authoritative. This effective tactic is still with us today, as the New Puritans in our midst ornament their arbitrary value judgments with the polysyllabic jargon common to identity studies departments on college campuses. How can you argue against their claims? They are scientific.

Posterity has rendered its verdict on both Boston's censorious moralism and Walt Whitman's literary talents, though it took quite some time for the wheel to turn. By 1905, the New England Society supported ten overlapping anti-obscenity statutes and helped prosecute dozens of violators.[6] Boston's libraries were forced to house banned literature behind locked doors. Booksellers conspired to shield the public from the works of immodest authors. Dramatic productions were bowdlerized for local audiences, and dime novels that became sensations around the country never found their way into the hands of young Bostonians.

And yet, these "victories" came at a cost. In 1915, the society rebranded itself the Watch and Ward Society in an effort to escape the controversial legacy of its spiritual founder, Anthony Comstock. And in 1926, H. L. Mencken's efforts to highlight the contradictions presented by the enforcement of Comstock laws made him famous and transformed Boston's moralists into objects of scorn and ridicule. Ultimately, "Banned in Boston" evolved from a warning against the consumption of impure thought to a powerful advertisement for it.

In the 1920s, the phrase entered the lexicon as shorthand for a titillating encounter with an artistic endeavor so taboo that you simply had to experience it for yourself. Affixing that slogan to a book or play was "sure to boost flagging sales in the rest of the country," Harvard University's Paul Boyer observed. "Boston's censorship became so ubiquitous that many began to view it with faint amusement as an inexplicable and even rather picturesque part of the Boston scene."[7]

So stifling was the intellectual climate in the heart of mainline Protestant New England that the city itself became a byword for prudery around the country. By the end of that decade, opponents of Boston's reflexive judgmentalism regularly engaged in gaudy displays of defiance. Students would costume themselves as characters from banned books and parade around campus with placards bearing their titles. Rallies were held in which censorship was "lampooned, ridiculed, and pilloried."[8] And, in the most effective protest of them all, consumers voted with their wallets, rewarding the creatives who offended the city's censors with serious commercial success. "Later," *Boston Globe* reporter Tania deLuzuriaga observed, "publishers actively sought to have books 'banned in Boston' to increase sales in the rest of the country."[9]

The same phenomenon is observable today, though the city of Boston has been replaced with the digital media landscape.

In 2020, Republic Book Publishers sought to advertise a forthcoming historical novel *Old Abe*, which followed Abraham Lincoln's travails during the Civil War. The publisher tried to drum up some sales by advertising the novel on Facebook—a request that was summarily rejected. Some anxious staffers at the social media network decided the book was dangerous because its cover featured a blurb by then vice president Mike Pence. It therefore violated Facebook's capricious policy of proscribing anything related to "Social Issues, Elections or Politics" in that tense election year. Republic promptly capitalized on its author's persecution, effectively labeling *Old Abe* "banned on Facebook." As you might imagine, sales of the book exploded as right-leaning audiences raced to get their hands on this dangerous literature.[10]

Following the attempt to brand the works of Theodor "Dr. Seuss" Geisel racist, an effort that was at least in part sanctioned by the children's author's estate, book-buying audiences saw fit to reward that very estate with a deluge of sales. Not long after a variety of schools, educational institutions, and even the Biden White House branded the books suspect, they took six of the top ten spots on *USA Today*'s list of bestselling works.[11]

In 2020, an activist campaign briefly succeeded in forcing

Amazon to delist the author Abigail Shrier's book warning of the dangers associated with reinforcing gender dysphoria in children, *Irreversible Damage: The Transgender Craze Seducing Our Daughters.* The American Civil Liberties Union, now wholly transformed into the very thing it was founded to fight, joined with those activists. One professor of English even encouraged people to steal and burn the book.[12] It became a bestseller.[13]

Amazon did the same thing to a book with similar themes, the political philosopher Ryan T. Anderson's *When Harry Became Sally: Responding to the Transgender Moment*, in 2021.[14] It, too, enjoyed more free publicity from that failed attempt at censorship than it would have received from a conventional public relations campaign.[15]

Senator Josh Hawley's missive against the "tyranny" of Big Tech was slated for publication by Simon & Schuster in 2021. But on January 6, 2021, the senator objected to the certification of the 2020 election results in several closely contested states—a cause that animated a mob that subsequently stormed the Capitol Building. Hawley's presumed complicity in that event led his publisher to sever their relationship. But the senator from Missouri soon found a new publisher and, when his book hit store shelves, it surged to number six on *Publishers Weekly*'s list of hardcover nonfiction titles. It's hard to imagine that a rather dry vehicle for a politician's national ambitions would have generated that kind of commercial traction without the intervention of his critics.[16]

In sum, it is this author's fondest hope that someone will try to cancel this book. Its critics will have drawn blood. Its fans will have all their worst suspicions confirmed about their enemies. And its writer will be well compensated. Everyone wins.

As Boston's experience over much of the nineteenth and early twentieth centuries attests, puritanism's moral and social prescriptions enjoyed a much longer half-life than you might expect given the historical briefness of the Puritan experiment. The Puritans who lived long enough to see the early 1700s would probably be surprised to find that their ideas had survived at all. From their perspective, the decline and collapse of their political philosophy occurred with disorienting speed.

The eighteenth century was still young when Increase Mather, the son of first-generation settlers in North America, surveyed the wreckage of the world he had tried to create. The Puritan experiment to which he had dedicated his life was over.

In the course of his eighty-four years, Mather witnessed the profound transformations overtaking intellectual life in the Western world. He was born into an all but unquestioned theocratic covenant in 1639. He departed the earthly plane in 1723 surrounded by devotees of the theory of natural law, secular liberalism, and religious pluralism. And Mather likely could not escape the nagging fact of his own contributions to the dissolution of his preferred social compact.

Increase Mather was still in his thirties in the late 1660s, when tensions between colonists and the native Wampanoag deteriorated precipitously. The uneasy alliance between the tribe and New England's colonists dissolved entirely after Metacom, who had taken the name Philip as was the custom amid the tribe's erstwhile friendly relations with the European settlers, ascended to tribal chief in 1662. Negotiations over a new peace agreement collapsed in 1675 when three Wampanoags were hanged in Plymouth Colony for the murder of a fellow tribesman, the Christian convert John Sassamon. Metacom retaliated, sending raiding parties to ransack and burn New England's frontier settlements.

What began as a series of skirmishes snowballed into a nearly three-year war involving every colony in New England and almost every native tribe, even those that initially sought to remain neutral. More than half of the European settlements in those colonies were destroyed, and roughly one in ten American colonists of military age were killed in the conflict.

By the time a new peace treaty was signed in 1678, the Wampanoag had been decimated, and their tribe was left landless. It was, in per-capita terms, the bloodiest conflict in American colonial history. It gave way to irreconcilable political differences among the previously united colonies and to a bitter dispute between them and their mother country.[17]

New England's isolation from the European affairs ended abruptly in the aftermath of King Philip's War—what posterity came to regard as the "First Indian War."

The war brought an end to London's laissez-faire approach to the conduct of American affairs. King Charles II had his fill of Massachusetts' independent streak, in particular. Between the colony's resistance to the Navigation Acts of 1651 and its puritanical hostility toward the Anglican Church, the Bay's stubbornness had become intolerable. Adding to Charles's frustration, mounting legal and territorial squabbles among the colonies made increasing demands on colonial administrators. Something had to be done. So, in 1683, Charles II inaugurated proceedings to vacate Massachusetts Bay Colony's charter and executed its annulment the following year.

The charter was replaced in 1686 with what many colonists regarded as an imperious infringement of their rights as Englishmen. That year, England imposed a new "Dominion" over New England and the Mid-Atlantic colonies, which effectively restructured what is today the entire northeastern United States into a single political entity. Land titles were revoked. Legislatures whose members had been elected by church members were tossed. Royal courts replaced local magistrates and juries. And worst of all, London took concrete steps to promote the Church of England over Congregationalism.

Puritans were enraged by the Crown's decision to annul their long-established legal and political conventions. But the Puritans' ordeal had only just begun.

Dominion was initially administered by a hardline royalist with little taste for dissension, Sir Edmund Andros. From the moment he assumed his charge, Andros enthusiastically set himself to the task of dismantling Puritan society. He harmonized laws throughout the colonies so they would more closely reflect those of England. He outlawed town meetings. He enforced odious British taxes. And almost anyone who resisted the new regime, including powerful landowners and ministers, he arrested.

In this period, European migration into New England took off, and religious pluralism in these formerly monolithic colonies became a de facto part of daily life. Massachusetts, which had been pleasantly undiversified, soon became home to droves of what Puritans regarded as impious Presbyterians, inscrutable Baptists, and downright demonic Quakers.[18]

Charles II died in 1685. He was briefly succeeded by James II, a Catholic, who ruled, as Charles had, by Royal Prerogative. In 1687, James II decreed and Andros enforced the "Declaration of Indulgence," which outlawed discrimination against Catholics. This, a devoted Puritan like Increase Mather could not abide. He published influential tracts against Andros's governance at considerable risk and eventually undertook the journey to England to personally petition the king for relief.

Parliament could not long abide both James II's Catholicism and his overbearing tendencies. In 1688, the king was deposed and exiled in the Glorious Revolution. But despite all this political tumult in England, British Dominion over the colonies persisted. Mather, now in England advocating on behalf of the Puritan cause, was instrumental in the crafting of a new royal charter reestablishing the legality of the Massachusetts colony. But the compromises he had to make in its pursuit contributed to Puritanism's downfall.

The new charter folded Plymouth Colony into Massachusetts' borders, expanding the power and influence of Puritanism's base in the New World. But the new franchise also brought the tightly coupled relationship between the Congregationalist church and Massachusetts's government to an end. The governor would henceforth be appointed by the Crown (Mather and his compatriots could recommend a new colonial manager suitable to them, but this was a one-time dispensation). The king would also have a veto over all laws and appointments. No longer would church membership and outward displays of godliness determine whether an individual was fit to participate in politics. Property ownership became the chief criterion enfranchising voters. Lastly, all Protestants regardless of their individual denominational affinities would henceforth enjoy religious liberty.[19]

The new charter preserved New England's proto-democratic character. It restored the rights of towns to organize, civilian juries to convene, and legislatures to be elected. But it plunged a dagger into the heart of the theocratic principles around which Puritan society had previously ordered itself. The new charter established, according to historian Michael G. Hall, "the constitutional framework for a pluralistic, secular society that would be inherited by John Adams."[20]

By the time Mather returned from England in early 1692, charter in hand, the old religious fervor that once typified Puritan society was rapidly being supplanted by political activism. And why not? After all, what we now regard as the conventional instruments of political authority were replacing the church as the mechanism through which social maxims were enforced and conflicts were mediated.

This tumult contributed to a general sense of instability. The old ways had fallen out from under the Puritans with such speed that it's hard to blame them for feeling a little insecure. Almost overnight, New England was transformed into an environment in which moral panics thrive. This unease produced an indelible stain on Puritanism's legacy: the Salem witch trials.

Previously, trials for those accused of witchcraft were relatively infrequent. The execution of the convicted was even rarer, and local authorities tended to use their power to invalidate rulings they believed to be unjust. But in 1692, amid profound political flux and confusion, the magistrates tasked with investigating the inexplicable fits that struck the daughter of Salem Village's minister made grave mistakes. In deference to this new age of political pluralism, the magistrates opened their preliminary hearings to the public. Those proceedings became a spectacle as the alleged victims put on performative displays of possession for the benefit of the audience. And that audience, having been whipped up into a terrorized frenzy, demanded indiscriminate bloodshed.

Though more sober authorities recognized the horrors over which they were presiding, they were constrained in their capacity to intervene. "Under the old charter," Michael Winship observed, colonial authorities "would have presided over appeals from the jury verdicts of the county courts where witchcraft cases like the ones in Salem were heard."[21] Now, however, they had neither the compunction nor jurisdiction to impose prudence on an anxious public.

"Perhaps they were chasing witches so aggressively to compensate for failing so abysmally to protect the colony from its satanic enemies on the Maine frontier, as was the magistrates' duty," Winship speculated of the aftermath of King Philip's War. "Whatever the reason for their lack of caution, the old Puritan order of things— magistrates serving as a brake on popular demands for witchhunting—had been flipped on its head." The unfolding drama took on a life of its own. The austere religious scholars who once governed these colonies were cowed or subordinated, and a proletarian mob now ruled in their place. The Salem witch trials were, Winship added somberly, "an expression of American puritanism in its fevered death throes."[22]

Not all the colony's authorities succumbed to populist passions. Increase Mather was among the many conscience-addled New Englanders to criticize the injustices he witnessed, but only well after the fact. Though he wrote that he "believed that witches did exist, and witch trials were justified," as was the general consensus of his time, Mather expressed serious reservations about the value of the "spectral evidence" that was the basis for their convictions. He eventually made it a point to speak directly with those accused of witchcraft and took them seriously when they claimed their confessions were made under duress.

In one of Mather's most famous sermons involving "cases of conscience concerning Evil Spirits," the minister advised his congregants that it was "better ten witches go free than the blood of a single innocent be shed." Thus, Mather articulated the logical basis upon which the famous jurist William Blackstone's ratio is predicated, which maintains that it is more ethical for ten guilty men to go free than for one innocent to die as punishment for a crime he did not commit.[23]

But Mather declined to denounce the proceedings while they were ongoing, and his objections came too late. Nineteen of the accused were hung. Another was pressed to death. Some of the executed died to the sound of the crowd's audible disfavor, as they met their fates well and with Christian love for the mob that was meting out such a brutal injustice. Mather's conversion was perhaps as much a product of a genuine change of heart as it was the fear that the populist sentiments engulfing his colony would take his family, too. After all, Mather's daughter was among the many women accused of witchcraft.

As public revulsion over this bloodletting mounted, the freshly empowered legal institutions established by the colony's new charter abandoned their restraint. In October 1692, warning of the "utter ruin and destruction of this poor country" that would follow if the mania on display in Salem was not tamed, the General Court of Massachusetts overrode the authority of the tribunals that had presided over such cruel persecution. Following this, Massachusetts' governor—the Maine-born sea captain William Phips, who coincidentally found religious faith along with his political appointment—suspended the court's authority in total. The governor acted with the political cover provided by the colony's legislative edict, but his heavy hand was surely moved as much by personal considerations. You see, Phips's wife, too, was identified as a possible witch.[24]

At the dawn of the eighteenth century, the Puritan order that had for so long governed life in New England was irreparably broken. Thriving commercial life in the colony's coastal outposts and cities brought with it unfamiliar cultures and activities that were, to put it mildly, incompatible with Puritan conceptions of piety. Immigration and religious liberty gave way to complexity, heterogeneity, and worst of all, tax exemptions for Baptists, Quakers, and Anglicans. The Congregationalist church and its sanctimonious prescriptions for what constituted a noble life resonated less and less with younger generations, for whom ambition was no longer a dirty word. And the lizard-brained panic that led what many colonists now understood to be the unjust execution of twenty innocent souls all but discredited the Puritan project.

By the early 1700s, Mather "no longer preached as if New England were a New Israel." Indeed, he barely recognized those whom he previously regarded as God's chosen people. "New England society as he came to know it during his last years had repudiated the great utopian vision of his Puritan ancestors," one reviewer noted, "and resembled more and more the ungodly world from which they had fled to America."[25]

The Congregationalist church to which Mather had committed himself was all but shorn of the absolute autonomy that was so central to its identity, and it lost the power to oversee in political affairs. Over the years, the church would come to resemble less a supreme theological institution and more a plain old church.

"Some Congregationalist churches in the early 1800s became Unitarian," author and newspaper columnist Joel Achenbach observed. "The Unitarian-Universalist Church and the United Church of Christ are among the most liberal, socially progressive religious denominations in America. We don't want to make too big a deal about this, or exaggerate, but you can't help but conclude that the Puritans basically became hippies."[26]

Puritanism fell victim to a generational backlash—a fate to which we all must one day succumb. Its inflexible codes of social conduct could not evolve with a changing world, and the inheritors of its strict commandments lacked their parent's fear of the temptations abundant in secular and commercial life beyond the village's bounds. Ultimately, Puritanism's blind zeal paved the way for its own demise.

And yet, while adherents of this unyielding doctrine were active for only a short time in the nation's history, they left behind a remarkably durable legacy. As we've seen throughout this book, Americans have unknowingly incorporated many of Puritanism's habits and conventions, though the Puritans themselves receive no credit for their contributions. They are more likely to be reviled and mocked than revered.

This is a cautionary tale—one which today's New Puritans would do well to take to heart.

The new puritanism, too, has enjoyed many successes in its moral crusade. Be it through persuasion or coercion, they have all but rid commercialism of its vulgar appeals to male sexual fantasies. They have compelled powerful institutions like the National Football League to bend to their demands, making the game more ethical without sacrificing its charm. And they have imposed on the corporate world a set of mores that compels captains of industry to treat everyone with decency and respect, and to stop looking the other way when their powerful compatriots do not. The question before us, however, is whether the New Puritans will be thanked for their efforts.

For all their successes, they have also suffered many setbacks and there is dissension within their ranks. This is a movement that has festooned itself with all the trappings of a religious cult. Whether it is deserved or not—and this book's thesis maintains that it is wholly deserved—their movement is tarred by the perception that their recipe for an equitable social contract comes at a cost. That cost will not be quietly absorbed forever. The price they demand of those who would contribute to their cause is the sacrifice of spontaneity, risk, frivolity, and carefree joy.

There's a reason why we don't remember the old Puritans fondly. Despite their noble works and lasting achievements, popular culture regards them as miserable parodies of themselves. When Puritanism lost its power, it also lost its moral authority and its capacity to stifle dissent. Once Puritanism and the Victorian tastes into which it evolved were defanged, the Puritans became objects of scorn. Those few who still exhibit the vestigial traits of a puritanical moralist are regarded with a mix of curiosity, pity, and contempt—even (perhaps especially) by those who unwittingly mimic their methods in the pursuit of their own brand of moralism.

For those of you who hope to impose some constraints on this new ethos and the power it has to rob life of enjoyment, this is both an observation and a means to an end.

Those activists who are most plainly exhibiting puritanical tendencies today are likely to be the most sensitive to the original connotation of the word *Puritan*, which was intended as an insult. The modern progressive is eager to rid themselves of puritanism's baggage.

In 2017, Harvard University—a school in which Increase Mather served as president until he was forced out of that role amid the changing of New England's cultural tides at the turn of the eighteenth century—attempted to rid itself of puritanism's legacy by excising the line "Till the stock of the Puritans die" from the school's 181-year-old alma mater.

The verdict was reached by the Presidential Task Force for Inclusion and Belonging and presented to students at an "Afternoon of Engagement on Inclusion and Belonging." You see, "diversity, inclusion, and belonging are fundamental to our missions and to our identity," and the old Puritan "stock" were not very inclusive. This announcement was followed by a parade of students offering sermons about their "personal experiences with 'belonging.'"[27] You may have detected a theme in the day's proceedings.

Even in the effort to shake off Puritanism's yoke, the sons and daughters of this tradition could not resist the comforting conformity it offers. Nevertheless, the lesson we should take from this episode is that proponents of the new puritanism are loath to be identified as such. And why wouldn't they be? We're talking about purists, after all. And the indefatigable purist is, to be frank, a spectacular pain in the neck.

The stereotypes that come to mind when we think about those who obsess over purity are not flattering. The purist is theatrically confounded by social and cultural evolution. He is ostentatious about the esteem with which he holds the obscure. She prefers the world not as it is today but as an ideal that exists only in her own head. They are judgmental and sanctimonious. They are snobby and classist. They believe themselves superior in their tastes and pretensions. And they will not let you forget it.

We are today at the precipice—the dawning of a new ethos that threatens to supplant the old. But we're not there yet. The old liberal vanguard of the sexual revolution hasn't disappeared. And while today's youngish militants do not mind offending their elders, they would strenuously object to the idea that theirs is a less open-minded generation than those that preceded them. Young progressive activists are likely to be deeply offended by the accusation that they seek the restoration of the priggish moral order their parents and grandparents worked so diligently to overthrow. But that is the fact, and they should be forced to reckon with it.

The bleeding edge of New Puritan thought believes itself to be boldly transgressive. Indeed, its members revel in their capacity to inspire fear in their targets. But this movement's members are only fearsome insofar as their prey provide them the power they wield. That goes some way to explain why progressive moral reformers spend so much time and attention imposing rigid codes of conduct on their fellow progressives.

Their movement enjoys the appearance of effectiveness because its members force those who already agree with them to bend the knee. After all, no one is going to take you all that seriously if you are easily ignored. Thus, the New Puritan creed lashes out at its allies as much as its adversaries—maybe even more.

This is as much a power play and an effort to prosecute professional jealousies as it is a moral crusade. At least, it is for now. The time will come when their work is complete, and the progressive movement is wholly overtaken by the New Puritan psychology. At that point, the movement will train its fire on harder targets outside the coalition.

That's an intimidating thought, but the executors of this vision today are not so intimidating. The New Puritans have made themselves into comic figures. They are the very portrait of fastidious busybodies. The consequences of their actions may be deadly serious, but these are not serious people.

They are worthy of mockery. Mock them.

That is all much more easily said (or written, as it were) than done. Given the threat posed by this revolutionary new social doctrine, simply pointing and laughing probably strikes you as both insufficient and an activity that involves more risk than reward.

And yet, we are talking about a paradigmatic shift, and there's no way to combat such a thing without a competing paradigm. The advantage of the one I offer is that it is less of a chore to maintain. It demands nothing more of you than the very toleration progressives pretend to preach.

The climate fostered by the New Puritan is both humorless and totalitarian, according to the word's dictionary definition. Like their puritanical forebearers, they seek to universalize their values. That mission is partly the result of a widespread misconception about what politics really is.

As the mind-set cultivated on campuses by critical theory and identity studies departments migrated out of academia and into the workplace, a certain type of activist has come to see the world through a political prism. So much of society has an unexplored political dimension to it, they believe. At least, it can be "deconstructed" and "interrogated" to the point that it gives up its hidden political dimensions. That has led those who are steeped in grievance studies to reach a miserable conclusion: everything is politics. This is a fallacy with real psychological downsides.

So much of what we talk about today as though it were politics is not politics at all. It's merely *political*. When "politics" is discussed on cable news or in pop-cultural forums, the conversation only occasionally revolves around the outcomes of elections or the conduct of legislative affairs in Washington, D.C., state capitals, or municipal governments. Instead, we're often imposing political themes on aspects of life that exist outside the legislative realm.

"Politics" looms over the brands you patronize, the food you eat, the art you enjoy, the commercials you watch, and the escapist television programs they interrupt. It determines your interpersonal associations, where you decide to put down roots and raise a family, and how you conduct yourself in public and private. Many of the issues we call politics are cultural ephemera to be forgotten no sooner than the moment you manage to wrap your mind around them. Politics and politicians have little influence over this sort of thing.

What I'm identifying is best described as a state of mass confusion, but there are many who are invested in our collective befuddlement. There is power in telling people that the cultural conditions they resent, which know no legislative remedy, *could* be resolved by politicians if only they had the guts to do what needs to be done. That is a morally bankrupt confidence game, but it has attracted many players.

This is an affliction to which both parties have recently succumbed, but the disorder is more advanced on the left. For years, Democrats were primed by their most influential leaders to view the conduct of politics as an emancipatory thing—the sort of "instrumental activism" to which Puritans were inclined. Not only were left-wing voters told that the conduct of politics was a source of identity and mission, they were also led to believe that political outcomes could bring about momentous transformations in the culture. That was a lie.

When Barack Obama assumed the presidency, one of the first acts he signed into law, the 2009 Lilly Ledbetter Fair Pay Act, was billed as an evolutionary leap forward. The Democratic president's allies insisted that it would contribute to a "cultural shift" in the American workplace.[28] Even today, President Joe Biden's White House maintains that this legislation was designed to "change the culture."[29] Those are grand claims to make of a law that did nothing more than relax the statute of limitations on civil litigation involving allegations of workplace discrimination.

Likewise, when Obama signed an extension of the Violence Against Women Act in 2013, he insisted that it, too, was transformative. "It changed our culture," he said of the VAW. "It empowered people to start speaking out." But as the #MeToo movement revealed four years later, women were still subjected to abuses, and the culture of silence in firms where abusers were ensconced long outlived this 1994 law. The stroke of a presidential pen did nothing to change that fact.

The Affordable Care Act (aka Obamacare) would similarly usher in a new era in which a "culture of coverage" had become the American "norm," wrote California Health Benefit Exchange board member Kim Belshe. The ACA did compel more people to buy insurance to avoid being penalized at tax time—at least, until that penalty was repealed by a subsequent Congress. But the rate of uninsured declined by only about 7 percent between 2010 when the law was passed and 2019.[30] Hardly a seismic shift.

Either the culture is far more inflexible than those who think it can be reformed by Congress believe, or the people making these sweeping claims are misleading their constituents.

The Biden White House has continued to play this flimflam game. The forty-sixth president and his allies in Congress have sought to place artificial barriers in the path of those who would participate in the so-called "sharing economy" to boost unionization rates. "Today's corporate culture treats workers as a means to an end and institutes policies to suppress wages," Biden's 2020 campaign website read.[31] This can only be remedied, labor activists claim, by encouraging a "culture of unionization" across the professional spectrum—even if it is fostered by the government's monopoly on coercive force.[32]

Similarly, the party-wide effort in 2021 to redefine "infrastructure" to mean anything and everything (well beyond simple roads and bridges) seemed intended to change the way left-leaning Americans thought about both infrastructure and government. As Senator Kirsten Gillibrand wrote, "Paid leave is infrastructure. Childcare is infrastructure. Caregiving is infrastructure."[33] Throwing trillions of dollars at these priorities, Democrats were told, has the potential to redefine American culture as we know it.

Why were there no federal mandates on businesses to provide paid time off? "America's individualist culture," the Prindle Institute's Emily Troyer insisted.[34] And Biden would change all that. Publisher Arianna Huffington and Harvard University dean Michelle Williams wrote that the president's preferred policies would encourage employers to build "well-being policies" into their "company culture."[35] "Government can help change the workplace culture," insisted the Rockefeller Institute of Government's Althea Brennan. Paid leave mandates will reshape "our culture and the way we view, treat, and employ women."[36]

No, they won't. Culture is not fabricated in Washington and imposed in a top-down fashion on the rest of the country. When Democratic politicians promised their voters that they could rewrite the American social compact at will, they were lying to their constituents and, quite probably, themselves.

Perhaps these politicians believed that reckless stakes-raising was a relatively harmless way to mobilize their base voters. But overpromising and underdelivering has consequences.

Those poor souls who foolishly bought into the gambit their incautious political representatives were peddling probably did believe the government could speed up the process of cultural evolution through legislation. Layer atop this misapprehension an all-consuming self-righteousness, and you have a recipe for psychological disaster. After all, we're not talking about something as tawdry as mere politics. The New Puritan's priorities are absolute moral imperatives. If the culture refused to bend, that only means you have to apply more pressure.

The American right is just as guilty of confusing the conduct of politics with culture warring, but at least they have pegged the sequence of events closer to the mark. In Andrew Breitbart's famous formulation, "politics is downstream from culture," which is to say that where the culture goes, so goes Washington. Eventually, at least.

This formulation leads the right into its own cognitive cul-de-sacs; notably, the flawed presumption that political reforms will not be successful if cultural forces are arrayed against them. That is manifestly untrue. Internalizing this untruth can lead to some unduly fatalistic conclusions about how American society operates. But at least this equation doesn't give right-wing activists the false impression that they can amend or annul cultural covenants via the legislative process.

Political activism can be quite fulfilling. By surrounding yourself with like minds in pursuit of a shared goal, political organizing provides its participants with a sense of community. The belief that you are engaged in a noble mission creates a shared sense of meaning, purpose, and identity. Those are invaluable properties. But political activism, fully apprehended, is not a transcendental experience. The work of politics in the United States is never going to be emancipatory.

Organizing coalitions is the result of compromise, and crafting legislation is a slog. Managing the valid but competing interests involved in that process is not a good time. Determining who wins and who loses in the game of life can be downright soul crushing. And that's just the work of crafting the language of legislation via regular order. Whatever that arduous process of compromise produces, the final product is destined to be watered down even further amid the negotiations with your political adversaries necessary to get the thing passed.

In the end, you must satisfy yourself with tinkering around the margins of a particular problem. In the United States, the government is designed to frustrate maximalists, narrow grandiose reforms, and thwart transformative initiatives in the absence of an overwhelming, bipartisan consensus. Overbroad goals are almost always out of reach. So, if you believe you're engaged in an almost spiritual mission to change the culture—to extirpate "systemic" problems from our midst—you're going to become frustrated fast. And for today's progressive activists, everything is "systemic."

"America has a long history of systemic racism," Vice President Kamala Harris asserted in 2021. President Joe Biden agreed. "The systemic racism is a stain on our nation's soul."[37] Oddly, this verdict followed another—a jury's verdict convicting former Minneapolis police officer Derek Chauvin of the statutory violations he committed on tape. If systemic abuses cannot be not remedied by the system itself even when the system is operating as designed and delivering desirable outcomes, it can never be reformed to the satisfaction of its critics.

If racism is systemic, so, too, is addiction to illicit substances. "It became clear to us that there is something systemic going on," Virginia Commonwealth University's Center on Society and Health director Steven Woolf said of drug abuse.[38] Know what else is systemic? "Poverty is systemic," the Southern Poverty Law Center's guideline for elementary-school teachers read. Impoverishment is "caused by systemic factors, not individual shortcomings."[39]

Corruption is systemic; a perverse form of "democratic responsiveness," according to Fordham University Law School professor Zephyr Teachout.[40] The Brady Campaign insists that gun violence won't be addressed without "upstream, systemic change."[41] Even obesity cannot be curtailed without reforms to "systemic problems" like the world's "increasingly commercialized food supply," per TakePart's Sophia Lepore.[42]

The picture is coming clearly into view now. The progressive activist class has steeped itself in messianic ideas about the nature of political activism. And yet, government never seems to respond to the urgency of our circumstances—not with the passion demanded of it by the activist class. And on the rare occasions that government behaves as progressives want it to, the culture stubbornly refuses to be transformed.

American politics, they reluctantly conclude, is woefully ill-equipped to deal with the myriad "systemic" problems confronting the nation. Its systems are indelibly corrupt, capable of delivering only incremental reforms wholly inadequate to the scale of the challenges before us.

It's enough to make anyone depressed. And that's precisely what's happening.

"Our belief in 'progress' has increased our expectations," the psychologist Bruce Levine observed in 2013. "The result is mass disappointment."[43] With that, Levine put his finger right on the progressive pulse. "I cannot continue to emotionally exhaust myself," wrote the British journalist and feminist speaker Reni Eddo-Lodge the following year.[44] In a 2016 *Washington Post* op-ed, Zack Linly concurred. "I've grown too disillusioned to be relieved and too numb to be frustrated," he wrote. "I'm just tired."[45]

Of course, these performatively exhausted activists are playing their own game. They are not so fatigued that they cannot bring themselves to editorialize on their favorite subject in the pages of big-city newspapers. But they are speaking for many who *have* been driven from the political arena in the interest of their own mental health.

You're unlikely to hear much from those for whom the promise of politics has given way to a sense of betrayal. The truly fatalistic are not interested in placing op-eds ruminating on their misery. But that's only half the picture. Those who have not dropped out of the political process to preserve their own sanity are likely to be the most zealous, the most radical, and the most committed to transforming the world around them.

They are imbued with an unquestioned belief in their own righteousness. They are confused about where culture ends and politics begins. They are convinced that America's problems are so deeply rooted that only deracinating the whole rotten structure will resolve them. This is a recipe for a totalistic political program, and it is busily making totalitarians of those who subscribe to it.

Sure, you say, but all this is academic. None of this helps anyone put the brakes on the transformations the New Puritans are trying to engineer, right?

Not necessarily. The first step toward solving this problem is diagnosing its proximate causes. Restoring a healthier understanding of what politics is and what politics can achieve is critical. Dissent is all well and good, but it won't deter those who are attracted to puritanical activism unless you can articulate where they've erred while advocating a healthier alternative.

The reconceptualization of politics as something narrower than what the progressive spiritualists believe it to be is an important first step, because the second step necessarily follows. That is, the understanding that governmental acts are not in and of themselves noble, particularly when they do more to empower the public sector than the actual public.

If there is an overarching theme to this book, it is one of tension. Tension between generations, as the young scratch out an identity and purpose all their own while their elders struggle to hold on to the cherished and familiar. Tension between geographies, with regions wrangling to preserve their beloved peculiarities in defiance of the pressure to acquiesce to sameness. Tension between entertainers and their audiences, when one seeks to take the other on a journey and their subjects resist that manipulation with all their subconscious might. Tension between religions and ideologies, as competing moral codes enter into and emerge from periods of conflict. And tension between the public and the authorities they trust to do what's right, even when what is right is difficult to discern and bitterly resented.

Tension is healthy. It tests and bends and shapes, and it ensures that this life will be an interesting one. It is a foundational precept upon which the Anglo-American political tradition is premised. Most marvelously, tension is difficult to maintain. It is uncomfortable and awkward. For most well-adjusted people, their instinct when they encounter tension is to defuse it as painlessly as possible. It's a miracle we've managed to preserve this condition for as long as we have.

It is a miracle, in part, because Puritans old and new desire nothing so much as they desire congruity. The diversity they like is almost entirely cosmetic, and their true desires are exposed whenever they encounter diversity of thought or disposition. Citing a "contemporary witticism," Michael Winship concluded: "A Puritan is such a one as loves God with all his soul but hates his neighbor with all his heart."[46] In much the same way, the puritanical progressive loves the public but just can't stand people.

"The modern world is not evil," the prolific and keen observer of human nature G. K. Chesterton observed. "In some ways the modern world is far too good. It is full of wild and wasted virtues."

In Chesterton's telling, mankind's "very power of enjoyment destroyed half his joys," because the "chief pleasure is surprise." The predictably ordered world is the enemy of that happiness, as is the arrogance associated with the presumption that we are capable of ordering anything indefinitely. Because, the author concluded, "the mightiest of the pleasures of man, is at bottom entirely humble. It is impossible without humility to enjoy anything—even pride."[47]

If history is any guide, this burst of moral enthusiasm will pass.

It will leave its marks on Western history; some virtuous, but most risible and excessive. And when future historians look back on our time, they will do so with condescension and pity. They will be navigating their own moral panics, of course. But they will also be confident in their own accumulated wisdom—enough, at least, to look upon us with embarrassment and to thank the stars for their own enlightened age. And the cycle explored in this book will begin again.

We can only hope that there will be someone around then to write about how truly awful we all were. That would be confirmation that the perennial tensions we find both so frustrating and exhilarating still exist. They are still shaping the generations, testing our moral commitments, and reconfirming foundational truths about how a democratic society should function. It is only the last and final release of that tension we should fear.

AFTERWORD

This book was conceived out of necessity. It was not, however, the urgency of the subject matter or the menace the New Puritan represents that moved me. The necessity was my own.

By December 2020, the unending monotony of the pandemic was broken up only by periodic reminders of its horrific death toll, the crushing economic and societal consequences associated with its mitigation, and occasional bouts of mass violence. It was not a fun time to be steeped in the news cycle, and I needed a way out.

What else could I possibly do? If I had my way, I'd spend my days talking to people in industries that I enjoy—many of which are far removed from the conduct of conventional politics: working comedians, chefs and gastronomes, authors and artists, sports broadcasters, and the like. But even if I could be so fortunate and make money doing it, I would still be unsatisfied. Politics had become so all-consuming that no industry existed outside of it anymore.

That's when my wife, Jaryn, had the idea for what became this book. Why not chronicle the ways in which these and many other previously apolitical aspects of life are being dragged into pop political debates, stripping them of their more carefree aspects in the process?

When the universe gives you a good idea, it's a safe bet that you're not the only person to be so lucky. In the months that followed the writing of this manuscript, a number of admirable thinkers and writers have attempted to chronicle the return of a vestigial puritanism to the fore of progressive political activism. It is my hope that this book is among the most comprehensive and irreverent treatments of the subject. After all, there is no cure for the ills of self-seriousness that involves even more sanctimony.

That is not to say that the subject matter addressed in this book doesn't have a serious dimension. While conducting interviews with the professionals directly affected by the rise of new puritanism, I found many who agreed with my premise but who did not share my conservative politics. What I also found, however, was that few were willing to risk professional consequences by talking to me on the record about their fears. Though they were candid about their concern that a small, censorious band of moral purists had taken over their industries, they were unwilling to risk their livelihoods by speaking out against them.

That is entirely understandable because it's entirely valid. Those who are seeking to impose a consistent moral framework on creatives in industries dedicated to the promotion of enjoyable cultural products wield sticks as well as carrots. You won't be surprised to learn, however, that living under constant threat is generating a lot of quiet resentment—resentment that will one day fuel a backlash.

The circumstances that will produce a rejection of new puritanism's joyless preening should be recognizable to anyone familiar with the neoconservative political movement. Neoconservatism was a creation of liberals who no longer recognized their fellow Democrats. Its members were almost all of the left. They supported the civil rights movement, Keynesian economic policies, and aggressive efforts to contain the spread of Communism abroad.

But as the Democratic Party began to integrate into its coalition elements of the countercultural left—outright supporters of the Vietcong, militant racial separatist groups like the Black Panthers, and quasi-socialists for whom a social safety net was no alternative to a cradle-to-grave welfare state—they fell out of love with their political tribe. Some gravitated away from the Democratic Party altogether. Others remained within it and sought to counter the influence of the New Left. But all formed the nucleus of a political juggernaut that became first an intellectual movement and, eventually, the dominant wing of America's governing party.

The outlines of another political realignment are visible in the resentment brewing among those who labor under the yoke of new puritanism. It has all the potential to incept something that the right has long sought but never brought about: a popular conservative counterculture.

Whether that hardens into a coherent sociopolitical force is anyone's guess. But all the ingredients are present for something spectacular. It is my fondest hope that just such a movement comes into being: a joyful crusade possessed of a genuine and unconditional love of humanity in all its variated forms and dispossessed of the pathologies that have overtaken the progressive activist class. If this book helps to catalyze that, it would be an honor to have modestly contributed to that happy outcome.

While that would be nice, it's hardly essential to my purposes. After all, what I set out to do when I began to write this book was have some fun. I got what I wanted. Hopefully, you did, too.

ACKNOWLEDGMENTS

This book would not have been possible without the contributions of a great many wonderful and important people in my life.

Foremost among them is my wife, Jaryn, who contributed mightily to the conceptualization of this book's thesis. As her reward for her innovation, she was saddled with my prolonged absence from the duties associated with parenting our two amazing boys, Jace Arnold and Elias Murphy. She deserves a vacation.

I would like to thank my editors, Eric Nelson and Hannah Long, and my agent, Andrew Stuart, for their dedication to molding this project from a rough idea into a salable product, as well as everyone at HarperCollins Publishers who believed in this book.

My parents, John and Patricia Rothman, are owed my undying gratitude for their guidance and editorial input—to say nothing of keeping me alive to the point of maturity.

The team at *Commentary* could not have been more accommodating and helpful throughout the writing process. A special thank-you is owed to John Podhoretz, Abe Greenwald, Christine Rosen, Stephanie Roberts, Carol Moskot, Kejda Gjermani, and Malkie

Beck. I would also like to thank my colleagues at MSNBC for their support and guidance.

I would have been lost without the assistance of Noam Dworman, who believed in this project from day one and who devoted considerable attention to my requests for his assistance only out of the goodness of his heart.

I am indebted to the many talented professionals who took the time to speak with me for this book. Among them, Ali Tate Cutter, Andrew Zimmern, Joe Concha, Judy Gold, P. J. O'Rourke, and Shane Gillis, as well as those who provided me with their insights on background.

Finally, I owe an incredible debt to the country that made it possible for me to think and write about politics and culture for a living. This book is, in part, a love letter to a nation with an exceptional history. Its capacity for vitality, resilience, and reinvention will long continue to astonish its doubters.

The United States remains the indispensable nation, and I am greatly indebted to the men and women who serve in and out of uniform.

NOTES

1: REVELATION: THE NEW RISE OF AN OLD MORALITY

1. Yascha Mounk, "Stop Firing the Innocent," *Atlantic*, June 27, 2020, https://www.theatlantic.com/ideas/archive/2020/06/stop-firing-innocent/613615/.

2. "Episode Notes: Global Greats," Holy Land Restaurant on Diners, Drive-Ins & Dives, season 25, episode 5, https://www.dinersdriveinsdiveslocations.com/holy-land-minnesota.html.

3. @MunaAzam, June 4, 2020, https://twitter.com/MunaAzam/status/1268434452193181696.

4. Yelp Review: Holy Land Midtown, Minneapolis, MN, https://www.yelp.com/biz/holy-land-midtown-minneapolis.

5. KSTP.com, "Midtown Global Market Terminates Holy Land's Lease After Racist Social Media Posts Resurface," June 4, 2020, https://kstp.com/minnesota-news/midtown-global-market-terminates-holy-lands-lease-after-racist-social-media-posts-resurface-june-4-2020/5751214/.

6. Hibah Ansari, "Holy Land Grocery CEO Faces Boycotts After Daughter's Past Racist Posts Resurface," MPR News, June 5, 2020, https://www.mprnews.org/story/2020/06/05/holy-land-grocery-ceo-fires-daughter-over-racist-social-media-posts.

7. Guardian Sport and Agencies, "Aleksandar Katai Cut by LA Galaxy over Wife's 'Racist and Violent' Instagram Posts," *Guardian*, June 5, 2020, https://www.theguardian.com/football/2020/jun/05/aleksandar-katai-wife-racist-social-media.

8. Jennifer Schuessler, "Poetry Foundation Leadership Resigns After Black Lives Matter Statement," *New York Times*, June 9, 2020, https://www.nytimes.com/2020/06/09/books/poetry-foundation-black-lives-matter.html.

9. Steve Rabey, "Religion Journal; A Chastened Singer Returns to Christian Basics," *New York Times*, May 11, 2002, https://www.nytimes.com/2002/05/11/us/religion-journal-a-chastened-singer-returns-to-christian-basics.html.

10. David D. Kirkpatrick, "Conservatives Urge Boycott of Procter & Gamble," *New York Times*, September 17, 2004, https://www.nytimes.com/2004/09/17/us/conservatives-urge-boycott-of-procter-gamble.html.

11. Brooks Barnes, "TV Watchdog Group Is on the Defensive," *New York Times*, October 24, 2010, https://www.nytimes.com/2010/10/25/business/media/25watchdog.html.

12. Meg James, "'Family Guy's' Seth MacFarlane Was Attacked by This Conservative TV Watchdog. Now They're Friends," *Los Angeles Times*, May 30, 2019, https://www.latimes.com/business/hollywood/la-fi-ct-col1-seth-macfarlane-parents-television-council-tim-winter-20190530-story.html.

13. Elizabeth Nash and Joerg Dreweke, "The U.S. Abortion Rate Continues to Drop: Once Again, State Abortion Restrictions Are Not the Main Driver," *Guttmacher Policy Review 22*, September 18, 2019, https://www.guttmacher.org/gpr/2019/09/us-abortion-rate-continues-drop-once-again-state-abortion-restrictions-are-not-main.

14. Jaclyn Diaz, "A Record Number of Americans, Including Republicans, Now Support Same-Sex Marriage," NPR, June 9, 2021, https://www.npr.org/2021/06/09/1004629612/a-record-number-of-americans-including-republicans-support-same-sex-marriage.

15. Noah Rothman, "Trump's Awful Conservative Ruse," *Commentary*, April 22, 2016, https://www.commentarymagazine.com/noah-rothman/trumps-awful-conservative-ruse/.

16. Pavel Somov, "4 Types of Perfectionism," *Huffington Post*, July 18, 2010, https://www.huffpost.com/entry/4-types-of-perfectionism_b_650438.

17. John McWhorter, "The Neoracists," Persuasion, February 8, 2021, https://www.persuasion.community/p/john-mcwhorter-the-neoracists.

18. Andrew Sullivan, "America's New Religions," *New York* magazine, December 7, 2018, https://nymag.com/intelligencer/2018/12/andrew-sullivan-americas-new-religions.html.

19. Michael Crichton, "Remarks to the Commonwealth Club," September 15, 2003, http://www.hawaiifreepress.com/Articles-Main/ID/2818/Crichton-Environmentalism-is-a-religion.

20. George McKenna, *The Puritan Origins of American Patriotism* (New Haven, CT: Yale University Press, 2007), 48.

21. B. C. Daniels, "Sober Mirth and Pleasant Poisons: Puritan Ambivalence Toward Leisure and Recreation in Colonial New England," *American Studies* 34, no. 1 (1993): 123–26.

22. McKenna, *The Puritan Origins of American Patriotism*, 123.

23. McKenna, *The Puritan Origins of American Patriotism*, 177.

24. McKenna, *The Puritan Origins of American Patriotism*, 203.

25. George Hukari, "The Eyes of the World Will Be upon You . . . ," Princeton University Posters Collection, Archives Center, National Museum of American History, https://sova.si.edu/details/NMAH.AC.0433#ref9848.

26. Woodrow Wilson, "Fifth Annual Message," University of Virginia, December 4, 1917, https://millercenter.org/the-presidency/presidential -speeches/december-4-1917-fifth-annual-message.

27. McKenna, *The Puritan Origins of American Patriotism*, 179–80.

28. McKenna, *The Puritan Origins of American Patriotism*, 305.

29. Bill Schneider, "Analysis and Insight into the Presidential Election," Landon Lecture Series on Public Issues, November 16, 2004, https://www.k-state .edu/landon/speakers/bill-schneider/transcript.html.

30. Bruce Bower, *The Victims' Revolution: The Rise of Identity Studies and the Closing of the Liberal Mind* (New York: Broadside Books, 2012), 65.

31. "A Ruling Inspired by U.S. Anti-Pornography Activists Is Used to Restrict Lesbian and Gay Publications in Canada," Human Rights Watch Free Expression Project, vol. 6, issue 1, February 1994, https://www .hrw.org/sites/default/files/reports/CANADA942.PDF.

32. Herbert Marcuse, "Repressive Tolerance," 1965, https://www.marcuse.org /herbert/publications/1960s/1965-repressive-tolerance-fulltext.html.

2: PIETY: THE WORK IS ITS OWN REWARD

1. Noah Rothman, "The Backlash Against Cop Shows Is a Moral Panic," *Commentary*, June 11, 2020, https://www.commentarymagazine.com /noah-rothman/the-backlash-against-cop-shows-is-a-moral-panic/.

2. Amanda Hess, "The Protests Come for 'Paw Patrol,'" *New York Times*, June 10, 2020, https://www.nytimes.com/2020/06/10/arts/television/protests -fictional-cops.html.

3. Hess, "The Protests Come for 'Paw Patrol.'"

4. Michael Winship, *Hot Protestants: A History of Puritanism in England and America* (New Haven, CT: Yale University Press, 2019), 50–55.

5. André Van Hoorn and Robbert Maseland, "Does a Protestant Work Ethic Exist? Evidence from the Well-Being Effect of Unemployment," *Journal of Economic Behavior & Organization* 91, (July 2013), https://www.sciencedirect .com/science/article/abs/pii/S0167268113000838.

6. Daniel Luzer, "The Protestant Work Ethic Is Real," *Pacific Standard*, June 14, 2017, https://psmag.com/economics/protestant-worth-ethic-real-65544.

7. Winship, *Hot Protestants*, 88.

8. E. C. Salibian, "Dear White People: What Is 'the Work' and How Do We Do It?," *Rochester Beacon*, July 9, 2020, https://rochesterbeacon.com/2020/07/09/dear-white-people-what-is-the-work-and-how-do-we-do-it/.

9. @ClintSmithIII, June 4, 2020, https://twitter.com/ClintSmithIII/status/1268640490070646785.

10. Nina Berman, "What Does It Mean When We Say Doing 'The Work'?," Fractured Atlas, October 30, 2020, https://blog.fracturedatlas.org/what-does-it-mean-when-we-say-doing-the-work.

11. B. C. Daniels, "Sober Mirth and Pleasant Poisons: Puritan Ambivalence Toward Leisure and Recreation in Colonial New England," *American Studies* 34, no. 1 (1993): 127–28.

12. Hakim Bishara, "SFMOMA Accused of Censoring Black Voices After Removing Comment by Former Employee," Hyperallergic, June 2, 2020, https://hyperallergic.com/568331/sfmoma-george-floyd-instagram-comments-disabled/.

13. Tony Bravo, "SFMOMA Director Apologizes for Deleting Critical Comment by Black Ex-Employee," *San Francisco Chronicle*, June 5, 2020, https://datebook.sfchronicle.com/art-exhibits/sfmoma-director-apologizes-for-deleting-critical-comment-by-black-ex-employee.

14. Carol Pogash, "Its Top Curator Gone, SFMOMA Reviews Its Record on Race," *New York Times*, July 22, 2020, https://www.nytimes.com/2020/07/22/arts/design/sfmoma-gary-garrels-resignation.html.

15. Sam Lefebvre, "Senior SFMOMA Curator Resigns Amid Reckoning with Institutional Racism," Hyperallergic, July 13, 2020, https://hyperallergic.com/576369/gary-garrels-resigns-sfmoma/.

16. Carolina A. Miranda, "Column: Are Art Museums Still Racist? The COVID Reset," *Los Angeles Times*, October 22, 2020, https://www.latimes.com/entertainment-arts/story/2020-10-22/art-museums-racism-covid-reset.

17. "A Snapshot of US Museums' Response to the COVID-19 Pandemic," American Alliance of Museums, July 22, 2020, https://www.aam-us.org/2020/07/22/a-snapshot-of-us-museums-response-to-the-covid-19-pandemic/.

18. Sarah Cascone, "Thousands of US Museums Could Close Forever as the Financial Effects of Lockdown Turn Existential, a New Report Finds," Artnet News, November 17, 2020, https://news.artnet.com/art-world/museums-shuttering-aam-report-1924371.

19. Peggy McGlone and Sebastian Smee, "Coronavirus Shutdowns and Charges of White Supremacy: American Art Museums Are in Crisis," *Washington Post*, October 12, 2020, https://www.washingtonpost.com/entertainment

/museums/american-art-museums-covid-white-supremacy/2020/10/11
/61094f1c-fe94-11ea-8d05-9beaaa91c71f_story.html.

20. Anonymous, "Anti-Racist Imperatives for the National Gallery of Art,"
    Last Plantation on the National Mall, 2020, https://lastplantationonthe
    nationalmall.wordpress.com/.

21. Daniels, "Sober Mirth and Pleasant Poisons," 130.

22. Gertrude Himmelfarb, *The De-moralization of Society: From Victorian Virtues
    to Modern Values* (New York: Vintage Books, 1996), 6.

23. Marva Hinton, "Little House, Big Problem: What to Do with 'Classic' Books
    That Are Also Racist," *School Library Journal*, May 28, 2020, https://www
    .slj.com/?detailStory=Little-House-Big-Problem-Little-House-Big-Problem
    -What-To-Do-with-Classic-Books-That-Are-Also-Racist.

24. Kat Chow, "Little House on the Controversy: Laura Ingalls Wilder's Name
    Removed from Book Award," NPR, June 25, 2018, https://www.npr.org
    /2018/06/25/623184440/little-house-on-the-controversy-laura-ingalls
    -wilders-name-removed-from-book-awa.

25. Hinton, "Little House, Big Problem."

26. Grace Hwang Lynch, "Is the Cat in the Hat Racist? Read Across America
    Shifts Away from Dr. Seuss and Toward Diverse Books," *School Library
    Journal*, September 11, 2017, https://www.latimes.com/entertainment-arts
    /books/story/2020-11-12/burbank-unified-challenges-books-including-to
    -kill-a-mockingbird.

27. Athens Bureau, "Massachusetts Teacher Says She Is 'Very Proud' to Have
    Removed Homer's Classic from School Curriculum," GreekCityTimes.com,
    December 31, 2020, https://greekcitytimes.com/2020/12/31/teacher-proud
    -removing-homer/.

28. John Podhoretz and Abe Greenwald, "Liberal Gaslighting," *The Commentary
    Podcast*, March 9, 2021, podcast audio 36:05–43:26, https://www
    .commentarymagazine.com/john-podhoretz/liberal-gaslighting/.

29. Rachel Poser, "He Wants to Save Classics from Whiteness. Can the Field
    Survive?," *New York Times*, February 2, 2021, https://www.nytimes
    .com/2021/02/02/magazine/classics-greece-rome-whiteness.html.

30. Amanda MacGregor, "To Teach or Not to Teach: Is Shakespeare Still
    Relevant to Today's Students?," *School Library Journal*, January 4, 2021,
    https://www.slj.com/?detailStory=to-teach-or-not-to-teach-is-shakespeare
    -still-relevant-to-todays-students-libraries-classic-literature-canon.

31. Stacy Schiff, "What a Witch Hunt Really Looks Like," *New York Times*,
    November 26, 2019, https://www.nytimes.com/2019/11/26/opinion
    /trump-witch-hunt.html.

32. Daniels, "Sober Mirth and Pleasant Poisons," 124–25.

33. Edmund S. Morgan, "Puritan Hostility to the Theatre," *Proceedings of the
    American Philosophical Society* 110, no. 5 (1966): 340, www.jstor.org
    /stable/986023, accessed June 18, 2021.

34. Winship, *Hot Protestants*, 92.

35. Sarah MacLeod, "The Dangers of Men in Women's Roles on the Renaissance Stage: An Analysis of William Prynne's Histrio-Mastix," University of British Columbia–Okanagan, 2007, 13, https://people .ok.ubc.ca/parthur/loughlin/MacLeod.doc.

36. Amber Roberts, "Dispelling the Myths About Trans People 'Detransitioning,'" *Vice*, November 17, 2015, https://www.vice.com/en/article/kwxkwz /dispelling-the-myths-around-detransitioning.

37. Liam Knox, "Media's 'Detransition' Narrative Is Fueling Misconceptions, Trans Advocates Say," NBC News, December 19, 2019, https://www .nbcnews.com/feature/nbc-out/media-s-detransition-narrative-fueling -misconceptions-trans-advocates-say-n1102686.

38. Janelle Griffith, "Scarlett Johansson Says She 'Mishandled' Transgender Casting Controversy," NBC News, November 19, 2019, https://www .nbcnews.com/feature/nbc-out/scarlett-johansson-says-she-mishandled -transgender-casting-controversy-n1092131.

39. Phaylen Fairchild, "No Scarlett Johansson, You Can't Play Trans," Phaylen. Medium.com, July 14, 2019, https://phaylen.medium.com/no-scarlett -johansson-you-cant-play-trans-134874dae29a.

40. Nick Romano, "Scarlett Johansson's Transgender Casting Is Part of an Issue Worth Revisiting," *Entertainment Weekly*, July 7, 2018, https://ew.com/movies /2018/07/07/scarlett-johansson-transgender-casting-controversy-rub-tug/.

41. Canela Lopez, "Halle Berry Said She's Going to Play a Transgender Man in an Upcoming Movie, Calling It a 'Female Story,'" Insider, July 6, 2020, https://www.insider.com/halle-berry-to-play-a-transgender-man-in -upcoming-film-2020-7.

42. MacLeod, "The Dangers of Men in Women's Roles on the Renaissance Stage," 9.

43. Jordan Simon, "The New Blackface Minstrelsy: When White Actors Voice Black Characters in Animation," Shadow and Act, July 5, 2018, https:// shadowandact.com/the-new-blackface-minstrelsy-when-white-actors-voice -black-characters-in-animation.

44. Edward Pinaula, "Are There Any Black Voice Actors That Play White Characters?," Quora, June 8, 2020, https://www.quora.com/Are-there -any-black-voice-actors-that-play-white-characters.

45. @CathyReisenwitz, May 3, 2021, https://twitter.com/CathyReisenwitz /status/1389078255517327361.

46. Stephen Galloway, "'Late Night' and the Decline of Comedy at the Box Office: Is Netflix Really to Blame?," *Hollywood Reporter*, June 18, 2019, https://www.hollywoodreporter.com/news/comedy-box-office-dwindles -but-is-netflix-blame-1219121.

47. Galloway, "'Late Night' and the Decline of Comedy at the Box Office."

48. Gary Thompson, "Don't Laugh: Movie Comedies Are Disappearing,"

Philadelphia Inquirer, June 12, 2019, https://www.inquirer.com
/entertainment/movies/death-of-movie-comedies-anchorman
-booksmart-shaun-of-the-dead-20190712.html.

49. Kyle Buchanan, "How Will the Movies (as We Know Them) Survive the
    Next 10 Years?," *New York Times*, June 20, 2019, https://www.nytimes
    .com/interactive/2019/06/20/movies/movie-industry-future.html.

50. Ann Hornaday, "Sex Is Disappearing from the Big Screen, and It's Making
    Movies Less Pleasurable," *Washington Post*, June 7, 2020,
    https://www.washingtonpost.com/lifestyle/style/sex-is-disappearing
    -from-the-big-screen-and-its-making-movies-less-pleasurable
    /2019/06/06/37848090-82ed-11e9-933d-7501070ee669_Story.Html.

51. Lindsey Bahar, "In a New Series, TMC Takes a Look at 'Problematic'
    Classics," Associated Press, March 3, 2021, https://apnews.com/article
    /tcm-reframed-classics-ccac676ad469ca3932a0890b0dd4e67a.

52. Jasmin Bull, "'Misogynistic, Sexist and a Bit Rapey': Calls for Iconic Movie
    Grease to Be Banned," MSN.com, March 1, 2021, https://www
    .msn.com/en-nz/entertainment/movies/misogynistic-sexist-and-a-bit
    -rapey-calls-for-iconic-movie-grease-to-be-banned/ar-BB1crn1T.

53. Jen Yamato, "At Netflix, 'Cobra Kai' Broke Out. Now Its Whiteness Is
    Under a New Spotlight," *Los Angeles Times*, January 8, 2021, https://www
    .latimes.com/entertainment-arts/tv/story/2021-01-08/netflix-cobra-kai
    -season-3-diversity.

54. Cady Lang, "The Bachelor Finally Cast a Black Man. But Racism in the
    Franchise Has Overshadowed His Season," *Time*, January 11, 2021, https://
    time.com/5926330/the-bachelor-diversity-matt-james/.

3: PRUDENCE: HERESIES OF THE UNCONSCIOUS MIND

1. Noah Rothman, *Unjust: Social Justice and the Unmaking of America*
   (Washington, DC: Regnery Gateway, 2019), 131–32.

2. Ashok Selvam, "Acclaimed Fat Rice Topples After Outcry from Employees,"
   Eater: Chicago, June 17, 2020, https://chicago.eater
   .com/2020/6/17/21288547/fat-rice-chicago-closes-employees-claim
   -mistreatment-abe-conlon.

3. @Evystadium, November 18, 2020, https://twitter.com/EVYSTADIUM
   /status/1329110893133783040.

4. Mira Miller, "New Toronto Clothing Store Ditches Broth Bar After Cultural
   Appropriation Complaints," BlogTo, November 18, 2020, https://www.
   blogto.com/eat_drink/2020/11/toronto-clothing-store
   -ditches-broth-bar-cultural-appropriation-complaints/.

5. Michael Winship, *Hot Protestants: A History of Puritanism in England and
   America* (New Haven, CT: Yale University Press, 2019), 31–33.

6. Winship, *Hot Protestants*, 31–33.

7. Jeremiah Boroughs, "Self-Denial," from *The Rare Jewel of Christian Contentment*, APuritansMind.com, 1657, https://www.apuritansmind.com/puritan-favorites/jeremiah-burroughs-1599-1646/self-denial-by-jeremiah-burroughs/.

8. George McKenna, *The Puritan Origins of American Patriotism* (New Haven, CT: Yale University Press, 2007), 41.

9. H. de Coninck et al., "Strengthening and Implementing the Global Response," in *Global Warming of 1.5°C*, Intergovernmental Panel on Climate Change (IPCC) report, 2018, https://www.ipcc.ch/site/assets/uploads/sites/2/2019/02/SR15_Chapter4_Low_Res.pdf.

10. Damian Carrington, "Huge Reduction in Meat-Eating 'Essential' to Avoid Climate Breakdown," *Guardian*, October 10, 2018, https://www.theguardian.com/environment/2018/oct/10/huge-reduction-in-meat-eating-essential-to-avoid-climate-breakdown.

11. Stephanie Strom, "Obama Sees New Front in Climate Change Battle: Agriculture," *New York Times*, May 9, 2017, https://www.nytimes.com/2017/05/09/dining/obama-climate-food-milan.html.

12. Kendra Pierre-Louis, "No One Is Taking Your Hamburgers. But Would It Even Be a Good Idea?," *New York Times*, March 8, 2019, https://www.nytimes.com/2019/03/08/climate/hamburgers-cows-green-new-deal.html.

13. Cory Stieg, "Study Suggests Eating Less Red and Processed Meat May Not Improve Your Health—But There's a Catch," CNBC, October 1, 2019, https://www.cnbc.com/2019/10/01/eating-less-red-meat-does-not-improve-according-to-controversial-new-health-study.html.

14. Jonathan Safran Foer, "Jonathan Safran Foer: Why We Must Cut Out Meat and Dairy Before Dinner to Save the Planet," *Guardian*, September 28, 2019, https://www.theguardian.com/books/2019/sep/28/meat-of-the-matter-the-inconvenient-truth-about-what-we-eat.

15. Frank Bruni, "Is the Burger Nearing Extinction?," *New York Times*, March 6, 2021, https://www.nytimes.com/2021/03/06/opinion/sunday/beef-meatless-burger.html.

16. Jan Dutkiewicz and Gabriel N. Rosenberg, "The Sadism of Eating Real Meat over Lab Meat," *New Republic*, February 23, 2021, https://newrepublic.com/article/161452/sadism-eating-real-meat-lab-meat.

17. Max Esterhuizen, "Virginia Tech Researchers Find That Removal of Dairy Cows Would Have Minimal Impact on Greenhouse Emissions," Virginia Tech, January 6, 2021, https://vtnews.vt.edu/articles/2020/12/cals-white-research.html.

18. Environmental Protection Agency, "Inventory of U.S. Greenhouse Gas Emissions and Sinks: 1990–2017," April 2019, https://www.epa.gov/sites/production/files/2019-04/documents/us-ghg-inventory-2019-chapter-executive-summary.pdf.

19. USDA/Agricultural Research Service, "Exploring a World without Food Animals," ScienceDaily, accessed June 18, 2021, www.sciencedaily.com /releases/2017/12/171206222218.htm.

20. Bradley C. Johnston et al., "Unprocessed Red Meat and Processed Meat Consumption: Dietary Guideline Recommendations from the Nutritional Recommendations (NutriRECS) Consortium," *Annals of Internal Medicine*, November 19, 2019, accessed June 18, 2021, http://annals.org/aim/article /doi/10.7326/M19-1621.

21. Gina Kolata, "Eat Less Red Meat, Scientists Said. Now Some Believe That Was Bad Advice," *New York Times*, September 30, 2019, https://www .nytimes.com/2019/09/30/health/red-meat-heart-cancer.html.

22. Arnold Huis et al., "Edible Insects: Future Prospects for Food and Feed Security," Food and Agriculture Organisation of the United Nations, FAO Forestry Paper 171, 2013, http://www.fao.org/3/i3253e/i3253e00.htm.

23. Cayte Bosler, "To Save the World, Eat Bugs," *Atlantic*, February 25, 2014, https://www.theatlantic.com/health/archive/2014/02/to-save-the-world -eat-bugs/283970/.

24. Joy Shulammite Yu, "Bug Appétit: Eating Bugs to Save the Planet?," Massachusetts Institute of Technology, Angles, 2015, http://cmsw.mit .edu/angles/2015/bug-appetit-eating-bugs-to-save-the-planet/.

25. Lisa DesJardins, "The Buzz Around Eating Insects: The Argument for Adding Bugs to Our Diet," NPR, May 2, 2016, https://dianerehm.org /shows/2016-05-02/eating-insects-the-pros-and-cons-of-adding-bugs -to-our-diets.

26. Steve Hopkinson, "Eat Insects, Save the World," Natural History Museum, London, https://www.nhm.ac.uk/discover/eat-insects-save -the-world.html.

27. Noah Rothman, "Over-Population: The Malthusian Myth That Refuses to Die," *Commentary*, June 20, 2018, https://www.commentarymagazine.com /noah-rothman/the-malthusian-myth-that-refuses-to-die/.

28. Jason Goodyer, "Eating Insects Could Help Us Save the Planet," Science Focus, May 11, 2019, https://www.sciencefocus.com/news/eating-insects -could-help-us-save-the-planet/.

29. Susan Shain, "Could Feeding Your Dog Bugs Save the Planet?," Mic, January 4, 2021, https://www.mic.com/p/could-feeding-your-dog-bugs-save-the -planet-53890000.

30. Angela Garbes, "These 6 Filipinx Recipes Turn Pantry Staples into a Cozy Winter Menu," *Bon Appétit*, February 19, 2021, https://www.bonappetit .com/gallery/melissa-miranda-filipinx-pantry-recipes.

31. Mackenzie Chung Fegan, "What to Know Before Buying Saffron," *Bon Appétit*, July 26, 2020, https://www.bonappetit.com/story/how-to-source-saffron.

32. Leanne Italie, "Epicurious Attempts to Right Cultural Wrongs One Recipe at a Time," Associated Press, December 24, 2020, https://www.huffpost

.com/entry/epicurious-rewriting-racist-recipes_l_5fe4e61dc5b66809cb30
aee2.

33. Aimee Levitt, "Bon Appétit Apologizes for Lack of Sensitivity, Promises More 'Archive Repair Efforts,'" Takeout, February 12, 2021, https:// thetakeout.com/bon-appetit-apologizes-for-lack-of-sensitivity-promise -1846259526.

34. Helier Cheung, "Cultural Appropriation: Why Is Food Such a Sensitive Subject?," BBC, April 13, 2019, https://www.bbc.com/news/world-us -canada-47892747.

35. Theresa Braine, "Chef Gordon Ramsay Hits Back at Critics Accusing Him of Cultural Appropriation in New Asian-Themed Restaurant," *New York Daily News*, April 15, 2019, https://www.nydailynews.com/news/national/ny -asian-eatery-restaurant-gordon-ramsay-cultural-appropriation-20190416 -eeojagnbwndpnob3cbcimt2ali-story.html.

36. Raj Patel, "Food Injustice Has Deep Roots: Let's Start with America's Apple Pie," *Guardian*, May 1, 2021, https://www.theguardian.com /environment/2021/may/01/food-injustice-has-deep-roots-lets-start-with -americas-apple-pie.

37. Shana McCann, "The Cultural Appropriation of Food," Solid Ground, April 15, 2019, https://www.solid-ground.org/cultural-appropriation-of-food/.

38. Maria Godoy and Kat Chow, "When Chefs Become Famous Cooking Other Cultures' Food," NPR, March 22, 2016, https://www.npr.org/sections /thesalt/2016/03/22/471309991/when-chefs-become-famous-cooking -other-cultures-food.

39. "Did Chef Rick Bayless Just Claim 'Reverse Racism' When Confronted by Critics?," Latino Rebels, March 22, 2016, https://www.latinorebels.com /2016/03/22/did-chef-rick-bayless-just-claim-reverse-racism-when -confronted-by-critics/.

40. Tim Carman, "Should White Chefs Sell Burritos? A Portland Food Cart's Revealing Controversy," *Washington Post*, May 26, 2017, https://www .washingtonpost.com/news/food/wp/2017/05/26/should-white-chefs -sell-burritos-a-portland-restaurants-revealing-controversy/.

41. Alex Frane, "The Pok Pok Empire Has Officially Fallen," Eater: Portland, Oregon, October 30, 2020, https://pdx.eater.com/2020/10/30/21542119 /pok-pok-closed.

42. Eddie Kim, "Andy Ricker, the Most Famous Thai Chef in America, Is Burnt Out," *Mel* magazine, August 23, 2018, https://melmagazine.com/en-us /story/andy-ricker-the-most-famous-thai-chef-in-america-is-burnt-out.

43. Damian Carrington, "Plant-Based Diets Crucial to Saving Global Wildlife, Says Report," *Guardian*, February 3, 2021, https://www .theguardian.com/environment/2021/feb/03/plant-based-diets-crucial -to-saving-global-wildlife-says-report.

44. Ligaya Mishan, "The Activists Working to Remake the Food System," *New

York Times, February 19, 2021, https://www.nytimes.com/2021/02/19/t-magazine/food-security-activists.html.

45. The World Bank, "Zero Hunger," 2017, https://datatopics.worldbank.org/sdgatlas/archive/2017/SDG-02-zero-hunger.html.

46. Sun Ling Wang et al., "Agricultural Productivity Growth in the United States: Measurement, Trends, and Drivers," United States Department of Agriculture, Economic Research Report 189, July 2015, https://www.ers.usda.gov/webdocs/publications/45387/53417_err189.pdf?v=0.

47. "Are Genetically Modified Crops the Answer to World Hunger?," National Geographic Resource Library, January 28, 2020, https://www.nationalgeographic.org/article/are-genetically-modified-crops-answer-world-hunger/.

48. Erica Chayes Wida, "White Women Are Paying Thousands of Dollars to Confront Their Racist Beliefs Over Dinner," *Today*, July 1, 2020, https://www.today.com/food/organization-aims-dismantle-racism-over-dinner-t185504.

49. Matt Donnelly and Kathy Zerbib, "Comedians Dump Campus Gigs: When Did Colleges Lose Their Sense of Humor?," The Wrap, August 23, 2015, https://www.thewrap.com/comedians-avoiding-campus-when-did-universities-lose-their-sense-of-humor/.

50. Nimesh Patel, "I Was Kicked Off Stage by College Students. Did I Deserve It?," *New York Times*, December 7, 2018, https://www.nytimes.com/2018/12/07/opinion/columbia-nimesh-patel-comedian-kicked-offstage.html.

51. Rob Picheta, "Sarah Silverman Says She Was Fired from a Movie for an Old Blackface Sketch," CNN, August 12, 2019, https://www.cnn.com/2019/08/12/entertainment/sarah-silverman-blackface-scli-intl.

52. Jon Gabriel, "Welcome to America, the Land of the Perpetually Whiny and Offended," AZ Central, August 17, 2019, https://www.azcentral.com/story/opinion/op-ed/2019/08/17/cancel-culture-spreading-left-right-perpetually-offended/2009132001/.

53. Megh Wright, "New SNL Hire Shane Gillis Has a History of Racist and Homophobic Remarks," *New York* magazine, September 12, 2019, https://www.vulture.com/2019/09/snl-shane-gillis-racist-homophobic-remarks.html#_ga=2.30670527.1053214948.1615318520-1868932046.1615318520.

54. Tara Edwards, "Shane Gillis Will Not Join SNL After His Racist Comments Were Discovered," Refinery 29, September 16, 2019, https://www.refinery29.com/en-us/2019/09/8412429/saturday-night-live-shane-gillis-racist-homophobic-jokes.

55. Brian Flood, "Sarah Silverman Says Progressives Don't Offer a 'Path to Redemption' for Victims of Cancel Culture," Fox News, October 26, 2020, https://www.foxnews.com/entertainment/sarah-silverman-says-progressives-dont-offer-a-path-to-redemption-for-victims-of-cancel-culture.

56. Will Sloan, "The Limits of Liberal Comedy," Current Affairs, December 10, 2020, https://www.currentaffairs.org/2020/12/the-limits-of-liberal-comedy.

57. Bill Burr, "The Joe Rogan Experience," episode 1,575, podcast, 1:39:30–1:41:00, https://open.spotify.com/episode/2RYuGMhdQCk6FFoFJzKUR1.

58. Barbara Maranzani, "Lenny Bruce's Obscenity Trial Challenged First Amendment Rights and Paved the Way for Other Socially Conscious Comedians," Biography, May 10, 2019, https://www.biography.com/news/lenny-bruce-obscenity-trial.

59. Tim Ott, "How George Carlin's 'Seven Words' Changed Legal History," Biography, May 2, 2019, https://www.biography.com/news/george-carlin-seven-words-supreme-court.

60. "A Pryor Restraint," Washington Post, September 14, 1977, https://www.washingtonpost.com/archive/lifestyle/1977/09/14/a-pryor-restraint/b90f2673-29c1-4cc0-bcf7-48690916cfef/.

61. James McPherson, "The New Comic Style of Richard Pryor," New York Times, April 27, 1975, https://www.nytimes.com/1975/04/27/archives/the-new-comic-style-of-richard-pryor-i-know-what-i-wont-do-says-the.html.

62. Cassie da Costa, "The Funny, Furious Anti-Comedy of Hannah Gadsby," New Yorker, May 2, 2018, https://www.newyorker.com/culture/culture-desk/the-funny-furious-anti-comedy-of-hannah-gadsby.

63. Jane Howard, "Hannah Gadsby's Nanette Dares to Dream of a Different Future—for Ourselves and for Comedy," Guardian, June 26, 2018, https://www.theguardian.com/tv-and-radio/2018/jun/27/hannah-gadsbys-nanette-dares-to-dream-of-a-different-future-for-ourselves-and-for-comedy.

64. Aja Romano, "Why Hannah Gadsby's Searing Comedy Special Nanette Has Upended Comedy for Good," Vox, July 5, 2018, https://www.vox.com/culture/2018/7/5/17527478/hannah-gadsby-nanette-comedy.

65. Matt Zoller Seitz, "Bill Maher Is Stand-Up Comedy's Past. Hannah Gadsby Represents Its Future," New York magazine, July 12, 2018, https://www.vulture.com/2018/07/bill-maher-hannah-gadsby-stand-up-comedy.html.

66. Jerry Zolten, "Professor Explores American Culture Through Comedy's History," Penn State News, December 18, 2012, https://news.psu.edu/story/143653/2012/12/18/academics/professor-explores-american-culture-through-comedys-history.

4: AUSTERITY: AN UNADORNED LIFE

1. Michael Winship, Hot Protestants: A History of Puritanism in England and America (New Haven, CT: Yale University Press, 2019), 92.

2. John Simkin, "Tudor Sports and Pastimes," Spartacus Educational, September 1997, https://spartacus-educational.com/TUDsports.htm.

3. "President Questions Safety of Football," ESPN, January 27, 2013, https://

www.espn.com/nfl/story/_/id/8886528/president-barack-obama-not-sure
-allow-son-play-football.

4. Mallory Simon, "2,000 Players Unite in Suing NFL over Head Injuries,"
    CNN, June 7, 2012, https://edition.cnn.com/2012/06/07/sport/football
    /nfl-concussion-lawsuit/index.html.

5. Janine Armstrong, "NFL Concussion Protocol Explained: How Does
    It Work?," Sportscasting.com, January 18, 2021, https://www.sports
    casting.com/nfl-concussion-protocol-explained-how-does-it-work/.

6. "Malcolm Gladwell: Football Is a Moral Abomination," Bloomberg Video,
    November 12, 2014, https://sports.yahoo.com/video/malcolm-gladwell
    -football-moral-abomination-004743497.html.

7. Beth Daley, "Is It Immoral to Watch Football?," The Conversation,
    September 28, 2018, https://theconversation.com/is-it-immoral-to-watch
    -football-103081.

8. Nancy Struna, "Puritans and Sport: The Irretrievable Tide of Change," *Journal
    of Sport History* 4, no. 1 (1977): 3, https://www.jstor.org/stable/43611526.

9. Struna, "Puritans and Sport," 5.

10. Winship, *Hot Protestants*, 52.

11. B. C. Daniels, "Sober Mirth and Pleasant Poisons: Puritan Ambivalence
    Toward Leisure and Recreation in Colonial New England," *American Studies*
    34, no. 1 (1993): 129.

12. Victor Mather, "A Timeline of Colin Kaepernick vs. the N.F.L.,"
    New York Times, February 15, 2019, https://www.nytimes.com/2019
    /02/15/sports/nfl-colin-kaepernick-protests-timeline.html.

13. Clay Travis, *Republicans Buy Sneakers Too: How the Left Is Ruining Sports
    with Politics* (New York: Broadside Books, 2018), 115–16.

14. Kenneth Arthur, "Why Fan Reaction to NFL National Anthem Protests
    Is About Racism, Not Patriotism," *Rolling Stone*, September 26, 2017, https://
    www.rollingstone.com/culture/culture-sports/why-fan-reaction-to-nfl
    -national-anthem-protests-is-about-racism-not-patriotism-201838/.

15. Steven Ruiz, "Colin Kaepernick Was Loudly Booed by Bills Fans During
    Return to 49ers Lineup," For the Win, October 16, 2016, https://ftw
    .usatoday.com/2016/10/bills-fans-boo-colin-kaepernick-49ers-national
    -anthem.

16. Victoria M. Massie, "The Backlash over Colin Kaepernick Is Just Americans'
    Refusal to Acknowledge Racism—Again," *Vox*, October 16, 2016, https://
    www.vox.com/identities/2016/10/13/12710860/colin
    -kaepernick-anthem-protest-explained.

17. Will Brinson, "NFL Won't Let Cowboys Wear Decals Supporting Dallas
    Police in Regular Season," CBS Sports, August 11, 2016, https://www
    .cbssports.com/nfl/news/nfl-wont-let-cowboys-wear-decals-supporting
    -dallas-police-in-regular-season/.

18. Mike Jones, "Legalese, Mistrust and Late Negotiating: How Colin Kaepernick and the NFL Broke Apart on Workout," *USA Today*, November 21, 2019, https://www.usatoday.com/story/sports/nfl/2019/11/21/colin -kaepernick-nfl-workout-waiver-teams-quarterback/4259272002/.

19. Harriet Sherwood, "NFL Decision to Permit Kneeling Protest by Players Enrages Donald Trump," *Guardian*, June 6, 2020, https://www.theguardian .com/us-news/2020/jun/06/nfl-decision-to-permit-kneeling-protest-by -players-enrages-donald-trump.

20. Shawn Grant, "Source Sports: Shannon Sharpe Says Drew Brees Should Retire After His Kneeling Protest Statement," The Source, June 4, 2020, https://thesource.com/2020/06/04/shannon-sharpe-drew-brees-retirement/.

21. Tadd Haislop, "Chiefs, Texans Players Booed During Moment of Unity; Houston Stays in Locker Room for National Anthem," *Sporting News*, September 10, 2020, https://www.sportingnews.com/us/nfl/news/chiefs -texans-national-anthem/h5wq7122d6jm17yardgjjtkqq.

22. Michael Rand, "End Racism? Messaging from NFL, Booing from Fans Shows the Challenge," *Star Tribune* (Minneapolis), September 11, 2020, https:// www.startribune.com/end-racism-messaging-from-nfl-booing-from-fans -shows-the-challenge/572382472/.

23. Michael Ryan, "After Shameful Boos During Chiefs Opener, We All Should Do Some Soul Searching," *Kansas City Star*, September 11, 2020, https://www.kansascity.com/opinion/opn-columns-blogs/michael-ryan /article245657955.html.

24. Lydia Saad, "Farming Rises, Sports Tumbles in U.S. Industry Ratings," Gallup, September 8, 2020, https://news.gallup.com/poll/319256 /farming-rises-sports-tumbles-industry-ratings.aspx.

25. Tom Junod, "The Many Forms of White Privilege," The Undefeated, July 7, 2020, https://theundefeated.com/videos/the-many-forms-of-white -privilege/.

26. "Stephen A. on Nets Hiring Nash: 'This Is White Privilege,'" ESPN, September 17, 2020, https://www.espn.com/video/clip/_/id/29801128.

27. @ESPN, June 24, 2020, https://twitter.com/espn/status /1275935014417555463?lang=en.

28. Myron Medcalf, "Kentucky Basketball Coach John Calipari Says White Privilege Has Helped His Life and Career," ESPN, August 26, 2020, https:// www.espn.com/mens-college-basketball/story/_/id/29746705 /kentucky-basketball-coach-john-calipari-says-white-privilege-helped -life-career.

29. @ESPN, June 9, 2020, https://twitter.com/espn/status/1270438070 387703810/photo/1.

30. ESPN Staff, "Jazz's Korver Reflects on Racism, White Privilege," ESPN, April 8, 2019, https://www.espn.com/nba/story/_/id/26471707/jazz -korver-reflects-racism-white-privilege.

31. Jim Brady, "Inside and Out, ESPN Dealing with Changing Political Dynamics," ESPN, November 8, 2016, https://www.espn.com/blog /ombudsman/post/_/id/767/inside-and-out-espn-dealing-with-changing -political-dynamics.

32. Des Bieler, "ESPN's Jemele Hill Says She Stands by 'White Supremacist' Description of Trump," *Washington Post*, February 21, 2018, https://www .washingtonpost.com/news/early-lead/wp/2018/02/21/espns-jemele -hill-says-she-stands-by-white-supremacist-description-of-trump/.

33. James Andrew Miller, "James Andrew Miller: Jemele Hill Waves Goodbye to ESPN and Hello to 'Places Where Discomfort Is OK,'" *Hollywood Reporter*, October 1, 2018, https://www.hollywoodreporter.com/news /jemele-hill-interview-leaving-espn-joining-atlantic-1148171.

34. Kevin Draper, "ESPN Employees Say Racism Endures Behind the Camera," *New York Times*, July 13, 2020, https://www.nytimes.com/2020/07/13 /sports/espn-racism-black-employees.html.

35. @ErickFernandez, July 18, 2019, https://twitter.com/ErickFernandez /status/1151943048101814273.

36. Brian Steinberg, "Dan Le Batard Tests ESPN's—and Jimmy Pitaro's— No-Politics Policy," *Variety*, July 19, 2019, https://variety.com/2019/tv /news/dan-le-batard-espn-politics-jimmy-pitaro-1203273101/.

37. @BenJStrauss, July 24, 2019, https://twitter.com/benjstrauss/status /1154067491297136640.

38. Christopher Palmeri, "With Shut-In Kids Flocking to Streaming, Disney Channel Retools," Bloomberg, April 17, 2020, https://www.bloomberg.com /news/articles/2020-04-17/with-shut-in-kids-flocking-to-streaming-disney -channel-retools?sref=PuSbyecd.

39. Dade Hayes, "Disney and ESPN 'Uniquely Positioned' to Move Sports Fully into Streaming—Analyst," Deadline, June 24, 2020, https://deadline .com/2020/06/disney-espn-should-move-sports-to-streaming-1202968442/.

40. @Ourand_SBJ, July 25, 2019, https://twitter.com/Ourand_SBJ/status /1154362771527614464.

41. Jerry Brewer, "Our Sports Need a Healthier Version of Masculinity, and Men Need to Create It," *Washington Post*, February 22, 2021, https://www .washingtonpost.com/sports/2021/02/22/toxic-masculinity-sports-sexism -don-mcpherson/.

42. Amanda Ripley, "The Case Against High-School Sports," *Atlantic*, October 15, 2013, https://www.theatlantic.com/magazine/archive/2013/10/the-case -against-high-school-sports/309447/.

43. Erica Bloom, "How Many Scholarships Could We Fund if We Eliminated College Sports? Hint: A Lot," Urban Wire, April 11, 2018, https://www .urban.org/urban-wire/how-many-scholarships-could-we-fund-if-we -eliminated-college-sports-hint-lot.

44. Peter Bolton, "Post-Covid, We Should Take a Leaf Out of Cuba's Book and Abolish Professional Sports," CounterPunch, January 22, 2021, https://www.counterpunch.org/2021/01/22/post-covid-we-should-take-a-leaf-out-of-cubas-book-and-abolish-professional-sports/.

45. Imran Amed et al., "The Influence of 'Woke' Consumers on Fashion," McKinsey & Company, February 12, 2019, https://www.mckinsey.com/industries/retail/our-insights/the-influence-of-woke-consumers-on-fashion.

46. Ryan Parker and Kimberly Nordyke, "Nike's Polarizing Colin Kaepernick Ad Wins Emmy for Best Commercial," *Hollywood Reporter*, September 15, 2019, https://www.hollywoodreporter.com/news/nikes-colin-kaepernick-protest-ad-wins-emmy-best-commercial-1239853.

47. Cedric Thornton, "Nike's Value Up $26 Billion Since Colin Kaepernick Endorsement," Black Enterprise, November 26, 2019, https://www.blackenterprise.com/nike-value-up-26-billion-since-colin-kaepernick-endorsement/#:~:text=Nike's%20stock%20reportedly%20rose%20over,value%20at%20nearly%20%20%24146%20billion.

48. Abha Bhattarai, "Levi Strauss CEO Takes a Side on Gun Control: 'It's Inevitable That We're Going to Alienate Some Consumers,'" *Washington Post*, September 10, 2018, https://www.washingtonpost.com/business/2018/09/10/levi-strauss-ceo-takes-side-gun-control-its-inevitable-that-were-going-alienate-some-consumers/.

49. "Levi Strauss & Co. Reports Fourth-Quarter and Full Year 2019 Earnings," Businesswire, January 30, 2020, https://www.businesswire.com/news/home/20200130005816/en/Levi-Strauss-Co.-Reports-Fourth-Quarter-and-Full-Year-2019-Earnings#:~:text=Levi%20Strauss%20%26%20Co.'s,net%20revenues%20were%20%20%245.8%20billion.

50. William Perry Pendly, "Trump Wants to Free Up Federal Lands, His Interior Secretary Fails Him," *National Review*, September 25, 2017, https://www.nationalreview.com/2017/09/secretary-interior-ryan-zinke-monuments-review-trump-executive-order-antiquities-act-environmentalists/.

51. Abha Bhattarai, "I'm Not Going to 'Let Evil Win': Patagonia's Billionaire Owner Says He Plans to Sue Trump," *Washington Post*, December 5, 2017, https://www.washingtonpost.com/news/business/wp/2017/12/05/im-not-going-to-let-evil-win-patagonias-billionaire-owner-says-he-plans-to-sue-trump/.

52. Kati Chitrakorn, "Woke Brands Walk a Thin Line with 'Moral Merch,'" Vogue Business, January 22, 2020, https://www.voguebusiness.com/companies/woke-brands-balenciaga-noah-nike-moral-merch.

53. "China: 83 Major Brands Implicated in Report on Forced Labour of Ethnic Minorities from Xinjiang Assigned to Factories Across Provinces; Includes Company Responses," Business & Human Rights Resource Centre, March 1, 2020, https://www.business-humanrights.org/en/latest-news/china-83

-major-brands-implicated-in-report-on-forced-labour-of-ethnic-minorities
-from-xinjiang-assigned-to-factories-across-provinces-includes-company
-responses/.

54. Ana Swanson, "Nike and Coca-Cola Lobby Against Xinjiang Forced Labor
Bill," *New York Times*, November 29, 2020, https://www.nytimes.com
/2020/11/29/business/economy/nike-coca-cola-xinjiang-forced-labor-bill
.html.

55. Sarah Laskow, "The Hidden Rules of the Puritan Fashion Police," Atlas
Obscura, July 10, 2017, https://www.atlasobscura.com/articles/sumptuary
-laws-puritan-fashion-colonies-modesty.

56. Daniels, "Sober Mirth and Pleasant Poisons," 131.

57. Ink Mendelsohn, "We Were What We Wore," *American Heritage* 39, no. 8
(December 1988), https://www.americanheritage.com/we-were-what-we
-wore.

58. George McKenna, *The Puritan Origins of American Patriotism* (New Haven,
CT: Yale University Press, 2007), 38–39.

59. Dorothy Mays, *Women in Early America: Struggle, Survival, and Freedom in a
New World* (Santa Barbara, CA: ABC-CLIO, 2004), 384.

60. Mays, *Women in Early America*, 384.

61. Mendelsohn, "We Were What We Wore."

62. Emily Wells, "Rudi Gernreich: Fearless Fashion Renegade and Los Angeles
Icon," Perfect Number, June 5, 2019, https://mag.perfectnumber.co/rudi
-gernreich-fearless-fashion-renegade-and-los-angeles-icon/.

63. Wells, "Rudi Gernreich."

64. Mendelsohn, "We Were What We Wore."

65. Antonia Opiah, "Why the Conversation About Cultural Appropriation
Needs to Go Further," *Teen Vogue*, May 24, 2017, https://www.teenvogue
.com/story/why-the-cultural-appropriation-conversation-needs-to-go
-further.

66. Jamé Jackson, "3 Hairstylists on Braids, Cultural Appropriation and Media's
Erasure of Black Women," Fashionista, November 9, 2018, https://fashionista
.com/2018/01/black-hair-braids-cultural-appropriation-media-erasure.

67. Tom Gerken, "YouTuber Nikita Dragun Faces Backlash over Hairstyle,"
BBC, September 9, 2019, https://www.bbc.com/news/blogs-trending
-49635136.

68. BBC Staff, "Comme Des Garçons: Row over White Fashion Models'
Cornrow Wigs," BBC, January 19, 2020, https://www.bbc.com/news
/world-51166873.

69. Ruby Pivet, "Hoop Earrings Are My Culture, Not Your Trend," *Vice*,
October 10, 2017, https://www.vice.com/en/article/j5ga5x/hoop
-earrings-are-my-culture-not-your-trend.

70. Lena Finkel, "'Vogue' Just Gave a Bunch of White Girls Credit for the Gold Hoop Earrings Trend and It's Not OK," Femestella, August 2, 2017, http://www.femestella.com/1928-vogue-cultural-appropriation/.

71. Latino Rebels, "A Message from the Latinas Who Made the 'White Girl, Take OFF Your Hoops' Mural," Latino Rebels, March 14, 2017, https://www.latinorebels.com/2017/03/14/a-message-from-the-latinas-who-made-the-white-girl-take-off-your-hoops-mural/.

72. Elliot Dordick, "Pitzer College RA: White People Can't Wear Hoop Earrings," *Claremont Independent*, March 7, 2017, http://claremontindependent.com/pitzer-college-ra-white-people-cant-wear-hoop-earrings/.

73. Seacoast Online, "Are Torn Designer Jeans Cultural Appropriation of Blue-Collar Maine Workers? Gallery Opens 'Provocative' Exhibit," *Bangor Daily News*, November 12, 2018, https://bangordailynews.com/2018/11/12/news/are-torn-designer-jeans-cultural-appropriation-of-blue-collar-maine-workers-gallery-opens-provocative-exhibit/.

74. Erin Schwartz, "Class Appropriation in Fashion Is Real, and Impossible to Talk About," *Vice*, May 17, 2018, https://garage.vice.com/en_us/article/xwmxgj/class-appropriation-in-fashion.

75. Sohan Judge, "Here's How to Avoid Cultural Appropriation with Your Festival Outfit Choices," *BuzzFeed*, May 6, 2018, https://www.buzzfeed.com/sohanjudge/cultural-appropriation-festival-fashion.

76. Rachel Tashjian, "In Fashion, Who Will Cancel the Cancelers?," GQ, July 1, 2020, https://www.gq.com/story/diet-prada-kanye.

77. Jonah Engel Bromwich, "We're All Drinking Diet Prada Now," *New York Times*, March 14, 2019, https://www.nytimes.com/2019/03/14/fashion/diet-prada.html.

78. Lifestyle Desk, "Diet Prada Calls Out Problematic Vogue Covers, Including One Featuring Deepika Padukone," *Indian Express*, June 17, 2020, https://indianexpress.com/article/lifestyle/fashion/diet-prada-calls-out-problematic-vogue-covers-including-one-featuring-deepika-padukone-6463838/.

79. Vanessa Friedman and Sui-Lee Wee, "The Crash and Burn of Dolce & Gabbana," *New York Times*, November 23, 2018, https://www.nytimes.com/2018/11/23/fashion/dolce-gabbana-china-disaster-backlash.html.

80. Colleen Berry, "Dolce&Gabbana Seeks over $600M Damages from 2 US Bloggers," Associated Press, March 6, 2021, https://apnews.com/article/dolce-gabbana-sues-diet-prada-over-600m-26f639d44796a5aa5ae9673bd988b46f.

5: FEAR OF GOD: THE EVIL OF BANALITY

1. Robert Regoli, "Racism, Racism Everywhere: Looking Inside the Hobby of Baseball Card Collecting," *Race and Society* 3, no. 2 (July 2000): 183–92,

https://www.sciencedirect.com/science/article/abs/pii
/S1090952401000286.

2. @NYTimes, December 13, 2020, https://twitter.com/nytimes/status
/1337990647006056449?lang=en.

3. Lindsey Bever, "A University President Held Dinner for Black Students—
and Set the Table with Cotton Stalks and Collard Greens," *Washington Post*,
September 19, 2017, https://www.washingtonpost.com/news/grade-point
/wp/2017/09/19/a-university-president-held-a-dinner-for-black-students
-and-set-the-table-with-cotton-stalks-and-collard-greens/?wpisrc=nl
_most&wpmm=1.

4. Cory Collins, "When Décor Is More Than Décor," Learning for Justice,
September 21, 2017, https://www.learningforjustice.org/magazine/when
-decor-is-more-than-decor.

5. Karen Templer, "2019: My Year of Color," Fringe Association, January 7,
2019, https://fringeassociation.com/2019/01/07/2019-my-year-of-color/.

6. Carley Marston, "Racism in the Knitting Community," Medium, January 24,
2019, https://medium.com/carleys-corner/racism-in-the-knitting
-community-696dc3d9114f.

7. Jaya Saxena, "The Knitting Community Is Reckoning with Racism," *Vox*,
February 25, 2019, https://www.vox.com/the-goods/2019/2/25/18234950
/knitting-racism-instagram-stories.

8. George McKenna, *The Puritan Origins of American Patriotism* (New Haven,
CT: Yale University Press, 2007), 275–78.

9. McKenna, *The Puritan Origins of American Patriotism*, 275.

10. Michael Winship, *Hot Protestants: A History of Puritanism in England and
America* (New Haven, CT: Yale University Press, 2019), 82.

11. McKenna, *The Puritan Origins of American Patriotism*, 49.

12. Jonathan Edwards, "Sinners in the Hands of an Angry God. A Sermon
Preached at Enfield, July 8th, 1741," ed. Reiner Smolinski, University of
Nebraska, Lincoln, Digital Commons, Electronic Texts in American Studies,
54, https://digitalcommons.unl.edu/etas/54.

13. Winship, *Hot Protestants*, 87–88.

14. McKenna, *The Puritan Origins of American Patriotism*, 124.

15. Winship, *Hot Protestants*, 160.

16. Jeff Mirus, "Ghosts of Christmas Past," Catholic Culture, January 6, 2012,
https://www.catholicculture.org/commentary/ghosts-christmas-past/.

17. B. C. Daniels, "Sober Mirth and Pleasant Poisons: Puritan Ambivalence
Toward Leisure and Recreation in Colonial New England," *American Studies*
34, no. 1 (1993): 124.

18. Classroom Resource, "A Racial Justice Guide to the Winter Holiday Season

for Educators and Families," Center for Racial Justice in Education, https://centerracialjustice.org/resources/racial-justice-guide-holidayseason/.

19. Maisha Z. Johnson, "What Privilege Really Means (and Doesn't Mean)—to Clear Up Your Doubts Once and for All," Everyday Feminism, July 21, 2015, https://everydayfeminism.com/2015/07/what-privilege-really-means/.

20. Paul Kivel, "Living in a Christian Dominant Culture: An Exercise," PaulKivel.com, 2004, https://christianhegemony.org/wp-content/uploads/2009/12/Christian_Hegemony_Exercise_5_31_10.pdf.

21. Jordan Uhl, "Dear White People, the Holiday Season Is the Best Time to Tell Our Grandparents to Stop Being Racist," Independent, November 23, 2016, https://www.independent.co.uk/voices/how-talk-about-race-white-person-relatives-holidays-thanksgiving-christmas-a7434886.html.

22. Mika Doyle and Mia Mercado, "PSA: These 10 Halloween 'Costumes' Will Always Be Offensive," Bustle, September 23, 2018, https://www.bustle.com/life/10-culturally-appropriative-halloween-costumes-you-should-never-wear-11941912.

23. Sachi Feris, "Moana, Elsa, and Halloween," Raising Race Conscious Children, September 5, 2017, http://www.raceconscious.org/2017/09/moana-elsa-halloween/.

24. Noah Rothman, Unjust: Social Justice and the Unmaking of America (Washington, DC: Regnery Gateway, 2019), 130.

25. Osamudia James, "Can a White Child Dress as a Halloween Character from Another Race?," Washington Post, October 30, 2017, https://www.washingtonpost.com/news/posteverything/wp/2017/10/30/can-a-white-child-dress-as-a-halloween-character-from-another-race/.

26. John F. Muller, "Halloween Is More Political Than You Think," Politico, October 31, 2018, https://www.politico.com/magazine/story/2018/10/31/halloween-politics-racial-divides-milwaukee-221955/.

27. Nicole Breedlove, "Happy National Genocide (Thanksgiving) Day!," Huffington Post, November 25, 2013, https://www.huffpost.com/entry/thanksgiving-pequot-massacre_b_4337722.

28. Amanda Morris, "Teaching Thanksgiving in a Socially Responsible Way," Learning for Justice, November 10, 2015, https://www.learningforjustice.org/magazine/teaching-thanksgiving-in-a-socially-responsible-way.

29. Classroom Resource, "Thanksgiving Mourning," Learning for Justice, https://www.learningforjustice.org/classroom-resources/lessons/thanksgiving-mourning.

30. Classroom Resource, "Relearning Thanksgiving," Arts and Justice, http://www.artsandjustice.org/relearning-thanksgiving-2/.

31. Chelsea Ritschel, "Thanksgiving: Why Some Americans Don't Celebrate the Controversial Holiday," Independent, November 25, 2020, https://www.independent.co.uk/life-style/thanksgiving-day-meaning-america-what-b1761971.html.

32. Natalia Mehlman Petrzela, "Jogging Has Always Excluded Black People," *New York Times*, May 12, 2020, https://www.nytimes.com/2020/05/12 /opinion/running-jogging-race-ahmaud-arbery.html.

33. Josie Glausiusz, "Is Dirt the New Prozac?," *Discover*, June 13, 2007, https:// www.discovermagazine.com/mind/is-dirt-the-new-prozac.

34. James Wong, "Weeding Out Horticulture's Race Problem," *Guardian*, June 14, 2020, https://www.theguardian.com/lifeandstyle/2020/jun/14/james-wong -weeding-out-the-race-problem-in-horticulture.

35. Harry Howard, "BBC Presenter James Wong Under Fire for Claiming British Gardening Culture Is 'Racist' Due to Its Use of Terms Like 'Heritage' and 'Native,'" *Daily Mail*, December 12, 2020, https://www.dailymail.co.uk /news/article-9047499/BBC-presenter-James-Wong-criticised-claiming -British-gardening-culture-racist.html?ito=social-twitter_dailymailUK.

36. J. Walton, "Reclaiming Victory Gardens from Our Racist History," Green America, April 21, 2020, https://www.greenamerica.org/blog /reclaiming-victory-gardens-our-racist-history.

37. Darryl Fears, "The Racist Legacy Many Birds Carry," *Washington Post*, June 3, 2021, https://www.washingtonpost.com/climate-environment /interactive/2021/bird-names-racism-audubon/.

38. Joel Johnson, "Reading the Water for Racism in Fishing," *Angling Trade*, August 4, 2020, https://www.anglingtrade.com/2020/08/04/reading -the-water-for-racism-in-fishing/.

39. Jesus Garcia, "Car Guys—Are We Unintentionally Sexist?," DriveTribe.com, December 15, 2016, https://drivetribe.com/p/car-guys-are-we -unintentionally-UtUzft21R5mSqq_Mt-HQqQ?iid=cOh0lomZSJ6 -0XPApAGFsQ.

40. Kea Wilson, "Streetsblog 101: Car Culture Is a Toxic Masculinity Problem," Streetsblog, February 27, 2020, https://usa.streetsblog.org/2020/02/27 /streetsblog-101-car-culture-is-a-toxic-masculinity-problem/.

41. Quoctrung Bui and Amanda Cox, "Surprising New Evidence Shows Bias in Police Use of Force but Not in Shootings," *New York Times*, July 11, 2016, https://www.nytimes.com/2016/07/12/upshot/surprising-new -evidence-shows-bias-in-police-use-of-force-but-not-in-shootings .html.

42. Alex Hider, "Cops Can Pull Over Drivers in Minnesota, Other States for Hanging Air Fresheners on Rearview Mirrors," Denver Channel, April 13, 2021, https://www.thedenverchannel.com/news/america-in -crisis/cops-can-pull-over-drivers-in-minnesota-other-states-for-hanging -air-fresheners-on-rearview-mirrors.

43. "This Month in Physics History. October 1958: Physicist Invents First Video Game," *American Physical Society* 17, no. 9 (October 2008), https://www. aps.org/publications/apsnews/200810/physicshistory.cfm.

44. Shannon Symonds, "Death Race and Video Game Violence," National

Museum of Play, May 15, 2012, https://www.museumofplay.org/blog
/chegheads/2012/05/death-race-and-video-game-violence.

45. Newt Gingrich, *Congressional Record* 145, no. 94 (June 29, 1999), https://
www.govinfo.gov/content/pkg/CREC-1999-06-29/html/CREC-1999-06
-29-pt1-PgE1427-2.htm.

46. Jill Disis, "The Long History of Blaming Video Games for Mass Violence,"
CNN, March 8, 2018, https://money.cnn.com/2018/03/08/media/video
-game-industry-white-house/index.html.

47. Timothy Bella, "Politicians Suggest Video Games Are to Blame for the
El Paso Shooting. It's an Old Claim That's Not Backed by Research,"
Washington Post, August 5, 2019, https://www.washingtonpost.com
/nation/2019/08/05/kevin-mccarthy-dan-patrick-video-games-el-paso
-shooting/.

48. Chris Ferguson et al., "News Media, Public Education and Public Policy
Committee," *Amplifier Magazine*, June 12, 2017, https://div46amplifier
.com/2017/06/12/news-media-public-education-and-public-policy
-committee/.

49. Kevin Draper, "Video Games Aren't Why Shootings Happen. Politicians
Still Blame Them," *New York Times*, August 5, 2019, https://www.nytimes
.com/2019/08/05/sports/trump-violent-video-games-studies.html.

50. Seth Schiesel, "The Real Problem with Video Games," *New York Times*,
March 13, 2018, https://www.nytimes.com/2018/03/13/opinion/video
-games-toxic-violence.html.

51. Jordan Minor, "Video Games Owe Black Players More Than Just Talk," *PC
Magazine*, June 18, 2020, https://www.pcmag.com/opinions/video
-games-owe-black-players-more-than-just-talk.

52. Nadine Dornieden, "Leveling Up Representation: Depictions of People of
Color in Video Games," PBS, December 22, 2020, https://www.pbs
.org/independentlens/blog/leveling-up-representation-depictions-of
-people-of-color-in-video-games/.

53. Keza MacDonald, "Is the Video Games Industry Finally Reckoning with
Sexism?," *Guardian*, July 22, 2020, https://www.theguardian.com/games
/2020/jul/22/is-the-video-games-industry-finally-reckoning-with-sexism.

54. Noah Smith, "Racism, Misogyny, Death Threats: Why Can't the Booming
Video-Game Industry Curb Toxicity?," *Washington Post*, February 26, 2019,
https://www.washingtonpost.com/technology/2019/02/26/racism-misogyny
-death-threats-why-cant-booming-video-game-industry-curb-toxicity/.

55. Peter C. Mancall, "Why the Puritans Cracked Down on Celebrating
Christmas," The Conversation, December 17, 2020, https://theconversation
.com/why-the-puritans-cracked-down-on-celebrating-christmas-151359.

56. Winship, *Hot Protestants*, 186.

57. Nancy Struna, "Puritans and Sport: The Irretrievable Tide of Change,"
Journal of Sport History 4, no. 1 (1977): 16.

58. Struna, "Puritans and Sport," 3.

59. David Harley, "The Beginnings of the Tobacco Controversy: Puritanism, James I, and the Royal Physicians," *Bulletin of the History of Medicine* 67, no. 1 (1993): 36–38, accessed June 21, 2021, http://www.jstor.org /stable/44444167.

60. Dan Ahrens, *Investing in Vice: The Recession-Proof Portfolio of Booze, Bets, Bombs & Butts* (New York: St. Martin's Press, 2004), 83.

61. Otho T. Beall, Jr., and Richard H. Shryock, *Cotton Mather: First Significant Figure in American Medicine* (Worcester, MA: American Antiquarian Society, 1953), 91, https://www.americanantiquarian.org/proceedings /44817435.pdf.

62. Records and Files of the Quarterly Courts of Essex County, volume II, University of Virginia, 384, http://salem.lib.virginia.edu/Essex/vol2 /images/essex384.html.

63. U.S. Department of Health and Human Services, "Reducing Tobacco Use: A Report of the Surgeon General," Centers for Disease Control and Prevention, National Center for Chronic Disease Prevention and Health Promotion, Office on Smoking and Health, 2000, https://collections.nlm. nih.gov/ocr/nlm:nlmuid-101584932X181-doc.

64. U.S. Department of Health and Human Services, "A Historical Review of Efforts to Reduce Smoking in the United States," Chapter 2, "Reducing Tobacco Use: A Report of the Surgeon General," https://www.cdc.gov /tobacco/data_statistics/sgr/2000/complete_report/pdfs/chapter2.pdf.

65. P. Hajek et al., "A Randomized Trial of E-Cigarettes Versus Nicotine Replacement Therapy," *New England Journal of Medicine* 380, no. 7 (2019): 629–37, https://www.nejm.org/doi/full/10.1056/NEJMoa1808779.

66. Noah Rothman, "The War on Vaping," *Commentary*, July/August 2020, https://www.commentarymagazine.com/articles/noah-rothman/the-war -on-vaping/.

67. Emily Baumgaertner, "Trump Administration Imposes Ban on Some, but Not All, Vaping Flavors in Retreat on Earlier Plan," *Los Angeles Times*, January 2, 2020, https://www.latimes.com/politics/story/2020-01-02/trump -administration-retreats-from-vaping-flavor-ban.

68. Ashley Gardner, "Clearing the Air: Vaping for Fun Quickly Became an Addiction," *Texarkana Gazette*, August 20, 2019, https://www .texarkanagazette.com/news/texarkana/story/2019/aug/31/clearing -air-vaping-fun-quickly-became-addiction/793023/.

69. Amy Morin, "Should Parents Be Concerned about Vaping?," Very Well Family, June 27, 2020, https://www.verywellfamily.com/what-parents -need-to-know-about-vaping-4154189.

70. University of Texas at San Antonio, "Vaping Is Linked to Adolescents' Propensity for Crime, Study Shows," ScienceDaily, May 28, 2019, https:// www.sciencedaily.com/releases/2019/05/190528193030.htm.

71. Aliyya Swaby and Jolie McCullough, "Students Face Felony Charges, Expulsions as Texas Schools Ramp Up Fight Against Vaping," *Texas Tribune*, December 17, 2019, https://www.texastribune.org/2019/12/17/texas-schools-vaping-surge-expulsions-felony-charges/.

72. Billy Binion, "Cops Tased and Beat Teens While Enforcing a Local Vaping Ban," Reason, June 14, 2021, https://reason.com/2021/06/14/ocean-city-maryland-police-viral-video-teens-vaping/.

6: TEMPERANCE: SOBER, CHASTE, AND PENITENT

1. Todd Spangler, "Vox Media Editorial Director Lockhart Steele Fired for Sexual Harassment," *Variety*, October 20, 2017, https://variety.com/2017/digital/news/vox-media-lockhart-steele-fired-sexual-harassment-1202595146/.

2. Matt Labash, "Millennials Have Officially Killed the Holiday Office Party," *Washington Examiner*, December 7, 2017, https://www.washingtonexaminer.com/weekly-standard/millennials-have-officially-killed-the-holiday-office-party.

3. "2018 Holiday Party Survey: Fewest Planned Parties Since the Recession Recovery," Challenger, Gray & Christmas, Inc., https://www.challengergray.com/blog/2018-holiday-party-survey-fewest-planned-parties-recession-recovery/.

4. "2018 Holiday Party Survey."

5. B. C. Daniels, "Sober Mirth and Pleasant Poisons: Puritan Ambivalence Toward Leisure and Recreation in Colonial New England," *American Studies* 34, no. 1 (1993): 128.

6. Michael Winship, *Hot Protestants: A History of Puritanism in England and America* (New Haven, CT: Yale University Press, 2019), 51–52.

7. Winship, *Hot Protestants*, 166.

8. Daniels, "Sober Mirth and Pleasant Poisons," 123.

9. Dean Albertson, "Puritan Liquor in the Planting of New England," *New England Quarterly* 23, no. 4 (1950): 478–90.

10. George McKenna, *The Puritan Origins of American Patriotism* (New Haven, CT: Yale University Press, 2007), 219.

11. Daniels, "Sober Mirth and Pleasant Poisons," 130.

12. Carl N. Degler, "Were the Puritans Puritanical?," in *Out of Our Past: The Forces that Shaped Modern America* (New York: Harper & Row, 1959), 28–37, http://frickman.pbworks.com/w/file/fetch/68983867/AP%20US%20History%20-%20Puritans.pdf.

13. Albertson, "Puritan Liquor in the Planting of New England," 486–87.

14. Rachel Fleming, "Those Loose Ladies: An Examination of Scandalous

Puritan Women in Massachusetts from 1635 to 1700" (honors thesis, Salem State University, 2015), 7–8, https://digitalcommons.salemstate.edu /honors_theses/48.

15. McKenna, *The Puritan Origins of American Patriotism*, 219.

16. McKenna, *The Puritan Origins of American Patriotism*, 220.

17. Leah Rae Berk, "Temperance and Prohibition Era Propaganda: A Study in Rhetoric," Brown University Library Center for Digital Scholarship, Fall 2004, https://library.brown.edu/cds/temperance/essay.html.

18. *Battle for Whiteclay*, directed by Mark Vasina (2008), https://www .youtube.com/watch?v=HDAdhOxuTwk&ab_channel=Publius4321.

19. Grant Schulte, "SD Tribe's Lawsuit Against Beer Stores Dismissed," Associated Press, October 2, 2012, https://www.cnbc.com/2012/10/02 /sd-tribes-lawsuit-against-beer-stores-dismissed.html.

20. Nicholas Kristof, "A Battle with the Brewers," *New York Times*, May 5, 2012, https://www.nytimes.com/2012/05/06/opinion/sunday/kristof-a-battle -with-the-brewers.html.

21. Opinion, "Alcohol and the Reservation: Anheuser-Busch's View," *New York Times*, May 8, 2012, https://www.nytimes.com/2012/05/09/opinion /alcohol-and-the-reservation-anheuser-buschs-view.html.

22. Tamika C. B. Zapolski, "Less Drinking, Yet More Problems: Understanding African American Drinking and Related Problems," *Psychological Bulletin* 140, no. 1 (January 2014), doi: 10.1037/a0032113, https://www.ncbi.nlm .nih.gov/pmc/articles/PMC3758406/.

23. Ed Butler and Edwin Lane, "The Impact of Banning Alcohol During Covid-19," BBC, September 17, 2020, https://www.bbc.com/worklife /article/20200917-the-impact-of-banning-alcohol-during-covid-19.

24. Katherine J. Karriker-Jaffe, Sarah C. M. Roberts, and Jason Bond, "Income Inequality, Alcohol Use, and Alcohol-Related Problems," *American Journal of Public Health* 103, no. 4 (April 2013): 649–56, doi: 10.2105 /AJPH.2012.300882, https://www.ncbi.nlm.nih.gov/pmc/articles /PMC3673268/.

25. James I. Daley et al., "The Impact of a 25 Cent-per-Drink Alcohol Tax Increase: Who Pays the Tab?," *American Journal of Preventative Medicine* 42, no. 4 (April 2012): 382–89, doi: 10.1016/j.amepre.2011.12.008, https:// www.ncbi.nlm.nih.gov/pmc/articles/PMC3794433/#.

26. Megan Gambino, "During Prohibition, Your Doctor Could Write You a Prescription for Booze," *Smithsonian*, October 7, 2013, https://www .smithsonianmag.com/history/during-prohibition-your-doctor-could -write-you-prescription-booze-180947940.

27. Ken Dowell, "Prohibition as Class Warfare," Off the Leash, December 19, 2017, https://offtheleash.net/2017/12/19/prohibition-as-class-warfare.

28. Fred Thys, "Dartmouth College Bans Hard Liquor," WBUR, January 29,

2015, https://www.wbur.org/news/2015/01/29/dartmouth-hard-liquor
-ban.

29. Jake New, "Banning Booze," Inside Higher Ed, April 8, 2015, https://www
.insidehighered.com/news/2015/04/08/can-college-bans-hard-liquor-be
-effective.

30. Damien Fisher, "Sharp Increase in Sexual Assault Reports at Dartmouth,"
New Hampshire Union Leader, October 6, 2019, https://www.unionleader
.com/news/crime/sharp-increase-in-sexual-assault-reports-at-dartmouth
/article_ba8f2987-27f5-5042-a7c5-dd2abef003d6.html.

31. Hannah Jinks, "A Deep Dive into Dartmouth's Judicial System," *The
Dartmouth*, October 30, 2020, https://www.thedartmouth.com/article
/2020/10/a-deep-dive-into-dartmouths-judicial-system.

32. German Lopez, "Europe Has Lower Drinking Ages Than the US—and
Worse Teen Drinking Problems," *Vox*, January 26, 2016, https://www
.vox.com/2016/1/26/10833208/europe-lower-drinking-age.

33. Nicola Carruthers, "Binge Drinking Falls by 25% in Europe," Spirits
Business, October 1, 2019, https://www.thespiritsbusiness.com/2019/10
/binge-drinking-falls-by-25-in-europe/.

34. Alexander Ahammer, "Minimum Legal Drinking Age and the Social
Gradient in Binge Drinking," VoxEU/CEPR, March 27, 2021, https://voxeu
.org/article/minimum-legal-drinking-age-and-social-gradient-binge-drinking.

35. NPR Staff, "After Years of Blackouts, a Writer Remembers What She 'Drank to
Forget,'" NPR, June 21, 2015, https://www.npr.org/2015/06/21/415748050
/after-years-of-blackouts-a-writer-remembers-what-she-drank-to-forget.

36. Jessica Bliss, "Police, Experts: Alcohol Most Common in Sexual Assaults,"
Tennessean, October 28, 2013, https://www.usatoday.com/story/news
/nation/2013/10/28/alcohol-most-common-drug-in-sexual-assaults
/3285139/.

37. Danny Shaw, "Men with Alcohol Problems 'Six Times More Likely to
Abuse Partner,'" BBC, December 23, 2019, https://www.bbc.com/news
/uk-50887893.

38. Wynford Ellis Owen, "Alcohol Is a Feminist Issue," CAIS, 2015, https://
www.cais.co.uk/news/alcohol-is-a-feminist-issue/.

39. German Lopez, "More Than One-Third of Americans Blame Alcohol for
Family Problems," *Vox*, August 8, 2014, https://www.vox.com/xpress
/2014/8/8/5979901/alcohol-family-troubles.

40. *Prohibition*, episode 2, "A Nation of Drunkards," directed by Ken Burns and
Lynn Novick, aired October 2, 2011, on PBS, 10:30–11:19, https://www.pbs
.org/kenburns/prohibition/.

41. "The Home Protection Ballot and the Hinds Bill of 1879," Frances Willard
House Museum and Archives, https://franceswillardhouse.org/wp-content
/uploads/HST391-3-wctu.pdf.

42. Moira Donegan, "The Temperance Movement Linked Booze to Domestic Violence. Did It Have a Point?," *Guardian*, January 3, 2020, https://www .theguardian.com/commentisfree/2020/jan/03/women-alcohol-drink -culture-prohibition-temperance.

43. David Sharp, "Missionary Zeal from Non-Missionary Positions," *Lancet* 350, no. 9094 (December 20, 1997): 1862–63, https://www.thelancet.com /journals/lancet/article/PIIS0140-6736(05)63691-4/fulltext.

44. Winifred Gallagher, "Getting Serious About Sex," *Washington Post*, November 16, 1997, https://www.washingtonpost.com/archive/ entertainment/books/1997/11/16/getting-serious-about-sex/ed440dd2 -2cd7-4ec9-abf3-7efa44b3528e/.

45. Allan Sherman, *The Rape of the APE* (New York: Playboy Press, 1975), 12.

46. "The Playboy Philosophy," *Firing Line*, episode 26, September 12, 1966, 15:20–29:49, https://www.youtube.com/watch?v=71B6hqEbbYQ&t =914s&ab_channel=FiringLinewithWilliamF.Buckley%2CJr.

47. "The Playboy Philosophy."

48. P. C. Kemeny, "'Banned in Boston': Moral Reform Politics and the New England Society for the Suppression of Vice," *Church History* 78, no. 4 (2009): 820, www.jstor.org/stable/20618793.

49. McKenna, *The Puritan Origins of American Patriotism*, 216.

50. McKenna, *The Puritan Origins of American Patriotism*, 217.

51. Kemeny, "'Banned in Boston,'" 819.

52. Degler, "Were the Puritans Puritanical?," 32–33.

53. Natasha Lennard, "The Uses and Abuses of Politics for Sex," Logic, no. 2, July 1, 2017, https://logicmag.io/sex/the-uses-and-abuses-of-politics-for-sex/.

54. William Dale, "Foucault's Sexuality," Atlas Society, February 27, 2011, https://www.atlassociety.org/post/foucaults-sexuality.

55. Joseph Saunders, "French Philosopher and Founder of Woke Movement Accused of Sexual Abuse of Minors," *Los Angeles Injury Law News*, April 4, 2021, https://losangeles.legalexaminer.com/legal/french-philosopher-and -founder-of-woke-movement-accused-of-sexual-abuse-of-minors/.

56. Roger Horrocks and Jo Campling, "Contradictions in Sexuality," in *Freud Revisited* (New York: Palgrave, 2011), 111–125, https://link .springer.com/chapter/10.1057/9780333985441_9.

57. Dave Madden, "It's Time Politicians Embraced the Revolutionary Power of Sex," *Guardian*, February 18, 2020, https://www.theguardian .com/commentisfree/2020/feb/18/politicians-embrace-sexual-desires -patriarchy.

58. Olivia Goldhill, "Polyamory Is a Quietly Revolutionary Political Movement," Quartz, December 18, 2018, https://qz.com/1501725 /polyamorous-sex-is-the-most-quietly-revolutionary-political-weapon -in-the-united-states/.

59. Indiana Seresin, "On Heteropessimism," *New Inquiry*, October 9, 2019, https://thenewinquiry.com/on-heteropessimism/.

60. Christopher Lehmann-Haupt, "Rape as the Combat in a War," *New York Times*, October 16, 1975, https://www.nytimes.com/1975/10/16/archives /books-of-the-times-rape-as-the-combat-in-a-war.html.

61. Julie Bindel, "Without Porn, the World Would Be a Better Place," *Guardian*, October 24, 2014, https://www.theguardian.com/commentisfree/2014 /oct/24/pornography-world-anti-porn-feminist-censorship-misogyny.

62. Andrea Dworkin, *Intercourse* (New York: Basic Books, 1987), https://www .feministes-radicales.org/2013/08/05/andrea-dworkin-occupation -colaboration-intercourse-chap-7/.

63. Moira Donegan, "Sex During Wartime," Book Forum, February/March 2019, https://www.bookforum.com/print/2505/the-return-of-andrea-dworkin-s -radical-vision-20623.

64. Katie Way, "I Went on a Date with Aziz Ansari. It Turned into the Worst Night of My Life," Babe.net, January 14, 2018, https://babe.net/2018/01 /13/aziz-ansari-28355.

65. Michelle Goldberg, "Not the Fun Kind of Feminist," *New York Times*, February 22, 2019, https://www.nytimes.com/2019/02/22/opinion /sunday/trump-feminism-andrea-dworkin.html.

66. Ashe Schow, "Advocacy Group Distributes Sexual 'Consent Contracts' to College Students," *Washington Examiner*, July 7, 2015, https://www .washingtonexaminer.com/advocacy-group-distributes-sexual-consent -contracts-to-college-students.

67. \ "The NCHERM Group Continues to Advocate for Affirmative Consent Policies in Colleges and Schools Across the Nation," PR Newswire, October 10, 2014, https://www.prnewswire.com/news-releases/the-ncherm-group -continues-to-advocate-for-affirmative-consent-policies-in-colleges-and -schools-across-the-nation-278778841.html.

68. Maura Lerner, "University of Minnesota to Adopt 'Affirmative Consent' Rule for Sex Partners," *Star Tribune* (Minneapolis), July 7, 2015, https:// www.startribune.com/university-of-minnesota-to-adopt-affirmative -consent-rule/311650821/.

69. Jake New, "The 'Yes Means Yes' World," Inside Higher Ed, October 17, 2014, https://www.insidehighered.com/news/2014/10/17/colleges-across -country-adopting-affirmative-consent-sexual-assault-policies.

70. Schow, "Advocacy Group Distributes Sexual 'Consent Contracts.'"

71. Jennifer Medina, "Sex Ed Lesson: 'Yes Means Yes,' but It's Tricky," *New York Times*, October 14, 2015, https://www.nytimes.com/2015/10/15/us/california -high-schools-sexual-consent-classes.html.

72. Ezra Klein, "'Yes Means Yes' Is a Terrible Law, and I Completely Support

It," *Vox*, October 13, 2014, https://www.vox.com/2014/10/13/6966847
/yes-means-yes-is-a-terrible-bill-and-i-completely-support-it.

73. Ashe Schow, "Judge Rules Campus Kangaroo Court 'Unfair,'" *Washington Examiner*, July 13, 2015, https://www.washingtonexaminer.com/judge
-rules-campus-kangaroo-court-unfair.

74. Anita Wadhwani, "Settling Sex Assault Lawsuits Costs Universities Millions," *Tennessean*, July 6, 2016, https://www.tennessean.com
/story/news/2016/07/06/settling-sex-assault-lawsuits-costs-universities
-millions/86756078/.

75. Jennifer Hirsch and Shamus Khan, "Researchers Found What Consent Looks Like Isn't Always Straightforward on College Campuses," *Teen Vogue*, January 3, 2020, https://www.teenvogue.com/story/what-sexual-consent
-really-looks-like-in-college.

76. National Center for HIV/AIDS, Viral Hepatitis, STD, and TB Prevention, "Trends in the Prevalence of Sexual Behavior and HIV Testing National YRBS: 1991–2015," Centers for Disease Control and Prevention, accessed June 24, 2021, https://www.cdc.gov/healthyyouth/data/yrbs/pdf/trends
/2015_us_sexual_trend_yrbs.pdf.

77. Christopher Ingraham, "The Share of Americans Not Having Sex Has Reached a Record High," *Washington Post*, March 29, 2019, https://www
.washingtonpost.com/business/2019/03/29/share-americans-not-having
-sex-has-reached-record-high/.

78. Ingraham, "The Share of Americans Not Having Sex Has Reached a Record High."

79. Christine Rosen, "No Sex, Please, We're American," *Commentary*, January 2020, https://www.commentarymagazine.com/articles/christine-rosen
/american-youth-celibate-but-fear-intimacy/.

80. Mica Lemiski, "We Asked Millennials Why Young People Are Having Less Sex," *Vice*, November 16, 2018, https://www.vice.com/en/article/qvqbmv
/we-asked-millenials-why-young-people-are-having-less-sex.

81. Yvonne Roberts, "The Sex Revolution of My Youth Wasn't So Great. Maybe Today's Celibacy Is a Sign of Progress," *Guardian*, April 7, 2019, https://
www.theguardian.com/commentisfree/2019/apr/07/sex-revolution-my
-youth-wasnt-great-maybe-celibacy-sign-progress.

82. Sarah Neilson, "Read Me: Angela Chen's *Ace* Challenges Us All to Reframe How We Talk About Sex," Them, September 15, 2020, https://www.them
.us/story/read-me-angela-chen-ace-interview.

83. Jamie Waters, "'I Don't Want Sex with Anyone': The Growing Asexuality Movement," *Guardian*, March 21, 2021, https://www.theguardian.com
/lifeandstyle/2021/mar/21/i-dont-want-sex-with-anyone-the-growing
-asexuality-movement.

84. Kirin, "Asexuality and Spirituality," Asexual Visibility and Education Network, June 12, 2012, https://www.asexuality.org/en/topic/75472 -asexuality-and-spirituality/.

7: ORDER: THE COMPANY WE KEEP

1. Michael Grynbaum, "New York Plans to Ban Sale of Big Sizes of Sugary Drinks," *New York Times*, May 30, 2012, https://www.nytimes .com/2012/05/31/nyregion/bloomberg-plans-a-ban-on-large-sugared -drinks.html.

2. Mark Oppenheimer, "The New Puritans," *New Republic*, July 15, 2013, https://newrepublic.com/article/113632/oregon-fluoridation-proof -liberals-are-new-puritans.

3. Arit John, "The New Puritan Parent," *Atlantic*, July 16, 2013, https://www .theatlantic.com/national/archive/2013/07/are-liberals-new -conservative-parents/313277/.

4. Lenore Skenazy, "'America's Worst Mom?,'" *New York Sun*, April 8, 2008, https://www.nysun.com/opinion/americas-worst-mom/74347/.

5. Hanna Rosin, "Police Investigate Family for Letting Their Kids Walk Home Alone. Parents, We All Need to Fight Back," *Slate*, January 16, 2015, https:// slate.com/human-interest/2015/01/maryland-parents -investigated-by-the-police-for-letting-their-kids-walk-home-alone.html.

6. Jessica Grose, "Parents Are Now Getting Arrested for Letting Their Kids Go to the Park Alone," *Slate*, July 15, 2014, https://slate.com /human-interest/2014/07/debra-harrell-arrested-for-letting-her-9-year -old-daughter-go-to-the-park-alone.html.

7. Lenore Skenazy, "Mom Briefly Left Kids Alone While She Grabbed Starbucks. Cop Accused Her of Child Abuse," Reason, August 31, 2016, https://reason.com/2016/08/31/mom-briefly-left-kids-alone-while-she-gr/.

8. Stephanie Clifford and Jessica Silver-Greenberg, "Foster Care as Punishment: The New Reality of 'Jane Crow,'" *New York Times*, July 21, 2017, https://www.nytimes.com/2017/07/21/nyregion/foster-care-nyc -jane-crow.html.

9. Vivek S. Sankaran and Christopher Church, "Easy Come, Easy Go: The Plight of Children Who Spend Less Than Thirty Days in Foster Care," Penn Law: Legal Scholarhsip Repository, 2017, https://scholarship.law .upenn.edu/cgi/viewcontent.cgi?article=1197&context=jlasc.

10. Michael Winship, *Hot Protestants: A History of Puritanism in England and America* (New Haven, CT: Yale University Press, 2019), 88–89.

11. Jack P. Greene, "Recent Developments in the Historiography of Colonial New England," *Acadiensis* 17, no. 2 (1988): 144, https://journals.lib.unb .ca/index.php/Acadiensis/article/view/12246/13090.

12. Greene, "Recent Developments in the Historiography of Colonial New England," 146.

13. Greene, "Recent Developments in the Historiography of Colonial New England," 147.

14. Winship, *Hot Protestants*, 186.

15. Winship, *Hot Protestants*, 186–87.

16. Greene, "Recent Developments in the Historiography of Colonial New England," 154.

17. Greene, "Recent Developments in the Historiography of Colonial New England," 154–56.

18. Greene, "Recent Developments in the Historiography of Colonial New England," 160.

19. Jonathan Haidt, "2017 Wriston Lecture: The Age of Outrage: What It's Doing to Our Universities, and Our Country," Manhattan Institute, November 15, 2017, https://www.manhattan-institute.org/html/2017 -wriston-lecture-age-outrage-10779.html.

20. Emily Bazelon, "The First Amendment in the Age of Disinformation," *New York Times*, October 13, 2020, https://www.nytimes.com/2020/10/13 /magazine/free-speech.html.

21. Bryan Mena and Duncan Agnew, "Republicans and Democrats Both Want to Repeal Part of a Digital Content Law, but Experts Say That Will Be Extremely Tough," *Texas Tribune*, January 21, 2021, https://www .texastribune.org/2021/01/21/section-230-internet-social-media/.

22. Andrew Marantz, "Free Speech Is Killing Us," *New York Times*, October 4, 2019, https://www.nytimes.com/2019/10/04/opinion/sunday/free-speech -social-media-violence.html.

23. Rafi Schwartz, "Why Is Facebook This Confused over Letting Donald Trump Back?," Mic, May 3, 2021, https://www.mic.com/p/why-is -facebook-this-confused-over-letting-donald-trump-back-76040098.

24. Dave Davies, "Unfettered Free Speech Is a Threat to Democracy, Journalist Says," NPR, October 20, 2020, https://www.npr.org/2020/10/20/925755387 /unfettered-free-speech-is-a-threat-to-democracy-journalist-says.

25. Erin Griffith and Taylor Lorenz, "Clubhouse, a Tiny Audio Chat App, Breaks Through," *New York Times*, February 15, 2021, https://www .nytimes.com/2021/02/15/business/clubhouse.html.

26. Imran Awan, "Social Media Helps Reveal People's Racist Views—So Why Don't Tech Firms Do More to Stop Hate Speech?," The Conversation, June 25, 2019, https://theconversation.com/social-media-helps-reveal-peoples-racist -views-so-why-dont-tech-firms-do-more-to-stop-hate-speech-140997.

27. Derald Wing Sue et al., "Racial Microaggressions in Everyday Life: Implications for Clinical Practice," *American Psychologist* 62, no. 4

(May–June 2007): 271–86, https://gim.uw.edu/sites/gim.uw.edu/files
/fdp/Microagressions%20File.pdf.

28. Winship, *Hot Protestants*, 52.

29. Winship, *Hot Protestants*, 53.

30. Steven Mintz and Susan Kellogg, *Domestic Revolutions* (New York: Free Press, 1988), 42.

31. Mintz and Kellogg, *Domestic Revolutions*, 42–48.

32. Mintz and Kellogg, *Domestic Revolutions*, 52–53.

33. Students for a Democratic Society, "Port Huron Statement," June 15, 1962, https://history.hanover.edu/courses/excerpts/111huron.html.

34. George McKenna, *The Puritan Origins of American Patriotism* (New Haven, CT: Yale University Press, 2007), 299.

35. Eva P. Dunn-Froebig, "All Grown Up: How the Counterculture Affected Its Flower Children" (master's thesis, University of Montana School of Journalism, 2006), 8, https://scholarworks.umt.edu/etd/5404.

36. Dunn-Froebig, "All Grown Up," 12.

37. Phineas Harper, "The Vision of the Home as a Tranquil Respite from Labour Is a Patriarchal Fantasy," Dezeen, April 18, 2019, https://www.dezeen.com /2019/04/18/nuclear-family-home-tool-repression-phineas-harper/.

38. Tom Kertscher and Amy Sherman, "Ask PolitiFact: Does Black Lives Matter Aim to Destroy the Nuclear Family?," PolitiFact, August 28, 2020, https:// www.politifact.com/article/2020/aug/28/ask-politifact-does-black-lives -matter-aim-destroy/.

39. Union Resolutions, "Resolution in Support of Black Lives Matter at School," United Federation of Teachers, November 18, 2020, https://www.uft.org /news/union-resolutions/resolution-support-black-lives-matter-school.

40. Union Resolutions, "Resolution in Support of Black Lives Matter at School."

41. Candi Finch, "The Puzzling Case of Maternal Feminism," Christian Examiner, March 9, 2016, https://www.christianexaminer.com/news /commentary-the-puzzling-case-of-maternal-feminism.html.

42. Kate Millett, chap. 2 in *Sexual Politics*, "Theory of Sexual Politics," https:// www.marxists.org/subject/women/authors/millett-kate/theory.htm.

43. Lukman Harees, *The Mirage of Dignity on the Highways of Human "Progress": The Bystanders' Perspective* (Bloomington, IN: AuthorHouse, 2012), 546.

44. Dolores Barclay, "The Family: College Professors Discuss the American Family," syndicated (AP), *Florence Morning News* (S.C.), August 21, 1977, http://unknownmisandry.blogspot.com/2011/08/anti-family-agenda-as -explained-in-1977.html.

45. Nicole Sussner Rodgers, "What Comes After the Nuclear Family?," *Nation*, February 24, 2020, https://www.thenation.com/article/society/nuclear -family-progressive-critique/.

46. Minyvonne Burke, "Private School Says Phrases Like 'Mom and Dad' Should Be Avoided," NBC News, March 11, 2021, https://www.nbcnews .com/news/us-news/private-school-says-phrases-mom-dad-should-be -avoided-n1260695.

47. Sarah Treleaven, "They're Single. They're Straight. They're Friends. And They're Having a Baby," *Marie Claire*, January 22, 2020, https://www .marieclaire.com/sex-love/a30517691/raising-a-child-with-your-best-friend/.

48. Deborah Linton, "'I Wanted to Meet a Mate and Have a Baby without Wasting Time': The Rise of Platonic Co-Parenting," *Guardian*, October 31, 2020, https://www.theguardian.com/lifeandstyle/2020/oct/31/i-wanted-to -meet-a-mate-and-have-a-baby-without-wasting-time-the-rise-of-platonic -co-parenting.

49. Jennifer Ludden, "Should We Be Having Kids in the Age of Climate Change?," NPR, August 18, 2016, https://www.npr.org/2016/08/18/479349760/should -we-be-having-kids-in-the-age-of-climate-change.

50. Elizabeth Bruenig, "I Became a Mother at 25, and I'm Not Sorry I Didn't Wait," *New York Times*, May 7, 2021, https://www.nytimes.com/2021 /05/07/opinion/motherhood-baby-bust-early-parenthood.html?smid =tw-nytimes&smtyp=cur.

51. Christine Rosen, "The Mother of All Meltdowns," *Commentary*, May 11, 2021, https://www.commentarymagazine.com/christine-rosen/the-mother -of-all-meltdowns/.

52. Rosemary Ho, "Want to Dismantle Capitalism? Abolish the Family," *Nation*, May 16, 2019, https://www.thenation.com/article/archive/want-to -dismantle-capitalism-abolish-the-family/.

53. Tom Whyman, "Should We Abolish the Family?," Outline, July 25, 2019, https://theoutline.com/post/7717/family-abolition-sophie-lewis-full -surrogacy-now.

54. Sophie Silverstein, "Family Abolition Isn't About Ending Love and Care. It's About Extending It to Everyone," Open Democracy, April 24, 2020, https:// www.opendemocracy.net/en/oureconomy/family-abolition-isnt-about -ending-love-and-care-its-about-extending-it-to-everyone/.

55. Joe Gelonesi, "Is Having a Loving Family an Unfair Advantage?," Australian Broadcasting Company, May 1, 2015, https://www.abc.net.au /radionational/programs/philosopherszone/new-family-values/6437058.

56. M. E. O'Brien, "Six Steps to Abolish the Family," *Commune*, December 30, 2019, https://communemag.com/six-steps-to-abolish-the-family/.

57. Alan Ball, *And Now My Soul Is Hardened: Abandoned Children in Soviet Russia, 1918–1930* (Berkeley and Los Angeles, CA: University of California Press, 1996), https://publishing.cdlib.org/ucpressebooks /view?docId=ft700007p9&chunk.id=ch1&toc.depth=1&toc .id=ch1&brand=ucpress.

58. Becket Adams, "Make Up Your Mind, You Weird, Lazy Scolds," *Washington*

Examiner, March 10, 2017, https://www.washingtonexaminer.com/make
-up-your-mind-you-weird-lazy-scold.

59. Moley Tant, "The BBC Pundit's Children Video Is NOT FUNNY. It's
Patriarchy in a Nutshell," *New Statesman*, March 10, 2017, https://www
.newstatesman.com/politics/media/2017/03/bbc-pundits-children
-video-not-funny-its-patriarchy-nutshell.

8: REFORMATION: SLOWLY AT FIRST, THEN ALL AT ONCE

1. P. C. Kemeny, "'Banned in Boston': Moral Reform Politics and the New
England Society for the Suppression of Vice," *Church History* 78, no. 4
(2009): 835, www.jstor.org/stable/20618793.

2. Kemeny, "'Banned in Boston,'" 830.

3. Kemeny, "'Banned in Boston,'" 824.

4. Kemeny, "'Banned in Boston,'" 835.

5. Kemeny, "'Banned in Boston,'" 827.

6. Kemeny, "'Banned in Boston,'" 845.

7. Paul S. Boyer, "Boston Book Censorship in the Twenties," *American
Quarterly* 15, no. 1 (1963): 3, www.jstor.org/stable/2710264.

8. Boyer, "Boston Book Censorship in the Twenties," 22.

9. Tania deLuzuriaga, "Man from Ministry Bans Potter," Boston.com,
October 25, 2007, http://archive.boston.com/ae/books/articles
/2007/10/25/man_from_ministry_bans_potter/.

10. Ron Charles, "Did Facebook 'Cancel Abe Lincoln'? The Truth Is
Complicated—and Alarming," *Washington Post*, March 4, 2021, https://
www.washingtonpost.com/entertainment/books/facebook-old-abe
-cancel-culture/2021/03/03/ad9e01fc-7b98-11eb-a976-c028a4215c78
_story.html.

11. Hannah Yasharoff, "Dr. Seuss Dominates USA TODAY Bestseller's List
amid Controversy, Takes Six of Top 10 Spots," *USA Today*, March 4,
2021, https://www.usatoday.com/story/entertainment/books/2021
/03/04/dr-seuss-books-sales-spike-after-some-banned-racist-imagery
/6917679002/.

12. Abigail Shrier, "Does the ACLU Want to Ban My Book?," *Wall Street Journal*,
November 15, 2020, https://www.wsj.com/articles/does-the-aclu-want-to
-ban-my-book-11605475898.

13. @AbigailShrier, December 29, 2020, https://twitter.com/abigailshrier/status
/1344135903531266048?lang=en.

14. National Coalition Against Censorship, "Statement on Amazon's Removal of
When Harry Became Sally," March 4, 2021, https://ncac.org/news/amazon
-book-removal.

15. Josh Marcus, "Conservatives Outraged That Anti-Trans Book Removed from Amazon," *Independent*, February 26, 2021, https://www.independent.co.uk/news/world/americas/us-politics/amazon-transgender-book-ryan-anderson-b1805917.html.

16. Melissa Koenig, "Josh Hawley's 'Canceled' Book on Big Tech Is Now a Best-Seller," *Daily Mail*, May 17, 2021, https://www.msn.com/en-us/money/companies/josh-hawley-s-canceled-book-on-big-tech-is-now-a-best-seller/ar-BB1gO0wB?li=BB141NW3.

17. "1675—King Philip's War," Society of Colonial Wars in the State of Connecticut, https://www.colonialwarsct.org/1675.htm.

18. Guy Howard Miller, "Rebellion in Zion: The Overthrow of the Dominion of New England," *Historian* 30, no. 3 (1968): 439–45, www.jstor.org/stable/24441216.

19. Michael Winship, *Hot Protestants: A History of Puritanism in England and America* (New Haven, CT: Yale University Press, 2019), 280.

20. Michael G. Hall, *The Last American Puritan: The Life of Increase Mather, 1639–1723* (Middletown, CT: Wesleyan University Press, 1988), 251.

21. Winship, *Hot Protestants*, 284.

22. Winship, *Hot Protestants*, 283–85.

23. Meghan M. Brockmeyer, "The Puritan President," *Harvard Crimson*, October 21, 2011, https://www.thecrimson.com/article/2011/10/21/puritan-president-mather/.

24. Winship, *Hot Protestants*, 289.

25. Avihu Zakai, "Who Was the Last American Puritan?," *Reviews in American History* 18, no. 1 (1990): 35, accessed June 24, 2021, doi: 10.2307/2702723.

26. Joel Achenbach, "Tell It to the Puritans!," *Washington Post*, December 24, 1993, https://www.washingtonpost.com/archive/lifestyle/1993/12/24/tell-it-to-the-puritans/f1fa1e28-073a-409b-b678-4be723b1e13a/.

27. Mia C. Karr, "University to Change 'Fair Harvard' Lyrics," *Harvard Crimson*, April 6, 2017, https://www.thecrimson.com/article/2017/4/6/fair-harvard-lyrics-change/.

28. Michelle Wade and Susan Fiorentino, "Gender Pay Inequality: An Examination of the Lilly Ledbetter Fair Pay Act Six Years Later," *Advancing Women in Leadership* 37, (2017): 35.

29. White House, "Statement on the 12th Anniversary of the Lilly Ledbetter Fair Pay Act," January 29, 2021, https://www.whitehouse.gov/briefing-room/statements-releases/2021/01/29/statement-on-the-12th-anniversary-of-the-lilly-ledbetter-fair-pay-act/.

30. Office of the Assistant Secretary for Planning and Evaluation, "Overview of the Uninsured in the United States: A Summary of the 2011 Current Population Survey," September 13, 2011, https://aspe.hhs.gov/basic-report

/overview-uninsured-united-states-summary-2011-current-population
-survey#:~:text=According%20to%20the%20Census%2Bureaus,16.3%25%20
of%20the%20total%20population.

31. JoeBiden.com, "The Biden Plan for Strengthening Worker Organizing, Collective Bargaining, and Unions," 2020, accessed May 16, 2021, https://joebiden.com/empowerworkers/.

32. Kelcey Patrick-Ferree and Shannon Patrick, "The Freedom to Associate Through Unions Is Essential to the Labor Movement," *Iowa City Press-Citizen*, September 5, 2018, https://www.press-citizen.com/story/opinion/contributors/writers-group/2018/09/05/unions-freedom-union-labor-university-iowa-city-cogs-ui-graduate-student-union-colin-gordon/1198401002/.

33. @SenGillibrand, April 7, 2021, https://twitter.com/sengillibrand/status/1379773312482607106?lang=en.

34. Emily Troyer, "Paid Family Leave in Individualist America," Prindle Post, February 27, 2017, https://www.prindlepost.org/2017/02/paid-family-leave-america/.

35. Arianna Huffington and Michelle A. Williams, "5 Ways to Make Sure the Post-Pandemic Recovery Focuses on Women," Thrive Global, April 30, 2021, https://thriveglobal.com/stories/arianna-huffington-women-key-pandemic-economy-recovery/.

36. Althea Brennan, "Paid Family Leave Programs and Their Effectiveness in Changing Workplace Culture," Rockefeller Institute of Government, August 9, 2019, https://rockinst.org/paid-family-leave-programs-and-their-effectiveness-in-changing-workplace-culture/.

37. Noah Rothman, "The Problem with 'Systemic Racism,'" *Commentary*, April 21, 2021, https://www.commentarymagazine.com/noah-rothman/the-problem-with-systemic-racism/.

38. Tharon Giddens, "It's More than Opioids," *Richmond* magazine, February 8, 2018, https://richmondmagazine.com/life-style/health/declining-life-expectancy-in-united-states/.

39. "Issues of Poverty," Learning for Justice, https://www.learningforjustice.org/classroom-resources/lessons/issues-of-poverty.

40. Thomas Frank, "Zephyr Teachout's 'Corruption in America,'" *New York Times*, October 16, 2014, https://www.nytimes.com/2014/10/19/books/review/zephyr-teachouts-corruption-in-america.html.

41. "Gun Violence Is a Racial Issue," Brady Campaign to Prevent Gun Violence, https://www.bradyunited.org/issue/gun-violence-is-a-racial-justice-issue.

42. Sophia Lepore, "You're Welcome, World: America Is Behind Climbing Childhood Obesity Rates," TakePart, October 14, 2016, http://www.takepart.com/article/2016/10/13/2025-obesity-trend/.

43. Bruce E. Levine, "How Our Society Breeds Anxiety, Depression and Dysfunction," Salon.com, August 26, 2013, https://www.salon.com /2013/08/26/how_our_society_breeds_anxiety_depression_and _dysfunction_partner/.

44. Reni Eddo-Lodge, "Why I'm No Longer Talking to White People About Race," *Guardian*, May 30, 2017, https://www.theguardian.com/world/2017 /may/30/why-im-no-longer-talking-to-white-people-about-race.

45. Zack Linly, "It's Time to Stop Talking About Racism with White People," *Washington Post*, September 7, 2016, https://www.washingtonpost.com /posteverything/wp/2016/09/07/its-time-to-stop-talking-about-racism -with-white-people/.

46. Winship, *Hot Protestants*, 52.

47. G. K. Chesterton, *Orthodoxy* (New York: John Lane Co., 1908), https:// www.gutenberg.org/files/16769/16769-h/16769-h.htm.

INDEX

INDEX

ABOUT THE AUTHOR

NOAH ROTHMAN is the associate editor of *Commentary Magazine*, a journal of scholarly opinion and analysis that has been in continuous publication since 1945, and a contributor to MSNBC. His work has been published in *Townhall Magazine, USA Today, National Review, The Washington Examiner, The New York Post, The New York Times, The Atlantic*, and *The Washington Post*. He is the author of *Unjust: Social Justice and the Unmaking of America*.

Mr. Rothman graduated from Drew University with a degree in Russian studies and political science (2004), and he earned a graduate degree from Seton Hall University on diplomacy and international relations with a focus on security policy in the former Soviet space (2010).

He lives in New Jersey with his wife and his two sons.